Evolutionary Epistemology
and Its Implications
for Humankind

SUNY Series in Philosophy and Biology
David Edward Shaner, Editor
Furman University

Evolutionary Epistemology and Its Implications for Humankind

Franz M. Wuketits

State University of New York Press

Published by
State University of New York Press, Albany

© 1990 State University of New York

For information, address State University of New York
Press, State University Plaza, Albany, N.Y., 12246

Library of Congress Cataloging-in-Publication Data

Wuketits, Franz M.
    Evolutionary epistemology and its implications for humankind / Franz M.
Wuketits.
        p.   cm. — (SUNY series in philosophy and biology)
    Includes bibliographical references.
    ISBN 0-7914-0285-1. — ISBN 0-7914-0286-X (pbk.)
    1. Evolution.   2. Knowledge, Theory of.   I. Title.
II. Series.
BD177.W85   1990
121—dc20   89-36315
                                                              CIP

10 9 8 7 6 5 4 3 2 1

There is grandeur in this view of life, with its several powers, having been originally breathed by the Creator into a few forms or into one; and that, whilst this planet has gone cyclic on according to the fixed law of gravity, from so simple a beginning endless forms most beautiful and most wonderful have been, and are being evolved.

Charles Darwin

To me the tragedy and comedy of life lie in the consequences, sometimes terrible, sometimes ludicrous of our persistent attempts to found our institutions on ideals suggested to our imaginations by our half-satisfied passions, instead of on a genuinely natural history.

George Bernard Shaw

Contents

Preface

Recently, there has been increasing interest in, and massive critique of, what is known as *evolutionary epistemology*, that is, an evolutionary theory of cognition and knowledge. Many philosophers have been shocked at the conclusion that human knowledge, even in its most sophisticated aspects including rational (scientific) knowledge, is a result of organic evolution.

The basic assumption of evolutionary epistemology is indeed that humans, like other living beings, result from evolutionary processes and that, consequently, their mental capacities are constrained by the mechanisms of biological evolution. This assumption is not new. It was formulated, with some accuracy, in the nineteenth century and should be familiar to everyone following the evolution controversies since Darwin's days. However, during the last fifteen years or so, interest in this old heresy has grown, and evolutionary epistemology has been intensively discussed by scientists and philosophers. Some of its advocates have portrayed evolutionary epistemology as a biological theory, others lay claim to its philosophical implications and consider it a new philosophy or even a new world view. Also, evolutionary epistemology has been said to mean a Copernican turn in science and philosophy and the solution to a host of scientific and philosophical problems. On the other side, critics have argued that this epistemology is just an inflated system of dogmas basing on an age-old and out-of-date materialism; that it is a tautology and cannot really solve any important philosophical problem; that it is unduly reductionistic; and that it leads to a rather one-sided view of human knowledge.

I am aware that I treat a subject currently popular but emotionally obscured. I do so, however, because I am convinced that the evolutionary view of (human) knowledge can indeed help us solve some venerable scientific and philosophical problems and that it can throw much light on human nature. Besides, what does seem clear (and what should be admitted even by the critics) is that evolutionary epistemology does the best job of generating the dialogue between naturalists and philosophers— and between American and European philosophical traditions. So, when David E. Shaner asked me to contribute to his Philosophy and Biology Series, I did not hesitate to take this opportunity to compose a full-length work on evolutionary epistemology, to present its foundation and implications, and to sketch my own view of the problems in question.

The aim of this book is to discuss, first, the scientific (biological) basis and, second, some philosophical consequences of the evolutionary theory of knowledge. I shall outline the importance of this theory as an up-to-date approach to different scientific and philosophical problems, particularly the problems of human knowledge: its origins, development, and possible dimensions. My thesis is that to take evolutionary epistemology seriously means to replace some old-fashioned philosophical views by what can be called a "new realistic philosophy" including new ways of thinking about humans and giving a fresh impetus to a group of philosophical disciplines and to the human and social sciences.

To be sure, at this stage evolutionary epistemology is not a monolith; rather, it comprises different views and covers different schools that hold in common only the thesis that (human) knowledge results from organic evolution and that, therefore, the study of evolution is relevant to an understanding of the phenomena of knowledge. In this book I shall, implicitly, give an account of these different views. However, I also shall try to draw the lines of a synthesis. This book is both a systematic treatment and a personal conclusion, although, as I hasten to say, such a conclusion can never be definite; it only can—and I hope that it will—stimulate further discussion and move the critics.

I have lived with evolutionary epistemology for more than a decade; I have watched its maturation, participated in endless discussions, and defended it against critics; I have lectured and written on its foundation, problems, and implications. It might be that, then, the present book is somewhat partisan. Indeed, it is written in a somewhat up-front, straightforward manner. However, I know that science and philosophy profit by discussions and not by the cementation of doctrines. Hence, my ambition is not simply to convince the reader of a "truth"— whatever that might be. Also, I do not want to withhold the limits and open problems of evolutionary epistemology from the reader. Thus, far from being the last word in this context—in fact, I do not believe that there can be something like the last word with regard to any scientific or philosophical problem—this volume explains one approach to the understanding of human knowledge, an approach that certainly is of some relevance. Besides, the book should eliminate some misconceptions and meet the critics.

I am greatly indebted to many friends and colleagues for stimulating discussions. Sometimes it is difficult, or even impossible, to say where the influence of colleagues upon one's own work starts and where it stops. However, I can say that my friends and former teachers Konrad Lorenz, Erhard Oeser, and Rupert Riedl have strongly influenced my intellectual development and particularly my interest in evolutionary epistemology. In their seminars and lectures, I became acquainted with the idea of an evolutionary theory of knowledge some fifteen years ago. Of course, this does not necessarily mean that they would agree to my conclusions in every respect. Of all the other people from whose conversation and exchange I have profited in the writing of this volume, I can only mention a few: Donald T. Campbell, Werner Leinfellner, Günter P. Wagner, and Eike M. Winkler. (Needless to say, no one but myself is responsible for any part of the book.) Furthermore, I wish to express my thanks to David E. Shaner who rather enthusiastically accepted evolutionary epistemology as an issue to be presented in his remarkable series. Last but not least, my thanks go to the staff of the State University of New York Press for the competent and efficient production of the present volume.

Prospectus: Approaching an Evolutionary Theory of Knowledge

> An evolutionary epistemology would be at mini-
> mum an epistemology taking cognizance of and
> compatible with man's status as a product of
> biological and social evolution.
>
> Donald T. Campbell

Charles Darwin, in *On the Origin of Species*, cautiously stated that from the idea of evolution by natural selection "much light will be thrown on the origin of man and his history" (Darwin [1859] 1958, p. 449). Thomas H. Huxley, his famous advocate—sometimes ironically called his "bulldog"—predicted that Darwin's work "is destined to be the guide of biological and psychological speculation for the next three or four generations" (Huxley [1863] 1968, p. 144). This prediction has proved true, and since Darwin, much light indeed has been thrown on the origins and history of humans. In his later books *The Descent of Man* (1871) and *The Expression of the Emotions in Man and Animals* (1872), Darwin himself offered most convincing evidence that humans stem from the animal kingdom and that even their mental capacities result from organic evolution. He worked out, with some insight, evolutionary principles in relation to human mental phenomena; that is, self-consciousness, language, and morality. Thus, he founded an *evolutionary psychology*. This evolutionary view of the human mind, which also was fostered by other evolutionists in the nineteenth century (e.g., Herbert Spencer), included an attempt to understand cognition

1

and knowledge as biologically constrained phenomena. Evolutionary psychology in the nineteenth century was the beginning of *evolutionary epistemology*.

However, even nowadays there is resistance to the evolutionist's view of humankind. Many people do not want to accept Darwin's message that humans came up from the ape. It is true that "if you take Darwin seriously . . . then the special status of Homo sapiens is gone for ever" (Ruse 1986, p. 104); and any powers we have, be they at the organic or mental level, are to be explained, then, as results of organic evolution. For psychological reasons, many people resist such conclusions, and they are taken aback.

Also, for *philosophical* reasons, many people have resistance to these claims. One might indeed argue that the theory of evolution is designated for universal explanations and that evolutionists argue as if their theory has unlimited explanatory power—but that, from a critical philosophical perspective, every theory has limits to what it can explain. Or, if one considers unlimited explanatory power, it might be that this leads to a reductio ad adsurdum. Take, for instance, quantum theory. One could indeed argue that any powers we have are to be explained as the results of processes covered by this theory. But what is actually explained if one says that, for example, our visual perception is a result of quantum-mechanical processes? Indeed, this general theory says little about particular phenomena like visual perception. The logically parallel argument that evolutionary theory explains everything is weak and insignificant for similar reasons. It, therefore, is necessary to specify what actually is meant by claims like "any powers we have, are to be explained as results of organic evolution." To put it briefly, by such claims, we evolutionary epistemologists—or, at least, I—mean that our organic and mental capacities have their roots in (organic) evolution so that it is interesting to study these roots to learn something about the genesis and development of our capacities. And this might help us gain a better understanding of how our capacities are constrained by their own history. Indeed, the biological theory of evolution does not tell us, for example, why I am writing this particular book. (I think that I have good reasons to write this book, reasons that are going beyond the compass of the *biological* theory of evolution.) But the theory tells us how the organs I am using (e.g., my fingers which control the typewriter) have evolved. This is to say that the theory offers an explanation of the *preconditions* (necessary preconditions!) of our abilities to write books and to do many other things.

From the scientific point of view the evolution of humans is simply a fact based on a host of empirical evidence. Human evolution has been studied successfully with many tools and by researchers working in different fields, from paleontology to biochemistry. The result of all these studies is that humans are animals modified by the mechanisms of organic evolution through millions of years. In other words: "The mutually sustaining efforts of biologists, paleontologists, and anthropologists have made the theory of the evolutionary descent (or rather ascent) of man impregnable. Whoever takes the effort to familiarize himself with the relevant evidence cannot doubt that humans have evolved from nonhuman ancestors" (Dobzhansky et al. 1977, p. 439). For most people, however, it is evident that our species, Homo sapiens, differs from the other 2 or 3 millions species now living with regard to our ability to critically reflect upon ourselves in our present situation, our past, and our future; and with regard to our language, our religious beliefs, and our moral systems. In short, the human mind has been said to be unique in the animal kingdom and unique on this planet or even in the universe. This supposed uniqueness of humanity has been explained as the result of God's action in the world. It has been frequently argued that humans are the favored creation of God and that they are His image. Then, in the nineteenth century, the evolutionists destroyed this comfortable belief.

Undoubtedly, humans exhibit some abilities that other living beings do not. Particularly, humans have invented culture: arts, writings, religions, moral systems, and so on. If now these abilities are not the creation of a benevolent God, how, we are then compelled to ask, are they to be explained? From an evolutionary point of view the answer is appallingly clear: they evolved by means of natural forces. Here evolutionary epistemology starts to work. Campbell (1974a, p. 413) explicitly states that evolutionary epistemology is "an epistemology taking cognizance of and compatible with man's status as a product of biological and social evolution"; moreover, he argues that evolution itself is a cognition or knowledge process "and that the natural-selection paradigm for such knowledge increments can be generalized to other epistemic activities, such as learning, thought, and science." In later parts of this book I shall explain what "evolution as a cognition or knowledge process" actually means. For the moment it may suffice to stress that any living system is an information-processing system and that evolutionary epistemology regards information processing as a general characteristic of organic nature. Humans exhibit the most sophisticated type of gaining and preserving information about certain aspects of reality. However, information processing in humans, too, can be explained as an evolutionary phenomenon. At least, this is the ambition of evolutionary epistemologists. Insofar, if we take evolution seriously, we should take evolutionary epistemology seriously—and if we take evolutionary epistemology seriously, then the special status of our species with respect to knowledge is gone again.

Now, the reader might suspect that evolutionary epistemology has been destined to destroy the traditional picture of humans and, particularly, to ruin religion. This is not right, even if evolutionary epistemology indeed may imply such consequences. The main purpose of this epistemology is a scientific and philosophical[1]; that is, to meet the urgent need in science and philosophy for a comprehensive approach to the intriguing problems of knowledge that go beyond traditional disciplinary boundaries. Evolutionary epistemology is an interdisciplinary account for epistemic activities (Wuketits 1984a). It is a science-oriented epistemology whose advocates do justice to results gained in different fields of empirical research as far as these results are of some relevance to the problems of knowledge.

The background and the starting point of this epistemology is the biological theory of evolution. Furthermore, disciplines like neurobiology, sensory physiology, ethology, and developmental psychology contribute much to it; not to forget disciplines and theories like cognitive science and hierarchy theory (Plotkin 1987a). The possible applications of evolutionary epistemology go from immunology to the study of human intelligence (Deary 1988). In this book, therefore, we will have to consider a good deal of evidences from these disciplines.

Epistemology, however, is known as a branch of philosophy. Is, then, an *evolutionary* epistemology possible at all? Well, I do not think that philosophy exists independent of the sciences and that philosophers can do their work without reference to scientific explanations and theories. Philosophical problems cannot be solved by mere speculation, and philosophical reflections upon the nature of humans particularly require scientific (biological, anthropological, psychological) studies. Philosophy can profit greatly by scientific research, so that, in our special case, the philosopher should welcome and pick up all the results of empirical work concerning the nature of the "knowing subject," its genetic outfit, its anatomy, and its physiological capacities.

Thus, we aspire to a *naturalized epistemology* (Quine 1971). Evolutionary epistemology is the most consistent form of this epistemology, because it can explain the origins and development (evolution) of the knowing subject (Oeser 1987). I should say that evolutionary epistemology is not only possible but necessary, for it paves the way for a reorientation in the study of knowledge and gives us a fresh impetus to epistemological discussions (Wuketits 1984a) that, at least in the European (German) tradition, have made little progress since Kant.

Up to now, however, there have been two somewhat distinct programs of evolutionary epistemology (Bradie 1986). First is the attempt to account for cognitive mechanisms in animals and humans by the extension of the biological theory of evolution to those structures of living systems that are the biological substrates of cognition (brains, nervous systems, sense organs). Second is the attempt to explain culture (including ideas and scientific theories) in terms of evolution; that is, using models drawn from evolutionary studies in biology. Both programs indeed are interrelated, but they prompt us to make a distinction between two levels of evolutionary epistemology. The first level would be that of a natural history or biology of cognition-knowledge (Lorenz 1977; Riedl 1984a). At this level evolutionary epistemology would be a *biological* theory founded on results of ethology, sensory physiology, neurobiology, evolutionary biology, and so on. At the second level, evolutionary epistemology would become apparent as a *metatheory* explaining the development of ideas, scientific theories, and so on with resort to evolutionary models (see, among others, Popper 1972a, 1972b). Here, I discuss both evolutionary-epistemology programs and show their connections. By now I only want to hint at the compass of evolutionary epistemology by showing its subject(s) of research, the levels of organization which it deals with, and the intended results (see Table 1).

The starting point of evolutionary epistemology—at the first as well as at the second level—is the fact of evolution. Only someone who agrees that living systems (including humans)

Table 1. The Scope of Evolutionary Epistemology with Respect to Its Two Programs or Levels.

Subject of Research	Level of Organization	Intended Result
Cognitive capacities in organisims and their biological substrates (brain, nervous systems, sense organs)	All levels of animal organization (including humankind)	A biological theory of the evolution of cognitive capacities in animals (including humankind)
Human rational knowledge (ideas, scientific theories)	Human mental level	A metatheory of the evolution of human (rational) knowledge

have been modified through evolutionary processes and that any species now living on our planet is a result of a long-term evolution will be prepared to take evolutionary epistemology seriously. And someone who takes evolution seriously will reach the conclusion that evolutionary theory can be generalized to epistemic activities in animals and humans or, at least, that this theory is of some importance to the study of such activities. Thus, the central question of epistemology—What is knowledge and how does it arise?—becomes a subject to evolutionary explanations. No wonder that, then, some of its advocates (e.g., Vollmer 1975, 1984) have made the point that evolutionary epistemology means a truly Copernican turn.

This brief preview should illustrate some prerequisites and dimensions of evolutionary epistemology. I now hope that the reader is willing to follow me and enter into details. At this point I shall say something about the structure of the book and epitomize its plan. I begin with an exposition of biological aspects and move to a discussion of anthropological and philosophical problems.

In chapter 1, I briefly outline the biological background of evolutionary epistemology and discuss the most important aspects of the biological theory of evolution and its present situation. I try to draw the reader's attention to the relevance of a theory based on, but going beyond, Darwin's theory of natural selection; that is, a systems theory of evolution. Moreover, I sketch the wider domain of the theory of evolution and point to its implications for humankind. (The discussions will be continued in later chapters of the book.)

In chapter 2, I present the historical background of evolutionary epistemology, showing that, as already mentioned, some basic ideas of this epistemology were formulated in the nineteenth century and that, in the twentieth century, there have been two main streams of the evolutionary theory of knowledge.

Chapter 3 will encounter biological facts and figures. In this chapter I discuss the thesis that evolution is a cognition-knowledge process: that cognition increases an organism's fitness and that information processing at the prerational level is characterized as a cycle of experience and expectation.

In chapter 4, I continue discussing the biological founda-tions of evolutionary epistemology. Here, I explain the thesis that animals are "realists"; that is, for the sake of survival, they necessarily develop a "realistic" picture of certain aspects of the world. Furthermore, the individual organism's ("realistic") per-ception of certain sections of reality is the outcome of evolution by natural selection and the capacity of perception has been genetically stabilized. Thus, as I shall argue, any individual living system is equipped with a posteriori knowledge about various phenomena and this knowledge is laid down in its peculiar nucleotide sequence of the DNA. In addition, I argue that a nonadaptationist (systems-theoretical) view of the evolution of cognitive mechanisms is required. Finally, I explain that cognition is based on inborn "hypotheses" about reality and that these hypotheses result from evolutionary learning programs. The philosophical conclusion will be that the evolutionary epistemologist's attitude toward realism is that of a "hypothetical realist."

Chapter 5 concentrates on human knowledge. I examine the evolutionary origins of human rational knowledge and espouse the argument that human knowledge indeed is constrained by biological factors but that it also depends on cultural determi-nants. I argue that biological and cultural constraints to knowledge are interrelated.

Chapter 6 focuses particularly on cultural evolution. One of the major questions about the emergence of culture is whether it is to be explained in terms of organic evolution. I am sure that there are biological constraints upon cultural evolution but that culture is not ontologically reducible to organic entities. From the point of view of evolutionary epistemology, evolution is a universal cognition and learning process, and there is a nested hierarchy of such processes from unicellular animals to humans. I suppose that culture is to be understood as the most sophisticated learning process. The theory that culture is a sophisticated learning process might be trivial. But whereas some sociobiologists tend toward genetic determinism, most evolutionary epistemologists (including myself) defend a nonreductionist (and nondeterminist) view of cultural evolution.

In chapter 7 I try to show that evolutionary epistemology can help us understand the peculiar paths of the development (evolution) of scientific knowledge, but that analogies and metaphors are not enough. The evolution of scientific knowledge may be described as an information process based on, but at the same time transgressing the boundaries of, biological information processing. This chapter also includes some reflections upon the idea of progress in science and the question of limits to scientific knowledge.

Chapter 8 is a critical examination of philosophical consequences of evolutionary epistemology. This epistemology includes new approaches to some old philosophical problems (e.g., the mind-body problem, the problem of truth, and so on). I argue that this epistemology replaces some antiquated philosophical positions, like empiricism and rationalism. I also explain some connections between evolutionary epistemology and ethics.

In the epilogue, finally, I once more draft the anthropological consequences of evolutionary epistemology and speculate about a new (evolutionary) image of humankind.

During the last fifteen years evolutionary epistemology has developed rapidly and an increasing number of publications cover its general and particular aspects (see the evolutionary epistemology bibliography by Campbell, Heyes, and Callebaut 1987, which contains relevant books and articles published up to the 1980s). However, many problems remain to be solved and many objections need to be removed. I hope that this book at least can serve as a guide to the evolutionary-epistemology controversies and generate further discussion.

1

Taking Evolution Seriously

> I am fully convinced that species are not immutable; but that those belonging to what are called the same genera are lineal descendants of some other and generally extinct species, in the same manner as the acknowledged varieties of any one species are the descendants of that species. Furthermore, I am convinced that natural Selection has been the most important, but not exclusive, means of modification.
>
> Charles Darwin

The Biological Theory of Evolution

For a long time our world view was determined by the belief in a design of the universe and its creatures by an omnipotent and benevolent creator (God). It was argued that God created the world a few thousand years ago[1] and that it has not changed since. This view is contradicted by the evolutionary world picture according to which the universe, the earth, and the organisms have evolved over billions of years. From the evolutionary point of view, living systems, including humans, emerged by means of natural forces and do not depend on supranatural principles. If we take this view seriously then we have no reason to believe in a world created and organized for "higher purposes." Simpson (1963, p. 25) puts it bluntly:

> A world in which man must rely on himself, in which he is not the darling of the gods but only another, albeit extraordinary,

9

aspect of nature, is by no means congenial to the immature or the wishful thinkers. That is plainly a major reason why even now . . . most people have not really entered the world into which Darwin led—alas!—only a minority of us. . . . It is possible that some children are made happy by a belief in Santa Claus, but adults should prefer to live in a world of reality and reason.

To be sure, in a free society everybody is—and should be—allowed to live in the world in which he or she wants to live, be it the world of science or the world of superstition; but it can no longer be denied that these are two fundamentally different worlds and that the evolutionist's view is not compatible with that of the creationist. Hence, one who takes evolution seriously will be prompted to do without any kind of mythology. It, therefore, is a curiosity that in the twentieth century, hundred years after Darwin, some people have revived an antievolutionism, which they call *creation science*(!) (see on this, e.g., Barker 1985; Ruse 1982).

The evolutionary view was approached before Darwin by some naturalists and philosophers (see Glass, Temkin, and Straus 1959). Prominent among them is Jean B. de Lamarck who, in *Philosophie zoologique* (1809), substantiated the assumption that species are mutable and that there is an almost inevitable progression from lowest forms of life up to higher ones. However, it was through Darwin's work that the idea of evolution became popular—and shook the world. His *On the Origin of Species* (1859) is a long argument for evolution and the forces of natural selection. Darwin ([1859] 1958, p. 426) concluded:

> That many and serious objections may be advanced against the theory of descent with modification through variation and natural selection, I do not deny. I have endeavoured to give to them their full force. Nothing at first can appear more difficult to believe than that the more complex organs and instincts have been perfected, not by means superior to, though analogous with, human reason, but by the accumulation of innumerable slight variations, each good for the individual possessor.

But in the sequel, eliminating the objections, he emphatically wrote:

> Nevertheless, this difficulty, though appearing to our imagination insuperably great, cannot be considered real if we admit the

following propositions, namely, that all parts of the organisation and instincts offer, at least, individual differences—that there is a struggle for existence leading to the preservation of profitable deviations of structure or instinct—and lastly, that gradations in the state of perfection of each organ may have existed, each good of its kind. The truth of these propositions cannot, I think, be disputed.

I discuss Darwin's theory of natural selection later in this chapter, for the moment, it is important to look at the basic structure and the general propositions and implications of the biological theory of evolution.

Any theory of organic evolution has to encounter at least three problems (Wuketits 1988a):

1. The *fact* of evolution; that is, the transformation of species through the ages. (This transformation, however, is heavily documented by fossils and by evidence from comparative anatomy, biogeography, molecular biology, and so on, so that it no longer is considered a real problem.)

2. The *path* of evolution; that is, the process of transforming one species into another (evolutionary history), and the (evolutionary, genealogical) relationships among different organisms. This problem also includes the question whether there are particular laws of the evolutionary process.

3. The *mechanisms* of evolution; that is, the forces leading to a transformation of species. Statements about such mechanisms should provide a causal explanation of evolution. This is the most controversial subject even among today's evolutionists. (I am more explicit on this problem in following paragraphs of this chapter.)

In other words, we should separate the *theory* of evolution, which is concerned with mechanisms or causes, from the actual fact and particular path of (evolutionary) transformations (Ruse 1986). Likewise Ayala (1985) makes a distinction among three subsets of statements concerning evolution: first, general propositions stating that living beings are related by common descent; second, propositions with regard to the degree of relationship and the evolutionary history of organisms; third, propositions concerning the mechanisms by which evolution occurs. Therefore, it should be clear that it is not enough to demonstrate the fact of evolution—this fact *has* been massively demonstrated by a host of evidence from different biological disciplines—but that the most important problem to be solved by the (biological) theory of evolution is the question of mechanisms and forces directing evolutionary change. Since the nineteenth century different answers have been given to this question. Hence, there has not been just one theory of evolution but rather several theories. Anyway, the basic idea inherent in theories of organic evolution is that species are not immutable and that their transformation is due to *natural* forces (and not to any spiritual principle or God's action in the world). The difficulty in understanding these forces, however, does not alter the fact of evolution. This fact is well-established. Biology would be a headless torso without the idea of evolution: "Evolution is the overriding fact for biology, the comprehensive framework to which separate biological facts and functions are related" (J. Huxley 1958, p. 23). Or, as Dobzhansky (Dobzhansky et al. 1977, p. v) put it: "Nothing in biology makes sense except in the light of evolution."

I now concentrate on the problem of mechanisms of organic evolution; that is, on theories of evolution in a narrower sense. Darwin's theory of natural selection has been the most influential among these theories. Until recently it has served as a matrix to discussions concerning the causes of evolution. In the twentieth century, most biologists have adopted the Darwinian view, according to which natural selection is the principal factor directing the transformation of species. Also, this view can be regarded as the broader theoretical framework within which many advocates of evolutionary epistemology have developed their arguments. Therefore, I shall briefly outline Darwin's theory and the so-called *synthetic theory* of evolution based on Darwin's view and that can be regarded as a continuation of this view by supporting it with genetical and, particularly, population-biological arguments.

The Theory of Natural Selection

As mentioned previously, the idea of organic evolution was born before Darwin. Darwin's original contribution to biology, however, was the foundation of the theory of natural selection. This theory is the heart of his celebrated *On the Origin of Species* and it has been the starting point of many reflections upon mechanisms of evolution in the twentieth century. The theory can be summarized in Darwin's own words:

> The principle of preservation, or the survival of the fittest, I have called Natural Selection. It leads to the improvement of each creature in relation to its organic and inorganic conditions of life; and consequently, in most cases, to what must be regarded as an advance in organisation. Nevertheless, low and simple forms will long endure if well fitted for their simple conditions of life . . . Natural selection, on the principle of qualities being inherited at corresponding ages, can modify the egg, seed, or young, as easily as the adult. ([1859] 1958, p. 128)

Thus, natural selection is the main factor of organic evolution, the most important mechanism of the modification of species.

Much has been said about the structure of Darwin's theory, its foundations, development, and implications. (Recent discussions include Farrington 1982; Mayr 1982; Oldroyd 1986; Ruse 1982; Wuketits 1988a.) Darwin started with some observations and attained to particular conclusions (see Table 2). First, he observed that any individual of a species is unique; that is, there is a remarkable variety of individuals within any species. Second, he stated that organisms reproduce geometrically. Third, the resources are limited. (With respect to these observations he relied on Thomas R. Malthus.) These observations express

Table 2. The Main Components of Darwin's Theory of Natural Selection.

Observations:

Variety within species; uniqueness of the individual.

Tendency in living beings to reproduce geometrically; i.e., to produce more offspring than actually survive.

Conclusions:

Struggle for existence.

Survival of the fittest; the other organisms are eliminated by natural selection.

Natural selection causes a transformation of species.

---

universal laws. Darwin, then, tells us that a *struggle for existence* inevitably follows. His next conclusion is that through this struggle many organisms are eliminated and there is a *survival of the fittest*. Thus, natural selection appears to be the driving force, the motor of organic evolution. Again in Darwin's own words: "From the war of nature, from famine and death, the most exalted object which we are capable of conceiving, namely the production of the higher animals, directly follows" ([1859] 1958, p. 450). Obviously, this view is mechanistic and excludes the action of any teleological factor. Therefore, it should not come as a surprise that the Darwinian perspective has been a controversial issue in (natural) philosophy. But, at the moment, this is not my point.

If you, now, compare Darwin's theory to some other scientific theories (particularly the theories in the physical sciences), you will easily recognize that it is a rather simple idea. It is based on observations that are—or, at least, should be—accessible to any naturalist's mind. Who can doubt the fact that any species produces more offspring than actually survive or, to put it another way, that only a few of the young survive and produce the next generation, whereas the others are eliminated before they reach the reproductive age? And, if one looks at nature, can there be any doubt that there indeed is a struggle for existence? Also, it should be clear that only the fittest survive and pass on their properties to offspring. Hence, it can be—or should be—easy to understand that "subsequent generations . . . are more like the better adapted ancestors, and the result is a gradual modification or evolution" (Ghiselin 1969, p. 46). Darwin, however, was aware of the shortcomings of his theory so that, in his later writings, he even relied on Lamarck's doctrine of the inheritance of acquired characteristics.[2] It is true that Lamarck's and Darwin's ideas were not so antithetical as is commonly believed (Oldroyd 1986), but Darwin's most serious problem was his rather vague understanding of genetical mechanisms. He did not take any notice of Mendelian genetics; Mendel remained what is well-known, generally ignored by the evolutionists (and not only by the evolutionists) for decades, and had to be rediscovered at the beginning of the twentieth century.

During the first three decades of the twentieth century genetical knowledge grew rapidly, and many biologists began to realize the importance of genetical concepts and approaches to the study of evolutionary phenomena. However, as is often the case with rapidly developing disciplines and theories, the genetical theory of evolution turned out to be a one-sided view reducing the evolutionary processes to genes and mutations and, some way or other, contrasting with Darwin's phenotypic version of evolutionary theory (see, e.g., Hull 1974; Mayr 1982). There was the need for a synthesis. Such a synthesis was established in the early 1940s under the name *synthetic theory of evolution*.

The basic idea of this theory is Darwinian: the idea of natural selection. Insofar, the synthetic theory does not differ from Darwin's view; it is based on Darwin's theory, but it synthesizes Darwin's natural-selection theory with genetics. The synthesis became possible when some biologists recognized the compatibility of Darwin's view of evolution and classical (Mendelian) genetics. "Darwin had formulated his theory of evolution assuming that there must be some mechanism for the production and maintenance of the type of variation it required. Mendelian genetics was precisely that theory" (Hull 1974, p. 57). Besides the population-genetical approach, the study of genetical mechanisms in populations (i.e., reproductive communities) became of particular importance.

For the purpose of this book it may suffice to pick up just the central arguments inherent in the synthetic theory and not enter into details. To start with the relevance of population genetics, it is most evident that the advocates of this theory have considered populations to be the units of evolution. They have noticed that natural selection can operate only because of the supply of immense variation. This point can be found in Darwin's work, too; but Darwin's argument lacked the population-genetical foundation that has been regarded as the conceptual framework to the understanding of evolutionary dynamics. Ernst Mayr, one of the chief proponents of the synthetic theory, writes:

> Natural selection can operate successfully because of the inexhaustible supply of variation made available to it owing to the high degree of individuality of biological systems. No two cells within an organism are precisely identical; each individual is unique, each species is unique and each ecosystem is unique. Many nonbiologists find the extent of organic variability incomprehensible. It is totally incompatible with traditional essentialist thinking and calls for a very different conceptual framework: population thinking. (1978, p. 44)

From the viewpoint of the synthetic theory another important insight, then, is that individuals are organized into populations, and the major features of evolution can be studied at the level of populations: "Uniquely different individuals are organized into inbreeding populations and into species. All the members are 'parts' of the species, since they are derived from and contribute to a single gene pool. The population or species as a whole is in itself the 'individual' that undergoes evolution; it is not a class with members" (Mayr, 1978, p. 44).

Another, most important, argument concerns the mechanisms of evolution. The advocates of the synthetic theory consider *mutation, genetic recombination,* and *selection* the essential factors of evolutionary change. They have argued that mutation and genetic recombination are the sources of new (genetic) variation—and, thus, the raw material of evolution—and that natural selection is the directive principle (see Figure 1). Stebbins gives the following illustration:

> An evolutionary line of organisms which is changing through eons of time can be linked to an automobile being driven along the highway. Mutation then corresponds to the gasoline in the

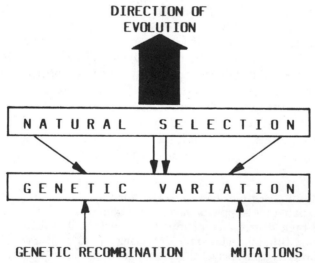

Figure 1. The meaning of natural selection in organic evolution. Genetic variation is produced by genetic recombination and mutations, natural selection acts upon the variants and causes certain directions of evolution.

tank. Since it is the only possible source of new genetic variation, it is essential for continued progress, but it is not the immediate source of motive power. This source is genetic recombination, through the shuffling of genes and chromosomes which goes on during the sexual cycle. Since this process provides the immediate source of variability upon which selection exerts its primary action it can be compared to the engine of the automobile. Natural selection, which directs genetic variability toward adaptation to the environment, can be compared to the driver of the vehicle. (1971, p. 3)

I think that this picture vividly illustrates the meaning of natural selection from the point of view of the synthetic theory. It should be obvious that this theory is essentially Darwinistic, although, by its (population-)genetical foundation, it transgresses Darwin's own theory. (On genetical aspects of modern evolutionary thought also see Ayala and Valentine 1979.)

The proponents of synthetic theory indeed have given much credit to Darwin's work. Rejecting Lamarck's notion of the inheritance of acquired characteristics, however, they have been more orthodox Darwinists than Darwin himself. To quote, once more, Mayr: "The new synthesis is characterized by the complete rejection of the inheritance of acquired characters, an emphasis on the gradualness of evolution, the realization that evolutionary phenomena are population phenomena and a reaffirmation of the overwhelming importance of natural selection" (1978, p. 44).

Two more elements of the synthetic theory can be seen now: first, the assumption that evolution occurs step by step, by *gradation*, and that there are no *saltations;* second, the argument that evolution is a process leading to *adaptation*. Both claims can be found in Darwin's *On the Origin of Species*, but emerged before 1859, however, reaching back to the early nineteenth century. Although gradualism is not discussed here, but the concept of adaptation deserves our attention, because it plays a role in evolutionary epistemology.

It has been argued that organisms are adapted to their environments, that there is a correspondence between structures in living systems and structures of their surroundings. This argument seems to be trivial. One should think that adaptation inevitably follows from evolutionary processes. "If an animal is placed in an environment which differs too greatly from that to which it is adapted, the equilibrium breaks down; a fish out of water will die" (Maynard Smith 1975, p. 15). In other words, the fish was fit into water, water is the particular environment to which it is adapted; and this adaption is a result of evolution by natural selection. Only an organism that is well adapted to its environment can be a fit organism and survive. Thus, we get the following relation:

natural selection ——> fitness <——> adaptation

Furthermore, we can say that adaptation is amply demonstrated by the fact that organisms from different classes have developed similar organs. For example, locomotion in water forces a particular kind of structure, which can be seen in the similarity of fish, penguins, seals, and whales and may be called *torpedo construction* (see Figure 2). "The problem of locomotion in an aquatic environment is," as Lewontin (1978, p. 169) states, "a real problem that has been solved by many totally unrelated evolutionary lines in much the same way. Therefore it must be feasible to make adaptive arguments about swimming appendages."

Yet another argument has been made about the relation between natural selection and adaptation. Adaptation has been explained as evolution's "answer" to specific environmental conditions, so that different kinds of organisms respond to similar (environmental) *selection pressures* with similar adaptations. (Look again at vertebrates living in an aquatic environment.) The key to an understanding of adaptation, then, would lie in the environmental selection. Darwin's theory and the synthetic theory include this argument: from the point of view of these theories natural selection operates as an *external* factor. Can Lamarck's doctrine be of some help? It is well worth spending a moment on this question.

As already mentioned, the advocates of the synthetic theory have dismissed the theory of the inheritance of acquired characteristics. Lamarck was an adaptationist, who argued that adaptation could be explained by use and disuse of organs. However, the adaptationist program inherent in the synthetic theory contrasts with Lamarck's view, according to which the consistent use of a particular organ would strengthen and modify it. The advocates of the synthetic theory have tried to offer evidence that this cannot be true; and they rely on results from molecular biology. They argue that any modification must be genetically programed. The German zoologists August Weismann stated that the germ cells exist independent of somatic cells, and

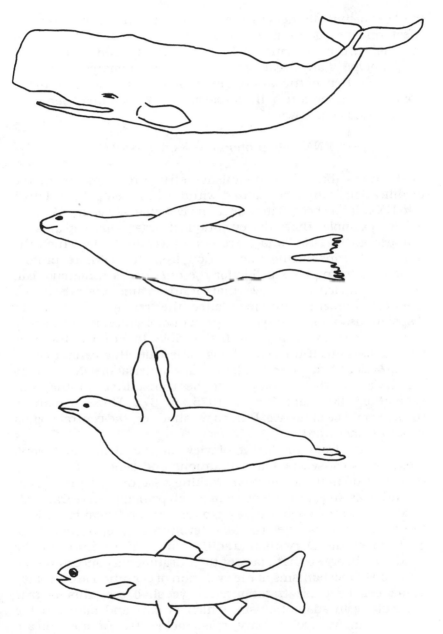

Figure 2. "Torpedo construction" in aquatic animals (whale, seal, penguin, fish).
Source: Adapted from Lewontin, 1978.

the "germ line" influences the "soma" but the "soma" has no effect on the "germ line." Some fifty years after Weismann established this doctrine, molecular biologists emphasized that the genotype of any organism influences its phenotype—and not *vice versa*. Hence, the flow of biological information is unidirectional. This is the core of the so-called *central dogma of genetics*, which reads as follows:

$$DNA \longrightarrow RNA \longrightarrow protein\ (\longrightarrow organism)$$

That means that, if an organism's structure is modified, the modification cannot be realized without first being "translated" into DNA. It has been flatly stated, by Dobzhansky et al. (1977, p. 30) for example, that "the evolution of organisms depends on changes in the DNA" and there is no mechanism by which the process of transmitting information from the DNA to protein structures (being responsible for the organism's functions) can be reversed. Hence it follows that "if an organism is raised in a new environment, this may alter the relative amounts or dispositions of different types of protein molecules, in such a way as to render the organism better able to survive the new conditions. But, if the central dogma is true, this cannot cause an equivalent change in the hereditary material or DNA, and so cannot cause the adaptation to be transmitted to the next generation" (Maynard Smith, 1975, p. 67). Thus, Lamarck's theory would be of no use. But, as we shall see, the central dogma is not the last word.

　　In sum, from the point of view of the synthetic theory, evolution is caused by blind mutations and genetic recombination, and by natural selection working as a directive force and operating as an external (environmental) principle. Like Darwin's view, the theory encompasses gradualism and adaptationism. Lamarck's view is rejected. Most evolutionary epistemologists grew up in the Darwinian tradition and the tradition of the synthetic theory so that many of their arguments concerning the question of mechanisms of the evolution of cognition are strongly influenced by these traditions. As we shall see, this is true particularly to adaptationism, which is part and parcel of the work of many evolutionary epistemologists. Because I am convinced that evolutionary epistemology requires a nonadaptationist view (see chapter 4), I now turn to conceptions that transgress the Darwinian frame.

Charles Darwin and Beyond

Suppose, for a moment, that natural selection indeed is just an outer mechanism, operating as an environmental principle that forces adaptations in living systems. These systems, then, seem to be nothing but playthings determined by environmental forces. I feel that this cannot be the whole story.

Since Darwin's days many naturalists—twenty-six of them are mentioned by Riedl (1979)—have proposed an "inner mechanism." Sometimes, however, this mechanism looks like the "life force" proposed by the vitalists. But the truth cannot lie in "vital principles" like Bergson's *élan vital* because, as Julian Huxley said, "ascribing evolution to an *élan vital* is like 'explaining' the movement of a train by an *élan locomotif"* (quoted after Simpson 1963, p. 199). Vitalism is a rather weak explanation: so, how things could be done better?

Remember that the synthetic theory tries to explain organic evolution by blind production of variation and by the somewhat "opportunist" and "short-sighted" external selection. These factors do not really explain the order and complexity of living systems; therefore, a third factor is needed. Such a factor has nothing to do with the vital forces, but is constituted by the regulatory principles of the organism itself. These principles are explained by Riedl in the following way:

> Order in the living world must rest on its molecular memory, which contains its own plans and the instructions for its assembly on the one hand, and the functional requirements of its structural expressions on the other. This is a feedback loop which not only forces structures to follow their molecular instructions, but also forces the DNA to "remember" the functional requirements of phene expression by means of superimposed decisions in the epigenetic system.[3] This process is propelled by tremendous selection pressure which is itself a feedback cycle between accessible adaptive niches in the environment as well as conditions within the organization of the organism. (1977, p. 363)

Continuing, Riedl writes:

> While mutation and environmental selection are "blind" and "short-sighted," this proposed third factor of evolution is far-sighted, although it can only look backwards, into the

> responses within its own organization. It operates . . . by
> selection, but the requirements of this selection differ from
> those of environmental selection, in the same manner as the
> patterns of organization within an industrial plant differ from
> the patterns of opinions and desires in the market. (p. 363)

What can be said at once is, first, that evolution is determined not only by external selection but by *intraorganismic constraints* upon evolutionary change, and second, that the flow of biological information is not unidirectional but bidirectional.

The second point does not mean that Lamarck is right and the central dogma is wrong. In a sense, both Lamarck's doctrine and the central dogma express the truth: the flow of biological information indeed is directed from the DNA to proteins, from the genotype to the phenotype, but the genotype must be "informed" about phenotypic requirements, so that, within the complex system of interrelations in the organism, there must be also a flow of information in the other direction:

genotype   phenotype
       $\longleftrightarrow$
   (DNA)   (protein)

This is a central argument of a theory of systems conditions of evolution that I shall explain next.

With regard to adaptation and external selection, Wagner (1985) made the point that an environmental change does not suffice as an "evolutionary pressure" and organic evolution exhibits patterns of its own dynamics (*Eigendynamik*) that goes beyond environmental constraints. Evolutionary processes are irreversible and no environmental change can "throw back" the organism to its previous state. Hence, it seems plausible that evolution is influenced by structures and functions of the organism itself.

Criticizing the adaptationist program, Gould and Lewontin (1984) come close to this point. They assume architectural and developmental constraints in organic evolution and compare organisms with complex buildings like the great central dome of St. Mark's Cathedral in Venice. They argue that any kind of adaptationism cannot really explain the evolutionary modification of complex systems exhibiting particular structures and functions that are linked together in a highly sophisticated way. I think that the failure of adaptationism indeed is the supposed dichotomy organism—environment. Considering the obvious fact that certain structures in organisms are adaptive, one should suppose that not only environmental forces have caused adaptations but that *adaptability* is a systems property of the organism itself. Therefore, we propose a flow of cause and effect in two directions and conclude that "organism and environment are co-determined" (Lewontin 1982, p. 169).

Finally, we reach a view that goes beyond the conceptual framework of Darwin's theory and the synthetic theory.

The Systems-Theoretical Approach to Evolution

Let me now summarize a theory that, some way or other, is a revised version of the Darwinian view (including Darwin's original theory and the synthetic theory), called a *theory of systems conditions* or a *systems theory of evolution* (Riedl 1977, 1979, 1982; Wagner 1983, 1985; Wuketits 1985b, 1987d, 1987e, 1988a). The theory is based on some of the central arguments inherent in a general systems theory in the sense of Bertalanffy (1973), who defined organisms as hierarchically organized open systems showing specific properties like self-regulation and self-maintenance. For brevity's sake I shall concentrate on the most important arguments and conclusions of this view.

1. Organisms are not simply molded by their environment. Any living system is an *active* system searching for, as Popper (1984) metaphorically put it, a "better world": better conditions of life. In other words, a living system is not a marionette hanging on the strings of its environment.

2. Any organism is a *hierarchically organized* system, a multilevel system organized in such a manner that its levels and parts are mutually related and linked together by feedback loops and regulatory principles. Not only the parts determine the whole organism, but the organism vice versa determines and constrains the structure and function of its parts in what can be called *downward causation* (Campbell 1974b).

3. The evolution of life results from *internal* (intraorganismic) and external (environmental) selection. Internal and external selection do not work independently but together build the systems conditions of evolutionary change. Hence, the

systems theory of evolution is a revised and extended version of the classical theory of natural selection.

Epistemologically the systems theory of evolution is founded on an extended notion of causality. The classical concept of causality that operates on the basis of (linear) causal chains does not suffice to explain complex systems like organisms. We should replace the one-way, causal paradigm that has hampered evolutionary explanations since Darwin with the concept of *feedback causality* or "network causality" (Riedl 1977, 1979; Wuketits 1981). Feedback causality is to be expected at every level of the organization of living systems, from the level of biological macromolecules to the level of the biosphere, because the parts (subsystems) of any system are mutually related. You cannot separate the functions of an organ from the functions of other organs; and, at the supraindividual level, you cannot separate the ecological functions of populations and species from those of other populations and species. (By definition an ecosystem consists of mutually related species!) The consequences of the notion of feedback causality are most obvious: "If it is true that feedback cycles can connect levels of different complexity . . ., then we must accept a flow of cause and effect in two directions, up and down the pyramid of complexity. Then we should also accept causality in living beings as a system in which effects may influence their own causes. Biology would then at last accept causality as a network rather than as a one-way chain" (Riedl 1977, p. 366). Considering these propositions, it now might be clear that, as emphasized earlier, in living systems information flows in two directions and the central dogma does not express the ultimate truth.

I wish to make another point here, which follows from a systems view of evolution. The point is that evolution is an "open process": "Only the genetic program of an organism (and of any species) contains goal-directedness towards survival; but there is no mechanism . . . that could anticipate any 'final result' of evolution" (Wuketits, 1987e, p. 55). From the thesis that evolution exhibits a particular *Eigendynamik* it follows that evolution creates its laws a posteriori and no a-priori principles prescribe certain paths. The laws of evolution are created by evolution itself—there is no preestablished harmony (in the sense of Leibniz's *Theodizee*). Take, for a moment, organic evolution as a game. You will probably agree to the conclusion that nothing is predetermined except the rules of that game (Eigen and Winkler 1975). The rules of the evolutionary game are physical and biological constraints upon the evolving organism that "canalize" evolution, so to speak, but that do not anticipate any final result or goal (e.g., the "omega point" proposed by Teilhard de Chardin).

This view has important implications for humankind (see Wuketits 1985a). If evolution is not predetermined, then the emergence and further development of humankind is not to be ascribed to any destiny. Rather, as rational animals, we are compelled to find our own goals. This might rescue something of the venerable idea of freedom. As Leinfellner (1984, p. 233) puts it: "We have to give up the deterministic view in favour of a fuzzy and indeterministic leeway, which has the great advantage for human societies of guaranteeing a certain freedom of choice for the individuals." As we shall see in Chapter 5, the idea of an open evolution is of some relevance to an understanding of human knowledge.

What is true to mechanisms of organic evolution in general also is true to mechanisms of the evolution of cognition in particular. Therefore, I propose the systems-theoretical approach as a conceptual framework to which evolutionary epistemology should be related (see Chapter 4).

Human Evolution: Some Facts and Figures

Thus far, I have sketched some prerequisites, problems, and perspectives of the biological theory of evolution. This discussion brings us conveniently to our own species, and I shall give a brief outline of the biological evolution of the species that has been called the *animal rationale* (Aristotle, Kant) and that is able to reflect upon its own past. To be sure, at the biological level, the principles of organic evolution apply fully to the human species; humans, like other organisms, result from organic evolution caused by genetic recombination, mutations, environmental selection, and—what should be emphasized once more— intraorganismic constraints.

Like some other naturalists in the nineteenth century, Darwin did not doubt that humans came up from the ape—and he and all the other naturalists who argued along these lines were right! Darwin was prepared to speculate on the looks of our ancestors, and in a short communication (1872) he remarked: "The early progenitors of man were no doubt once covered with hair, both sexes having beards; their ears were pointed and capable of movement; and their bodies were provided with a tail, having the proper muscles. Their limbs and bodies were also acted on by many muscles which now only occasionally reappear, but are normally present in the Quadrumana" (quoted by Barrett 1977, vol. 2, p. 168). Darwin was on the right track, although, as a matter of course, his view of human evolution has been changed with regard to many details.

Since Darwin's days human evolution has attracted many naturalists, and we have learned much about our own past. The study of human fossils has developed rapidly; and geneticists, biochemists, and researchers working in other disciplines have contributed much to an understanding of our evolutionary development. True, many problems are still to be solved and some questions have remained unanswered, but the main lines of human evolution have been reconstructed with some accuracy. (For recent accounts, see, e.g., Isaac 1983; Johanson and Edey 1981; Pilbeam 1984; Washburn 1978; Weaver and Brill 1985.) I focus only on some important aspects.

1. Our next relatives in the animal kingdom are the apes (chimpanzee, gorilla, orangutan) (see Figure 3). The lineage of "manlike creatures" (Hominidae) was separated from that of the apes (Pongidae) some 6 million years ago, or perhaps before that time.

2. Two genera of hominids are to be distinguished; namely, *Australopithecus* (including three fossil species) and *Homo* (including the fossil *Homo erectus* and the only living hominid species, *Homo sapiens*).

Appreciating the fossil record, we can date back the earliest hominids, the australopithecines, to at least 4 million years (little is known about their direct ancestors); *Homo erectus*, the antecedent of *Homo sapiens*, emerged some 1 million years ago; whereas modern man, *Homo sapiens sapiens*, has been around for the last 40,000 years of so. In Figure 4 human evolution is projected over the span of 4 million years, and you can see there the most significant changes with respect to the habitus of hominids.

An upright posture and bipedal locomotion are typical characteristics of hominids. However, the most striking feature of human evolution is the increase in brain size. Generally, the most distinctive trait in the evolution of primates "is the

ORANG-UTAN   GORILLA   CHIMPANZEE   HUMAN

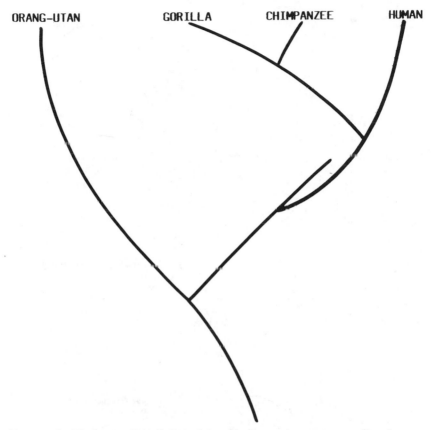

Figure 3. Phylogenetic relationship of humans to apes according to our present understanding.

tendency towards the development of a brain which is large in proportion to the total body weight, and which is particularly characterized by a relatively extensive and often richly convoluted cerebral cortex" (Le Gros Clark 1971, p. 227). This tendency is most obvious in human evolution. Within a few millions of years the cranial capacity in humans was trebled (see Table 3). The story of humans is virtually the story of the growth of the brain; the ascendance of humankind is due to the preeminence of the brain and not to bodily prowess (Dobzhansky et al. 1977). And therefore, as we shall see some evolutionary epistemologists pay much attention to the study of the brain, its structure and

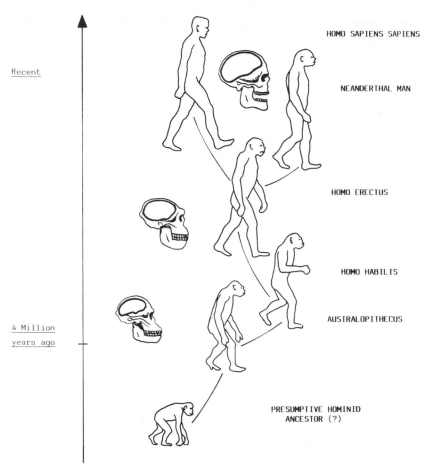

Figure 4. Human evolution from *Australopithecus* to *Homo sapiens sapiens* according to our present understanding. Note the evolution of the skull and the increase in cranial capacity.

function. Human mental capacities, we venture to say, have evolved as systems properties of the brain (see Chapter 5) and cannot be properly explained without knowledge about the human brain's evolution. (I admit that I have great difficulties to understand how, even nowadays, some philosophers continue to talk about the human mind and human cognitive capacities without giving credit to important biological research work.)

Despite some unsolved problems and frustrating gaps—for example, we have not yet clarified the relation of *Homo erectus* to

Table 3. Cranial capacity in higher primates.

Hylobates (gibbon)	110 cm^3
Pongo (orangutan)	450 cm^3
Gorilla (gorilla)	500 cm^3
Pan (chimpanzee)	400 cm^3
Australopithecus	550 cm^3
Homo erectus	1000 cm^3
Homo sapiens	1500 cm^3

Source: Data adapted from different authors.

the australopithecines—all the evidences from biological studies compel us to accept our "lower ancestry." Ruse (1986, p. 108) says: "If you are prepared to accept a natural explanation of human origins, you just cannot deny that we are animals and that we share a common origin with the rest of the organic world." (Unfortunately, some people are not prepared to accept natural explanations of human origins.)

However, another point needs to be made. Indeed one thing makes humans unique in the animal kingdom: our capacity for *culture*. The human species is the only one that has produced highly sophisticated artefacts, and it is justified to define us a *tool makers* (Oakley 1972). Due to our intellectual capacities we have been able to produce artefacts not only for immediate use but also for future service. Our early relatives, the australopithecines, produced rather primitive tools, but the capacity for tool making increased rapidly. This must have something to do with the increase of cranial capacity in human evolution. Is, then, evolution to be extended to culture? Can culture be explained in terms of organic evolution?

The Wider Domain of Evolutionary Theory: Mind and Culture

Biologists, anthropologists, and philosophers long have been prepared to speculate on the relations between organic and cultural evolution, a problem that will be discussed in Chapter 6. Here I want to give only some preliminary remarks.

First, I want to stress the thesis that culture relies upon specific brain structures and functions. It is the result of the peculiar development of the human brain and can be regarded as the most sophisticated expression of the brain's power. It might be trivial to say that culture cannot emerge without a functioning brain. However, the question arises whether (biological) explanations of the brain suffice to explain the particular paths of cultural evolution. This problem is not trivial.

If culture is defined as "the sum total of mental constructs and behaviors, including the construction and employment of artifacts, transmitted from one generation to the next by social learning" (Lumsden and Wilson 1981, p. 3), then I should attempt, first, to explain the origins of mental constructs and, second, to trace them back to the roots of social behavior. Taken for granted that mental constructs depend on a biological system (i.e., the brain) and that the same is true of social behavior, even in its most distinct aspects including moral behavior, then the biological approach is needed. Would this mean that cultural evolution indeed is to be explained in terms of organic evolution?

Anthropologists, social scientists, and philosophers have struggled against the conception of a "naturalized culture." And I agree that it is unwarranted to reduce the complex patterns of culture to the principles of organic evolution. Or, does anybody really believe that, for example, the rise and fall of ancient Roman civilization can be explained in biological terms? What I mean is that cultural evolution exhibits its own characteristics and systems conditions. However, I cannot doubt that the emergence of culture has been propelled by organic forces. The "organic forces" of culture are the potentials of the human brain; so that, after all, the biological approach is needed but not sufficient to explain the peculiar paths of cultural evolution.

Since the nineteenth century, evolutionary thought has been extended to cultural phenomena. Particularly, Darwin's theory of natural selection has been taken as a matrix to evolutionary explanations of culture and society and has influenced speculations in disciplines on the outside of biology; disciplines such as linguistics, archaeology, educational theory, and others (see, e.g., Oldroyd and Langham 1983). An unfortunate result of the extension of Darwin's theory to the human sciences was Social Darwinism. Darwin himself wanted to keep his theory separate from theorizing in sociology, but others took his theory as the background to their social beliefs and ideological claims.

Clearly, principles of organic evolution cannot be translated literally into explanations of culture and society or, vice versa, explanations of culture and society cannot be given in biological terms. Actually there is no adequate biological terminology for the rise and fall of ancient Rome, for the outbreak of World War I, and so on. Culture indeed has *evolved*, but the principles of cultural evolution are not the same principles we know from organic evolution. We can draw analogies between organic and cultural evolution, but analogies do not really explain the relation between these two types of evolution. So, how things could be done better?

On the one side, organic evolution, in particular the evolution of the (human) brain, is said to be the basis of cultural evolution. On the other side, however, the latter should not be reduced to the former. Let me just suggest that studying organic evolution brings us close to an understanding of the *preconditions* of cultural evolution, but that cultural evolution requires explanations beyond the biological theory of evolution in its strict sense. The term *evolution* applies to both the development of the organic world, from unicellular organisms to humans, and the development of culture, from primitive tools made by the australopithecines to modern technology, but we must make a distinction here between two types of evolutionary development. Hence, we have to take into account that culture, when explained in evolutionary terms, is not to be reduced to biological entities.

Evolutionary models are needed to explain cultural evolution, but these models cannot be drawn from studies of organic evolution. The preconditions of cultural evolution lie in organic evolution; hence, biology offers the necessary conditions of culture, but it does not offer the sufficient conditions. A two-level approach of evolutionary epistemology, mentioned earlier, gives us the tools to justify to both the peculiarities of organic evolution and the special features of cultural evolution (including the development of ideas and scientific theories).

Evolutionary Epistemology: A Consequence of Evolutionary Theory

I have already indicated that the starting point of evolutionary epistemology is the biological theory of evolution. Evolution-

ary epistemology has grown form theorizing on organic evolution, so that, as we shall see in the next chapter, some
evolutionists in the nineteenth century already advocated an
evolutionary approach to cognition and knowledge. If you accept
organic evolution, if you accept that humans originated from
organic evolution a few millions of years ago, then you should be
prepared to speculate on the evolutionary origins of cognitive and
mental phenomena. For if (organic) evolution has occurred—and,
undoubtedly, it *has*—then the human cognitive structures
necessarily follow from evolutionary processes (Mohr 1983a).
Hence, evolutionary epistemology is a consequence of the
biological theory of evolution. This is not to say that, therefore,
this epistemology is an epistemology in a strict philosophical
sense (see note 1 of the Prospectus). But, like almost every
comprehensive scientific theory, it has consequences for the field
of traditional (philosophical) epistemology, or at least, it contains
philosophically relevant ideas. However, the theory does not
explain only human cognition, but is concerned "with the origin
and development of cognitive structures and abilities, in a long
phylogenetic line stretching from amoeba to man" (Tennant
1983a, p. 33). It has already been pointed out, and will be argued
in chapter 3, that evolution itself can be described and explained
as a cognition process, so that studying cognition processes in
animals would be part of evolutionary theory. Insofar evolutionary epistemology is part of evolutionary theory, it has been
suggested that seeing organisms as cognition-knowledge systems is one way of founding a unified theory of evolution (Plotkin
1982).

However, some problems arise from different views of the
mechanisms of organic evolution. The Lamarckist's approach to
(organic) evolution leads to an evolutionary epistemology different from the evolutionary epistemology of the advocate of the
synthetic theory. And one who advocates the adaptationist view
will try to explain cognition and knowledge processes in terms of
adaptation and thus argue that adaptations actually are to be
considered "knowledge." Therefore, a comprehensive evolutionary epistemology is possible only if one takes into account the
different approaches to (organic) evolution and if these approaches are put together into an overall conceptual framework.
Otherwise we will have different "evolutionary epistemologies."
Up to now a synthesis has not been constructed, but I am
convinced that it is needed and possible. I believe that the

systems theory of evolution, just sketched, will provide a broad framework to evolutionary explanations of cognition-knowledge.

Enough has been said for the moment. In this chapter I was concerned with some prerequisites of evolutionary epistemology. Please remember just the following points:

1. Evolution is a fact, species are not immutable but have evolved over millions of years. The same is true of humans. Like any other species *Homo sapiens* is the result of long-term evolutionary processes; our emergence is not due to supranatural causes but to natural mechanisms accessible to scientific (biological) explanations.

2. From the fact of (human) evolution it inevitably follows that (human) mental capacities, our cognitive and knowledge capacities, result from evolutionary processes. The central problem of evolutionary epistemology is the reconstruction of the origins and evolution of these capacities.

3. The problem of the mechanisms of evolution should be separated from the fact of evolution. Any theory of evolution includes statements concerning the mechanisms or motors of evolution. Prominent among the theories of (organic) evolution has been Darwin's theory of natural selection, including an adaptationist view that is now inherent in the synthetic theory.

4. Appreciating intraorganismic factors—that is, intraorganismic constraints to evolution (internal selection)—we seek a systems theory of evolution that is based on Darwin's view (and the view of synthetic theory) but that, at the same time, goes beyond Darwinian claims. Such a theory would provide a comprehensive framework to an up-to-date evolutionary epistemology.

5. Cultural evolution (including the evolution of ideas and scientific theories) cannot be reduced to organic evolution, although it is based on organic structures (brain). The study of human evolution, that is, the study of the evolution of humankind as a biological species, can clarify the preconditions of cultural evolution but cannot explain the particular paths of culture. However, explaining culture requires a biological (evolutionary) background.

2

The Historical Background

And what in fluctuating appearance hovers, Ye
shall fix by lasting thoughts.

Johann Wolfgang von Goethe

As far as I know, the term *evolutionary epistemology* was
coined by Donald T. Campbell (although Campbell himself, as he
told me, is not sure about it). Campbell (1959) reflected upon
"biology and psychology of knowledge" and thus attained an evolutionary view of (human) knowledge processes. Thirteen years
later Popper (1972a) used the phrase *evolutionary epistemology*
with particular reference to Campbell's approach. The central
claims of evolutionary epistemology are rather old, however; they
are almost as old as the idea of (organic) evolution itself. As soon
as it was recognized that species are not immutable and that
humans, too, result from evolutionary processes, some naturalists and philosophers started to speculate on the evolutionary
origin of (human) knowledge. The framework for such speculations in the nineteenth century was a comprehensive "evolutionary cosmology" and a general "philosophy of evolution" (Oeser
1984, 1987). Hence, the very idea of evolutionary epistemology
has a venerable tradition, including philosophers as well as naturalists (see Campbell 1974a; Wuketits 1983a, 1983b, 1984a,
1987f). In this chapter I survey the tradition, starting with Herbert Spencer's philosophical system.

Spencer's Development Hypothesis

Herbert Spencer, one of the pre-Darwinian evolutionists, can be regarded as an eminent forerunner of evolutionary epistemology. He was one of the most discussed philosophers in Victorian England. His magnum opus, *The Synthetic Philosophy*, an impressive work of many volumes, is an attempt to establish a universal world picture on a scientific basis. Philosophy in his perspective is a synthesis of the fundamental principles of the sciences and thus a kind of *summa scientiae* to replace the thought systems of theologians. Spencer advocated the idea of progress in evolution and drew links between organic evolution and the development of society and culture (so that he has been considered an advocate of Social Darwinism). In defending the notion of evolutionary progress, he relies on a Lamarckian view; that is, the idea of the inheritance of acquired characteristics. But on the other side, he had discovered natural selection independent of and before Darwin and coined the phrase "survival of the fittest." Darwin, however, did not greatly appreciate Spencer's style of thinking—nor did he appreciate the man. In his *Autobiography* (1969, p. 109), Darwin says: "I am not conscious of having profited in my own work by Spencer's writings." But Darwin did not fail to see Spencer's important contributions to an evolutionary foundation of psychology. In *On the Origin of Species*, he announced: "Psychology will be securely based on the foundation already well laid by Mr. Herbert Spencer, that of the necessary acquirement of each mental power and capacity by gradation" (Darwin [1859] 1958, p. 449). So, let us see what Spencer really contributed to the formation of the idea of evolutionary epistemology.

Spencer believed in a universal evolution and extended his *development hypothesis* to the sphere of human social and mental structures. The development hypothesis expresses the idea that nature progresses toward complexity and heterogeneity arises from homogeneity. Spencer argued that the development of science can be explained by the same principle: science evolves from simple and concrete to more complex and abstract structures. In *Principles of Psychology*, he wrote:

> The law of the scales was known before the general law of the lever was known; the law of the lever was known before the laws of composition and resolution of forces were known; and these were known before the laws of motion under their universal forms were known. From the ancient doctrine that the curve in which the sun, the moon, and each of the planets, moves, is a

circle (a perfectly simple and constant figure); to the doctrine
. . . that each member of the planetary system describes an
ellipse (a much less simple and constant figure); and afterwards
to the doctrine . . . that the curve described by every heavenly
body is some conic section (a still less simple and constant
figure); the advance in generality, in complexity, in abstractness
is manifest. (Spencer 1870, vol. 1, pp. 461–462)

In these sentences Spencer shows that he is an advocate of the
idea of progress, a rather popular idea among philosophers in the
eighteenth and nineteenth century. Remember that Auguste
Comte, French philosopher, sociologists, and the founder of
positivism, already had established a "law of three stages",
according to which human thinking once started with theologi-
cal and metaphysical doctrines and went on to scientific
("positive") explanations of the world.

Moreover, in Spencer's work, a universal evolutionism can be
seen that explains phenomena like scientific knowledge in terms
of organic evolution. Hence, Spencer already pursued both
programs of evolutionary epistemology mentioned on p. 5: not
only was he convinced that human mental phenomena, cognition and thinking, evolved along with other aspects of life, but he
also looked at the development of culture, including science, from
an evolutionary point of view. In a way, he anticipated some
important aspects of today's evolutionary explanations of cognitive mechanisms in living systems. What can be criticized,
however, is his blatant adaptationism. Campbell (1974a, p. 437)
says: "Believing that an infinitely refinable and sensitive human
cognitive apparatus had in the course of evolution adapted
perfectly to the external evolution, he became a naive realist."
Spencer's view of the evolution of scientific knowledge has been
criticized as well. Certainly, Spencer was right in stating that the
history of scientific ideas is an evolutionary process; but he was
wrong in pretending that this process can be inferred from the
nature of organic evolution (Ruse 1986). Or, as Oeser (1984, p.
151) puts it: "Spencer, who regarded the evolution of science,
within the framework of his general development hypothesis, as
a direct sequel of biological evolution, failed to observe differences." The point is that the development of science, as we shall see
in chapter 7, is a process much faster and more complex than
organic evolution.

Nevertheless, Spencer's work is a cornerstone in the history
of evolutionary thinking and a decisive step toward an evolution-

ary theory of knowledge. In his *Principles of Psychology* he laid the foundation for an evolutionary view of psychic phenomena and, thus, influenced many speculations in psychology in the late nineteenth century. I should say that Spencer's work, notwithstanding its fallacies, includes the first comprehensively formulated version of evolutionary epistemology.

Darwin's Evolutionary Psychology

What is true of Spencer, is true of Darwin: he advocated an evolutionary psychology that, some way or other, anticipated the fundamentals of modern evolutionary epistemology. More than this, like Spencer, Darwin already championed an evolutionary epistemology without using the term. Darwin's evolutionist view of psychology is an original contribution to an important field of scientific research. Unlike Spencer, Darwin did empirical work in science, so that his (evolutionary) psychology to a larger extent is founded on empirical evidences. Unfortunately, it is not common knowledge that Darwin devoted a considerable part of his efforts to the study of animal and human behavior and that he is to be regarded as a forerunner of modern ethology. Ghiselin (1969, p. 187) wryly remarked: "Indeed, because the underlying frame of reference has been overlooked, Darwin's work on behavior has been interpreted as little more than miscellaneous observations—the casual study of a Sunday naturalist seeking relaxation from the strains of theoretical controversy."Of course, it is not true that Darwin was a "Sunday naturalist"; rather he was a full-blooded scientist trying to solve the problems of nature, using a mass of empirical evidence to substantiate his theoretical work.

There is continuity in Darwin's writings. His studies on behavior led to an evolutionary neurobiology and psychology that do not lack scientific rigor: "One may trace out the systematic development of a comprehensive system of neurophysiological theory, from its roots in the hypotheses of *The Origin of Species*, to its application as a fundamental component in the arguments of *The Descent of Man*. Without an understanding of this particular continuity, Darwin's later writings are largely unintelligible" (Ghiselin, 1969, p. 187). Most important among Darwin's later writings is *The Expression of the Emotions in Man and Animals*, published in 1872, ten years before his death. This book clearly shows Darwin's view of an evolutionary psychology—and an evolutionary epistemology. (By the way, in this book Darwin used photographs as illustrations, for the first time.)

In the introduction to this book Darwin explains the main routes of his argument for the evolutionary view of behavior:

> With mankind some expressions, such as the bristling of the hair under the influence of extreme terror, or the uncovering of the teeth under that of furious rage, can hardly be understood, except on the belief that man once existed in a much lower and animal-like condition. The community of certain expressions in distinct though allied species, as in the movements of the same facial muscles during laughter by man and by various monkeys, is rendered somewhat more intelligible, if we believe in their descent from a common progenitor. He who admits on general grounds that the structure and habits of all animals have been gradually evolved, will look at the whole subject of Expression in a new and interesting light. (Darwin [1872] 1965, p. 13)

As can be seen, Darwin knew that animal and human behavior can be properly understood only within the framework of evolution. This was the insight that paved the way to the foundation of modern ethology (Lorenz 1965, 1971; Tinbergen 1951). No wonder that, then, one of the roots of modern evolutionary epistemology can be found in the study of behavior. (I return to this fact later in the chapter.)

The argument that becomes visible in Darwin's work runs as follows: animal and human behavior depends on an evolutionary basis—human psychic and mental capacities and their expression are part of behavior—hence these capacities, too, are subject to evolutionary studies. Moreover, much of our behavior is conducted, so to speak, by archaic principles that developed millions of years ago. Therefore, our behavior, at least as to some traits, reflects its own evolutionary history. Who wonders that our experiencing and "knowing" the world is influenced by age-old mechanisms? Whoever takes Darwin seriously will be prepared to see that we humans exhibit ineradicable characters of our phylogenetic ancestors and that our "low ancestry" is documented not only by our anatomy but also by our behavior (Darwin 1871).

What Darwin told us concerning our own species has been apt to stimulate new approaches in different fields. Researchers working in physical anthropology indeed have grasped his ideas quickly. Psychologists, except for a few pioneers, long have ignored his important insights. Only recently have serious arguments for an evolutionary-founded psychology been developed (Bunge 1980; Bunge and Ardila 1987; Medicus 1985, 1987), and a synthesis of evolutionary thinking and psychology become possible. Such a synthesis is necessary to eliminate one-sided views in psychology. In any case, evolutionary psychology will be an integral part of evolutionary epistemology. And Darwin's ideas are still of greatest importance.

Other Predecessors

Spencer and, particularly, Darwin have strongly influenced the work of many naturalists and philosophers in the late nineteenth and in the early twentieth centuries. Some basic ideas of evolutionary epistemology thus can be found in the writings of many scholars.

Among biologists Thomas H. Huxley took up Darwin's ideas enthusiastically and defended the view according to which human intellectual capacities depend on organic structures and their evolution. He argued "that all functions, intellectual, moral, and others, are the expression or the result, in the long run, of structures, and of the molecular forces which they exert" (Huxley [1863] 1968, p. 141). Likewise Ernst Haeckel, the indefatigable popularizer of Darwin's ideas in Germany, clearly expressed the phylogenetic relativity of human mental capacities and interpreted human cognitive abilities by the means of the theory of natural selection (see Haeckel 1899, 1905). Haeckel, therefore, was a forerunner of a more recent version of evolutionary epistemology. However, his "biological philosophy," his "monism," on the whole, was a rather one-sided view, somewhat naive, and lacked rigor with regard to philosophical argument. Other biologists, for example George J. Romanes, were more explicit on the evolution of mental powers in animals and tried to substantiate the evolutionary view of psychology by showing that all mental capacities in humans developed by gradation, having their roots in the animal kingdom (see Romanes 1883). Similar ideas can be found in Drummond (1897), who, however, tried to link evolution with Christian belief. Also, some authors ventured to reconstruct the prehistory of humankind, particularly prehistoric religion and moral systems. Among these authors was Otto

Caspari, a German polyhistorian, who attempted to give evidence for natural causes of metaphysical and religious belief (see Caspari 1877). All these researchers anticipated at least some of the ideas of modern evolutionary epistemology and also some of its philosophical consequences.

Darwinism had a great impact on philosophy, too. This is a well-known fact. However, it may come as a surprise to some readers that a philosopher like Friedrich Nietzsche, better known for his nihilism, can be regarded as a predecessor of a biological theory of knowledge. As Smith (1987) amply demonstrates, Nietzsche's philosophical thought is of interest to those concerned with the development of evolutionary epistemology. "Although . . . his understanding of Darwinism was defective, his metaphysics can nevertheless be seen as consistent with and complementary to Darwin's biology" (Smith 1987, p. 88).

Other philosophers in the nineteenth century explicitly stated a relationship between Darwin's theory of natural selection and epistemology. Therefore Georg Simmel assumed that human knowledge has its origins in practical needs; that is, needs for preserving life. He argued that truth and usefulness are to be interpreted historically, along the lines of a natural selection epistemology.

> We, being also things in space, so to speak, learn very fast from the way other things react to our own actions to restrain any such "ease" of thought as soon as we act upon it. If inherent usefulness and purely psychic laws are the only real factors in the formation of thought, its end result must be at least to imagine and produce an objective reflection of reality. Since true thought could be the only basis for life-promotion action, the truth of an idea should be cultivated somewhat as muscle strength is. (Simmel [1895] 1982, p. 64)

Simmel anticipated an idea that, some decades later, was explained by Jakob von Uexküll and that has been vital to the development of evolutionary epistemology. This is the idea that the "worlds of animals" differ from each other, according to the different sense organs and to the different aspects of the world to which the animals are adapted. Uexküll (1928) stated that any organism shows its own "ambient," that what we can call the "world picture" differs from one species to another. Similar ideas can be found in Bergson (1907). (I return to these problems i·

Chapter 4.) It should be noted, however, that Bergson and Uexküll partly rejected Darwin's theory and continued the vitalist tradition. Also, it was Spencer's view of evolution toward cognitive perfection against which Bergson rebelled (Campbell 1974a). On the other side, Spencer had influenced thinkers like Ernst Mach.

Mach, a physicist and philosopher, tried to establish a physiological basis of psychic phenomena and stands in the tradition of evolutionary psychologists, which becomes apparent in *Analyse der Empfindungen* (first published in 1886).[1] In this work he relied heavily on Darwin, but the limitation of his evolutionary epistemology follows from his tendency to accept Spencer's idea of the completeness of cognitive evolution (Campbell 1974a). Nevertheless, his work as a whole contains much of a modern approach to evolutionary epistemology. The same is true to another physicist and philosopher, Ludwig Boltzmann, who was the successor to Mach at the University of Vienna and who, like Mach, defended an evolutionary interpretation of the history of science (Flamm 1987). (By the way, Mach's chair at the University of Vienna was the first chair of philosophy of science in a German-speaking country.)[2]

The idea that the development of scientific knowledge can be described in terms of evolution, by analogy to organic evolution, can be found in a couple of works in the nineteenth century. As already mentioned, Spencer was most explicit on this. One of the first to deal with this problem was William Whewell, who in *On the Philosophy of Discovery* (1860) argued that there are powers and faculties that seem fitted to endure. He also wrote: "The mind is capable of accepting and appropriating, through the action of its own Ideas, every step in science which has ever been made—every step which shall hereafter be made. . . . Can we suppose that the wonderful powers which carry man on, generation by generation, from the contemplation of one great and striking truth to another, are buried with each generation?" (Whewell [1860] 1972, p. 396). It is remarkable that Whewell's work contains a historical relativism of the Kantian a priori and, regarding the nature of hypotheses, an explanation similar to that of Popper (discussed later). Therefore, Whewell, in a sense, was an advocate of a trial-and-error model or a selective elimination model of scientific research. Other early advocates of such a model were Alexander Bain, Stanley Jevons, and Henri Poincaré (for details see Campbell 1974a). Obviously, philosophers and philosophers of science were attracted by the application of evolutionary theory to science itself.

Kant's Doctrine of the A Priori in a Biological Perspective

Konrad Lorenz, in his seminal essay (first published in 1941), wrote that the Kantian categories and forms of intuition have to be understood (or interpreted) in terms of evolution and adaptation and that they are for us "inherited working hypotheses." The truth-content of these hypotheses, thus Lorenz argued, "is related to the absolutely existent in the same manner as that of ordinary working hypotheses which have proven themselves just as splendidly adequate in coping with the external world" (Lorenz [1941] 1982, p. 133). Moreover,

> This conception . . . destroys our faith in the absolute truth of any a priori thesis necessary for thought. On the other hand it gives the conviction that something actual "adequately corresponds" to every phenomenon in our world. Even the smallest detail of the world of phenomena "mirrored" for us by the innate working hypotheses of our forms of intuition and thought is in fact pre-formed to the phenomenon it reproduces, having a relationship corresponding to the one existing between organic structures and the external world in general. ([1941] 1982, p. 133)

Expressed here is an attempt to interpret Kant's doctrine of the a priori from a biological (evolutionary) point of view: From this point of view any a priori is an a posteriori of evolution. This indeed has been one of the central theses of evolutionary epistemology.

In the introduction to his *Critique of Pure Reason* (1781) Kant firmly stated that the human intellect is in possession of cognitions a priori. He said:

> We might easily shew that such principles are the indispensable basis of the possibility of experiencing itself, and consequently prove their existence *a priori*. For whence could our experience itself acquire certainty, if all the rules on which it depends were themselves empirical, and consequently fortuitous? No one, therefore, can admit the validity of the use of such rules as first principles. But . . . we may content ourselves with having

established the fact, that we do possess and exercise a faculty of pure *a priori* cognition; and, secondly, with having pointed out the proper tests of such cognition, namely, universality and necessity. (Kant [1781] 1901, pp. 3–4)

Kant has been a leading figure in German philosophy, and his epistemology has been said to be the last word. From the evolutionary point of view, however, it is *not* the last word. Lorenz put the challenging question: "Is not human reason with all its categories and forms of intuition something that has organically evolved in a continuous cause-effect relationship with the laws of the immediate nature, just as has the human brain?" (Lorenz [1941] 1982, p. 122). The answer to this question, according to Lorenz and other evolutionists, is that human reason—and with it the a priori—indeed has evolved, so that the Kantian approach must be revised. The result of this revision is the "dynamization" of the a priori and of the whole corpus of Kantian epistemology.

We must be aware of the fact that some authors before Lorenz argued along these lines. Soon after the publication of Darwin's *On the Origin of Species* some biologists, at least those who were concerned with philosophical questions, too, attempted to give an evolutionary interpretation of the a priori (see, e.g., Wuketits 1987g). Again, Ernst Haeckel is to be mentioned. And it will not come as a surprise that Herbert Spencer already regarded Kant's categories and forms of intuition as products of evolution. Furthermore, for example, a book by Paul Flaskämper, published in 1913, has a chapter entitled "Biological Epistemology" and shows the author's attitude toward biological conceptions of knowledge transgressing the boundaries of Kantian philosophy.

Lorenz's essay, however, is the richer exposition of the subject. As far as I can judge it, Lorenz formulated his insight independent of the older conceptions, even though, teaching in Königsberg (Kant's province), he could (or should) have noticed the neo-Kantian tradition (Danailow and Tögel 1988). Early in his life he was concerned with problems of perception and, as he told in a symposium lecture (Lorenz 1987), believed that any phenomenon to be perceived is but a picture—however, a picture of something *real*. Thus, he has been a realist; not a naive realist, but a "hypothetical realist." As we shall see in Chapter 4, hypothetical realism is the realism that follows from the evolutionary approach to epistemology. Lorenz anticipated this conception in the 1940s and was able to consolidate it in later works.

What can be seen in Lorenz's works, furthermore, is the emphasis on the notion of the *innate*. He dismissed the doctrine of the tabula rasa, which was the core of the empiricist view and behaviorism, and replaced it by the thesis that no organism is initially a clean slate but is equipped with inborn dispositions that are the outcomes of evolution by natural selection. This thesis rests on a huge body of observations in ethology.

Another point to be mentioned is that Lorenz has taken an adaptationist view. He said that our central nervous apparatus is adapted to the real world "just as the hoof of the horse is adapted to the ground of the steppe which it copes with" (Lorenz [1941] 1982, p. 124). This adaptationist view up to now has been inherent in many conceptions of evolutionary epistemology and will be criticized in Chapter 4. It is true, however, that Lorenz's work, as a whole, was the first comprehensive exposition of the natural history of cognition in the twentieth century, and it revived old ideas on the basis of new approaches coming mainly for ethological research. Lorenz, particularly through his *Behind the Mirror* (1977), contributed much to the increasing interest in evolutionary epistemology.

Natural history or biology of cognition-knowledge has been one of the two mainstreams in evolutionary epistemology. The other mainstream comes from scientific methodology and philosophy of science and led to an evolutionary modeling of the development of scientific ideas. This modeling of science has been strongly influenced by the philosophy of Karl Popper.

Popper's Evolutionary View

Despite some older conceptions (Mach, Spencer, Whewell, and others), through Popper's work evolutionary epistemology became a metatheory of science (see p. 5). The most fundamental assertion in Popper's work is that science is a historical, evolutionary phenomenon (Radnitzky 1982). Therefore, the growth of scientific knowledge should be explained by analogy to organic evolution, particularly to evolution by natural selection: "The growth of our knowledge is the result of a process closely resembling what Darwin called 'natural selection'; that is, *the natural selection of hypotheses*: our knowledge consists, at every moment, of those hypotheses which have shown their (comparative) fitness by surviving so far in their struggle for existence; a competitive struggle which eliminates those hypotheses which are unfit" (Popper 1972a, p. 261). Popper, clearly, has advocated a "natural-selection epistemology": a "selective elimination model" of the development of (scientific) ideas. And he has been responsible for the view well known under the term *critical rationalism*.

Unlike Lorenz, Popper approached evolutionary epistemology as a philosopher of science and a historian of ideas; biology was not his primary concern. William W. Bartley, one of his former apostles, tells us that Popper's public discussion of biological problems is comparatively recent: that it started on November 15, 1960, when in his seminar at the London School of Economics Popper read a paper of his own that explicitly spoke of biology (Bartley 1976). On the other side, as Popper himself remembers in his *Autobiography* (1976, p. 167), he has "always been extremely interested in the theory of evolution, and very ready to accept evolution as a fact". However that might be, Popper early adopted a trial-and-error view of scientific theories and ideas in general. For him, science and philosophy consist mainly of *problems*: they start with problems to which we offer tentative solutions (theories) that are then criticized, "in an attempt at *error elimination* . . .; and . . . this process renews itself: the theory and its critical revision give rise to new *problems*" (Popper 1976, p. 133). He was concerned with these ideas by the 1930s and gave them a powerful expression in *The Logic of Scientific Discovery* (1959).

Popper's message has been that knowledge can never be absolute or perfect: all our knowledge is conjectural and a scientific theory must be formulated in a version that makes the theory *falsifiable*. Hence the growth of scientific knowledge is a cycle of conjectures and refutations (Popper 1972b). Thus, this process indeed is similar to the processes of organic evolution by natural selection. However, Popper has noted the intrinsic differences between organic evolution and the evolution of ideas, which he vividly illustrates by the following figure: "The difference between the amoeba and Einstein is that, although both make use of the method of trial and error elimination, the amoeba dislikes to err while Einstein is intrigued by it: he consciously searches for his errors in the hope of learning by the discovery and elimination. The method of science is the critical method" (Popper 1972a, p. 70). The point here is that errors in organic evolution can kill the respective organism, whereas a false theory—fortunately!—does not kill the scientist, who is able to learn from errors and correct them. In other words, falsification in organic evolution can be a case of death and extinction, but it does best service to the development of science.

From the viewpoint of Popper's thought the process of "knowing" can never start with nothing, so that he, like Lorenz, rejects the tabula rasa theory. He sententiously writes:

> The *tabula rasa* theory is absurd: at every stage of the evolution of life and of the development of an organism, we have to assume the existence of some knowledge in the form of dispositions and expectations. Accordingly, *the growth of all knowledge consists in the modification of previous knowledge—* either its alteration or its large-scale rejection. Knowledge never begins from nothing, but always from some background knowledge. (1972a, p. 71)

One final remark should be made here, although, on the one hand, Popper's evolutionary epistemology obviously rests on Darwin's theory; on the other hand, it contains a rather critical view of Darwinism. In particular, Popper has criticized Darwin's theory as an overall explanation of the mechanisms of evolution. Also, he has criticized the adaptationist view that has predominated in evolutionary thinking since Lamarck and that can be found in the work of both Spencer and Darwin (remember Chapter 1, p. 17). In his most recent writings on evolution and evolutionary epistemology, Popper (1984, 1987) pleads for a model of "active evolution," arguing that organisms are not just passive beings adapted to—and molded by—their environments (also see the critical comment on Popper's view by Perutz 1986). Thus, he has come close to a nonadaptationist version of evolutionary epistemology (see Chapter 4).

Epistemology Naturalized

The approaches sketched so far have but one argument in common: that cognitive abilities in animals and humans are results of organic evolution and, consequently, all human knowledge capacities are products of *natural* processes. Thus, epistemology as the study of these capacities becomes naturalized. A naturalized epistemology (Kornblith 1985; Quine 1971) is at variance with all epistemological systems that start with a priori ingredients of knowledge, abstract and immutable essences or ideas, and similar proposals. Those defending a naturalized epistemology undertake epistemological inquires by assuming that psychology and the natural sciences give us approximately valid knowledge of the world and that they can tell us something about humans, the knowing subjects (Campbell 1987b).

In *Treatise of Human Nature,* David Hume, the eminent representative of empiricism in eighteenth century, ventured to say: "It is certain, that the mind, in its perceptions, must begin somewhere; and that since the impressions precede their correspondent ideas, there must be some impressions, which without any introduction make their appearance in the soul . . . these depend upon natural and physical causes" ([1739] 1972, p. 37). I do not want to take Hume's philosophy in the tradition of evolutionary epistemologists or regard Hume as a precursor of evolutionary epistemology. However, if you remember that Hume argued that our causal thinking stems from *the way we are*—and not from divine principles (which might be, then, a priori in a particular sense)—you will become aware of his commitment to a kind of naturalistic epistemology. Therefore, Ruse (1986) is right that "Darwinian epistemology" grew from (British) empiricism. The advance of the Darwinian and the evolutionist in a general sense is in giving an evolutionary explanation to our causal thinking. Thus, we can complete Hume's argument, the "natural and physical causes" of the "impressions in our soul" are evolutionary principles.

Hence, the attempt to naturalize epistemology is rather old. Evolutionary epistemology is a more recent version of naturalized epistemology. It has become possible only on the basis of a comprehensive evolutionary view that regards humans, the knowers, as a product of long-term (evolutionary) processes. On the other side, a naturalized epistemology no longer is possible without appreciating the evolutionary view. This also would mean that evolutionary epistemology today is not only a type of naturalized epistemology, but that the latter inevitably follows from the former.

The evolutionists of the nineteenth century (Darwin, Haeckel,

Huxley, Spencer, and all the others) took a decisive step toward a "dynamization of knowledge," so to speak, for they regarded cognitive phenomena as *evolving* phenomena—and not as static, immutable principles. Knowledge, then, is to be defined as a *process* and, as a matter of course, as a "life preserving function." Ernst Mach explicitly states that the external world is represented in the sensations of the internal world—and that this representation is of certain survival value. (For a more profound analysis of Mach's statement see Leinfellner 1988.) Here again we see that Mach was a forerunner of modern approaches to evolutionary epistemology. But Mach was aware of Hume as a predecessor of his own view. Unlike Hume, however, he could refer to the evolutionary background. Therefore, his conclusions that gaining cognition helps preserve life is influenced mainly by Darwin's theory. Most recently, evolutionary epistemologists indeed have argued that cognition increases an organism's fitness. I shall return to this argument in the next chapter. What can be said now is that cognition, also in its most sophisticated forms in humans, cannot be separated from the set of "life functions." This was clear to the evolutionists in the nineteenth century and is clear to all who take an evolutionary view, whether or not concerned with particular epistemological questions. Some contemporary philosophers have realized this and claimed the naturalization of knowledge. The argument expounded, for example, by Lelas (1983) runs: the renunciation of ideal or divine knowledge implies that cognition is a natural phenomenon, from this follows a link between cognition and life. And, because life is an evolutionary phenomenon, cognition, too, is to be regarded as a product of evolution. However, some other philosophers (e.g., Löw 1984) still argue along "traditional lines." They try to rescue cognitive phenomena from biology and save a nonevolutionist, or even an antievolutionist, tradition; that is, they fall back into preevolutionary thinking. When doing so they obviously do not worry about the underdevelopment of epistemology. This, I should say, is an anomaly.

Every epistemologist interested in making progress in this discipline should focus on the possible links between the classical epistemological questions and the results of the sciences. In particular, it is important to grasp the results of physiology and neurobiology. Furthermore, our present knowledge about human evolution, and evolution in general, is to be noted. Finally, important aspects come from studying the development of cognitive phenomena in the individual; that is, from developmental psychology. This last demand brings us close to the work of Jean Piaget, who was concerned with the development of cognitive capacities in children and endeavored to reconstruct the "mental ontogenesis" in humans. Between 1920 and 1970 Piaget studied the development of conceptual thought, perception, representation of the external world, language, moral judgements, and so on. This search for an understanding the "mental world" and its development as a dynamically organized process found its expression in a *psychontogenetic* conception known under the term *genetic epistemology* (Piaget 1970, 1971).

Piaget clearly demonstrated the links among (developmental) psychology, genetics, and epistemology. His conception is the pendant to the evolutionary approach to knowledge. Note the following relations:

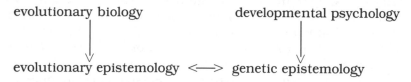

evolutionary biology   developmental psychology

evolutionary epistemology <—> genetic epistemology

In Piaget's work we can find another approach to naturalized epistemology. It is a science-oriented approach to solving epistemological questions and at the same time a plea for intensifying interdisciplinary studies. Piaget wrote: "The facts that have been ascertained, taken together, show that interdisciplinary collaboration is possible in the sphere of the epistemology of the human subject in general, and that this epistemology of natural thought links up with the great problems of the epistemology of scientific knowledge." (1973b, p. 65).

There has been resistance against genetic epistemology and generally against the alliance between psychology and epistemology. This has to do with many philosophers' claims to establish a rationally founded epistemology. Amundson (1983, p. 342), for one, says: "The goal of a *rationally* (and not just empirically) justified epistemology is not in principle beyond our reach." This might be true, but such an epistemology would stand apart from recognizing the status of humans as biological species, and such an epistemology would be obsolete. With regard to the links between psychology and epistemology, I should say that the latter can indeed profit from the former. Psychology assists *genetic* epistemology in the way that history of science assists philosophy of science (Kitchener 1987). More generally, psychology can assist epistemology in the same way. Genetic epistemology and evolutionary epistemology, taken together, furnish the underpinnings of an epistemology concentrating on *rational* knowledge. I have noticed—and I shall explain this in chapters 5–7—that (human) rational knowledge (including scientific thought) is not just biologically constrained. However, we need an explanation of the emergence of this type of knowledge; and such an explanation can be given on the basis of empirical studies in disciplines like biology and psychology.

In conclusion, I want to point once more to the possibility of making progress in epistemology by applying the tools of empirical sciences. We should take this opportunity. In particular, biology offers the most convincing evidence that we humans stem from the animal kingdom and result from natural processes. Therefore, knowledge—rational knowledge—cannot simply start by itself, but rather is generated by mechanisms older than any rational operation. This insight can no longer be ignored. Epistemologists before Darwin cannot be held responsible for their nonevolutionist view—today's epistemologists can.

Let me sum up. The historical overview given makes clear that the idea now called *evolutionary epistemology* has predecessors in the nineteenth century and is almost as old as evolutionary thinking itself. Although, until recently, there was no elaborated evolutionary epistemology, we can trace back the basic concepts and ambitions of this epistemology to the works of evolutionists in the nineteenth century.

1. Spencer argued that nature progresses toward increasing complexity (development hypotheses) and extended his arguments to the development of knowledge, including scientific knowledge.

2. Darwin gave strong empirical support to the view according to which all cognitive phenomena have developed by gradation (evolutionary psychology).

3. In the late nineteenth century, many naturalists and philosophers adopted the evolutionary approach to an understanding of knowledge, among them Ludwig Boltzmann, Ernst Haeckel, Thomas H. Huxley, and Ernst Mach.

4. In the twentieth century, Konrad Lorenz explicitly

formulated the idea that the Kantian a priori is to be regarded as an "evolutionary a posteriori" and added an ethological underpinning to evolutionary epistemology. At the same time, Karl Popper developed an evolutionary interpretation of the growth of scientific knowledge.

5. All this amounts to a naturalized epistemology, which David Hume already had in mind, but is now stronger, supported by results from different scientific disciplines, particularly biology and (developmental) psychology (Piaget).

3

Evolution as a Cognition Process

> The gaining of new information inexorably demands the breaking down of some previous knowledge which, up to that moment, had appeared to be final.
>
> Konrad Lorenz

One of the central claims of evolutionary epistemology is this: not only has evolution produced cognitive phenomena, but evolution itself can be described as a cognition process or, more precisely, a cognition-gaining process (Campbell 1974a; Lorenz 1977; Oeser 1987; Plotkin 1982; Riedl 1984a, 1987c; Tennant 1983b; Vollmer 1985; Wuketits 1984a, 1984c, 1986a, 1986b). In what way is evolution actually a cognition or cognition-gaining process? What does *cognition* mean in this context? In this chapter I examine these questions and give some biological explanations.

Organisms as Information-Processing Systems

Let us begin with a somewhat trivial observation. Organisms, particularly animals, accumulate information about their environments or, at least, about certain properties of their environment: they see, hear, and smell "something" and thus become informed about their surroundings. Hence, living systems generally may be characterized as information systems or information-processing systems. This is true even of plants that are able to react to many changes in the chemical nature of their environments, to changes in temperature and in light intensity. A plant's specific reaction to certain environmental influences lets us assume that the plant has gained some information about these influences. In particular, however, information-gaining and information-processing takes place in animals, which are to be regarded as information systems in a narrower sense. The following principles can be stated:

1. Animals are equipped with *perceptors;* that is, sense organs or, as it is the case at the level of unicellular living beings like the amoeba, special organelles. Further, in most animal phyla, a nervous system has been developed.

2. In their totality these organs constitute an animal's *perceiving apparatus.* This apparatus accumulates information about the animal's specific environment and functions in a way analogous to a calculation machine.

In a word, an animal's perceiving apparatus "models" certain structures of reality. Informationprocessing in animals, then, means the construction of models of particular aspects of the world.

Why not label these information-processing activities in animals *cognition?* To be sure, an animal does not *consciously* perceive its surroundings; it does not critically reflect upon reality or certain parts of it. On the other hand, any animal's information gaining is a process closely resembling what is called *knowledge.* Philosophical misunderstandings are due to the fact that evolutionary epistemologists are speaking of cognition and knowledge in a broader sense. (By the way, I do not make a distinction between the terms *cognition* and *knowledge.*) Of course, cognition in animals is not to be confused with (human) *rational* knowledge to which usually the philosopher's concept of knowledge applies. To make things clearer, let me say that, as I trust, no advocate of evolutionary epistemology would deny the peculiarity of (human) rational knowledge. What evolutionary epistemologists have in mind when they are speaking of cognition or knowledge is information processing that, however, is a universal character of living beings. Perhaps, it indeed would be better to use the term evolutionary *information theory* instead of evolutionary *epistemology* (Engels 1985) to better characterize the intentions of evolutionary epistemologists, at least at the first of the two levels distinguished in Table 1. But, in whatever manner the phrase *evolutionary epistemology* has come into use, and it is quite convenient in a particular sense, it expresses the idea that there are epistemic (cognitive) activities in all animals, although these activities are not identical with rational knowledge, and that cognition—generally, as information process-ing—is a result of evolution.

Now, we should be aware of different types or levels of information and information processing in the living world. According to Oeser (1984, 1987) three levels of information processing can be distinguished:

1. The *genetic level* refers to the development (ontogenesis) of living systems. Genetic information can be transmitted from one generation to the next only by inheritance. It indeed has the character of a "signal," but it is not to be confused with any kind of cognitive structure.

2. The *preconscious cognition level* in animals requires an information-processing system like the nervous systems. At this level occurs information processing by showing a certain similarity to human rational cognition processes (without being identical with them). Here, the information system is to be distinguished from that of genetic information "by the fact that it enables the individual organism to acquire and store information about certain individual situations in its environment" (Oeser 1984, p. 160).

3. The *rational knowledge level* in humans comes con-scious action. At this level we encounter intellectual information, which represents a particular state of (human) consciousness and is stored in—and transmitted through—exosomatic struc-tures (like writing). The conscious act of information processing no longer is identical with the information coded as a signal in the neurodynamic system; it processes "pure information" whose material basis had been eliminated.

Hence, we can see a hierarchy of information processing and also a hierarchy of cognition processing in the living world (for similar reflections also see Plotkin and Odling-Smee 1982). Human rational knowledge is the most sophisticated type of information processing. Appreciating the organisms' capability of individual *learning*, which is not a characteristic of plants but of most animals, we can say that life also is an information-*increasing* process: An animal increases its information about the environment through particular experiences and thus information processing means an increase of cognition.

Cognition, Fitness, and Survival

There is an important evolutionary aspect of information processing in organisms. Information processing—cognition gaining—is vital for any living being. "Thus, cognition (knowledge) is useful in a strict biological (evolutionary) sense. To put it in Darwinian terms: cognition increases the fitness of an organism" (Wuketits 1986a, p. 193). Hence, cognition might be explained in terms of (Darwinian) fitness, and even the emergence of human (rational) knowledge might be linked with fitness and survival because, as we might suppose, it was of a certain survival value to our ancestors (Mohr 1977, 1983a, 1983b). However, at the moment I shall say nothing about rational knowledge and focus only on some general aspects.

First, recall the meaning of the term *fitness*. *Fitness* simply means selective or adaptive value. In Darwin's sense—and in the sense of the synthetic theory (p. 15)—it is a product of various advantages (Dobzhansky et al. 1977): the carriers of one genotype may be more fertile than the carriers of another, or more viable, or reach the reproductive age sooner. In each case the advantages may increase (Darwinian) fitness; a certain advantage, or a combination of advantages, may confer upon the carriers of a certain genotype a (Darwinian) fitness higher than that of another genotype.

Second, we now contend that cognition may increase (Darwinian) fitness, that is to say that the carriers of a particular genotype may increase their fitness if they are able to better calculate their environment than the carriers of another genotype. Take, for example, a young rabbit that has difficulty recognizing dogs. Such a rabbit will not reach the reproductive age (unless it never meets a dog). The same is true of a leopard that cannot recognize its prey: this leopard will starve to death. Further examples are needless. As a rule, any organism able to acquire knowledge about its surroundings will be fitter than an organism without this ability. The better an organism's calculation of its environment, the better are its chances of survival. Thus, cognition indeed increases the fitness of organisms. "We can therefore speak of a fitness function . . . of particular organisms bearing specific knowledge structures" (Lumsden and Wilson 1981, p. 255). From the biologist's point of view this might be trivial.

Third, if there is a link between perceptors (sense organs) and the environment, then this link, by increasing the organism's fitness, is of evolutionary advantage. A good example is an animal's eye (see Table 4). Several *fits* in the eye have advantages in a biological sense. Similarly, there are fits in other sense organs; for example, the ear. These organs, then, because of their particular structure increase the organism's fitness. In a nutshell, "no fit, no knowledge," and the "*fit* increases the *fitness* (it is useful, functional, expedient) of an organism" (Vollmer 1984, p. 72). This brings us to the problem of the correspon-

Table 4. Useful fits in the eye.

Facts and Fits	*Advantage (survival value)*
The sensitivity of the retina coincides both with the "optical window" of the earth's atmosphere and with the area where the radiation of the sun has its maximum of intensity.*	Normal objects reflect sunlight and thus can be seen, caught, or avoided.
Different wavelengths are interpreted as different colors.	Objects are recognized and distinguished more easily and reliably.
A superposition of all wavelengths is not interpreted as a colorful medley, but rather as colorless (white) light.	Normal daylight does not carry information; only deviations from the normal distribution are informative and worthy of perception.
The lower limit of sensitivity for a photoreceptor in the retina is one photon. But only simultaneous excitation of several adjacent cells yields a sensation of light in consciousness. The wiring of the optical nerves thus censors the incoming stimuli.	Spontaneous activity of the retinal cells, occasional misfiring, and statistical fluctuations of the flow of photons ("noise") are devoid of information and are eliminated by the censorship.

Source: After Vollmer 1984

* Besides, as Campbell (personal communication) explains, the visual spectrum is such as to make transparency coincide with locomotor penetrability; the advantagae of this is that it enables vision to substitute for locomotor exploration.

dence between cognition and reality that will be discussed in the next chapter.

What I want to stress here is that information processing, cognition gaining, is an important biofunction and indeed can be regarded as a characteristic that increases the organisms' fitness in a Darwinian sense. Certainly, Darwin would agree to the formula "without cognition no survival."

The Evolution of Nervous Systems

Information processing in animals is most effectively managed by nervous systems. These systems enable multicellular animals to respond to changes in their external and internal environments. As already mentioned, plants also have the ability to obtain some information about certain aspects of their environment, but this ability has progressed little. In the animal kingdom, however, the ability to gather and process information has been advanced due to the "invention" of the nervous system that, then, was a decisive step in the evolution of life. "The nervous system constitutes a part of the body provided by heredity that is especially sensitive to environmental change" (Young 1958, p. 290). It enables the animal to respond to environmental changes in such a way that the organism can survive. Hence, the nervous system contributes much to an increase of fitness.

There are two types of nervous organization to be distinguished (see Figure 5):

1. *Nervous networks* appear in lower animals and consist of individual nerve cells and their connections. The mediation of environmental states and changes and the adequate behavior to these states and changes can be accomplished in the simplest manner by only two nerve cells, one for informational input, the other for instructional output.

2. *Nervous systems* in a narrower sense "are characterized by nerve cell aggregations . . . connected by current nerve cell processes and arranged in parallel strings along the longitudinal axis of the body" (Seitelberger 1984, p. 125). Moreover, these systems are distinguished by the presence of large nerve cell groups near the oral pole of an animal. The most advanced

 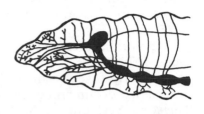

Figure 5. The two types of nervous organization in animals. Left: Nervous network of a hydra. Right: Nervous system of an earthworm (front part).

nervous system is the *central nervous system* (CNS) of vertebrates, which emerged some 400 million years ago.

Understandably, there is no fossil record of the evolution of nervous organization. However, the main lines of this evolution can be deduced from studies on recent animals, from comparative anatomy and physiology. At least, some general conclusions are possible:

> In the course of evolution the nervous processes have become increasingly complicated. Once a network of neurons for the conduction of excitation was developed . . ., the behaviour of animals could be controlled by an increasing number of reflexes. Later, the development of nerve-centres made possible the origin of complicated instincts with a genetic basis and the increasing utilization of associations and experience. The higher the animal in the animal kingdom, the more the fixed hereditary instincts are reduced in favour of actions guided by experience. (Rensch 1958, p. 181)

Generally, the evolution of animals and, particularly, the evolution of nervous organization exhibits three advances (phylogenetic trends) (Rensch 1958):

1. Increase in complexity.
2. Increase in rationalization and centralization of functions.
3. Increase in autonomy and plasticity of behavior.

The vertebrates' central nervous system deserves our special attention, because with this system the evolution of nervous organization has reached the highest level. Rationalization and centralization of functions, and autonomy and plasticity of behavior in vertebrates are due to the *brain* (see also Delbrück 1978, 1986).

The brain is to be regarded as a part of the CNS. Primitive types of brain occur in invertebrate animals, too; arthropods (particularly insects) are the most advanced group of invertebrates, as documented by their complex forms of behavior. However, "vertebrates are generally able to obtain and process much more complicated signals and to produce a much greater variety of responses than the arthropods" (Dobzhansky et al. 1977, p. 515). The vertebrates' brain exhibits an enormous number of nerve cells or neurons. Progress in the ability to gather and process information is correlated with the emergence of the *neopallium*, which first appeared in reptiles and has developed to the *cerebral cortex* in mammals.

The mammalian brain is the most progressive in the vertebrate lineage; within a span of about 150 million years it increased in relative size and in complexity. In Figure 6, brains of some recent mammals are shown to demonstrate the differences between the brains of more primitive mammals and those of the most progressive group, the primates including the human. Most characteristically, the *encephalization*, the shift of information processing from the periphery to the CNS resulting in the increase of brain size, has been an evolutionary trend in mammals (Jerison 1976; Seitelberger 1984). An important step of encephalization was the evolution of the visual system, which provided an interaction with the senses of hearing and smell in newly formed areas of the cortex.

The most general conclusion with respect to the evolution of nervous organization in animals is that, over many millions of years, more and more complex information-processing organs have been developed. In this sense, evolution generally has been an information-increasing process and, some way or other, a cognition process. From the sociobiologist's point of view, Barash (1979, p. 203) writes: "Evolution . . . is the result of innumarable experiences, accumulated through an almost unimaginable length of time." This will be examined in the next paragraphs of the present chapter.

What can be stated at once is that evolution has produced more and more complex organs that serve as information-

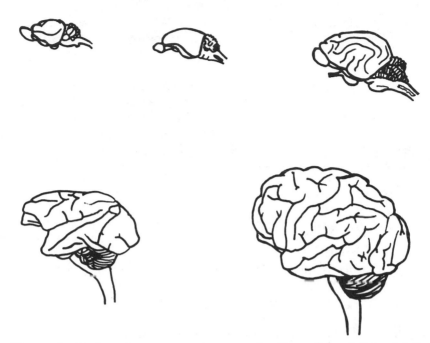

Figure 6. Brains of some recent mammals. Above (from left to right): Opossum, rabbit, cat. Below (left): Macaque. Below (right): Chimpanzee.

gathering and information-processing structures. Moreover, clearly animal behavior has developed together with the evolution of these structures. And, thus, evolutionary epistemologists argue, cognition is a particular function of these structures so that, as a rule, their increase in complexity has increased the animals' capability of cognition. The nervous organization has been the material basis of cognitive abilities; the evolution of these abilities actually is the evolution of nervous systems. For this reason an understanding of nervous structures and functions is of great significance to the evolutionary epistemologist. Cognitive phenomena cannot be separated from their material basis, just as one cannot separate walking from the locomotory apparatus. Likewise Rensch (1985, p. 170), although he does not explicitly advocate an evolutionary epistemology, argues that "psychic" phenomena in the widest sense "are explainable by the basic corresponding sense and brain processes, but not by purely psychic characteristics or processes." Similar arguments are inherent in the sociobiologists' program (see, e.g., Barash 1979; Lumsden and Wilson 1981). (On some connections and differences between sociobiology and evolutionary epistemology see chapter 6.)

In sum, the evolution of nervous organization has been a particular feature of animal evolution. Increasing complexity of nervous systems has made possible an everincreasing radius of action in animals. In a way, animals' horizons have been extended through the evolution of nervous systems. Therefore, these systems are to be regarded as vehicles, as it were, of the expansion of the animals' "view of the world."

The Ratiomorphic Apparatus

As mentioned earlier, no animal—except for the human—is able to consciously reflect upon itself and its surroundings. Information gathering and information processing in animals occur at a preconscious (prerational) level. True, some higher animals, particularly mammals, exhibit complex patterns of behavior such as insight learning and self-exploration that, some way or other, are similar to rational behavior. However, no animal reflects upon its own past and future; and no animal acts in a really teleological manner, anticipating the future and executing goal-intended behavior. This is not to say that humans, on the other side, always act consciously. Many of our actions are conducted by prerational mechanisms—a truism that has been stated for many centuries.

Like other animals, humans are not consciously aware of many activities of their body or of certain organs. Popper gives the following example:

> If I am standing quietly, without making any movement, then . . . my muscles are constantly at work, contracting and relaxing in an almost random fashion . . ., but controlled, without my being aware of it, by error-elimination . . . so that every little deviation from my posture is almost at once corrected. So I am kept standing, quietly, by more or less the same method by which an automatic pilot keeps an aircraft steadily on its course. (1972a, p. 245)

This example might illustrate Popper's assertion that every organism is always engaged in solving problems. The point is that the organism is not consciously aware of the problem or the method by which the problem is solved. Hence, something like a "logic of life" must be functioning in a way analogous to consciousness without being identical with it. The sum-total of these logiclike or reasonlike mechanisms is called the *ratiomorphic apparatus* (a term coined by the psychologist Egon Brunswik and now often used by evolutionary epistemologists). The ratiomorphic apparatus comprises all organs involved in information gathering and information processing (sense organs, nervous system). It functions for the sake of survival through information processing (cognition) and, as stated earlier, generally increases an organism's fitness.

Let me explain just two points that often cause misunderstanding. First, the use of the concepts consciousness and conscious, and ratiomorphic require some explanation. To be sure, the term *consciousness* (*conscious*) is used in an ambiguous manner. (For different definitions see, e.g., Löwenhard 1981.) I use the term *consciousness* to describe *self-awareness* including *teleological* (i.e., goal-intended) actions and the reflection upon these (and other) actions (which leads to moral judgements) (Wuketits 1985a). Insofar, I use consciousness synonymously with *self-consciousness*, which, according to Bunge and Ardila (1987), applies to individuals that are able to recall correctly some of the past situations and to imagine (even wrongly) their future. Thus, my concept of consciousness is restricted to humans and the capability of rational knowledge (see chapter 5). Animals, particularly mammals, exhibit complex behavioral activities including self-exploration, which might be considered a first step towards consciousness, but which is not identical with (self-)consciousness in its strict sense. Hence, the mass of behavioral capacities listed in Table 5 belongs to ratiomorphic capacities. The term *ratiomorphic* must not be confused with any concept denoting any kind of rational behavior. As stated earlier, this term applies to an animal's (or a human's) activities that are of certain survival value but do not require a consciousness. (I would like to use the term *instinct* to characterize these activities, but this term, unfortunately, has become somewhat blurred.) I hope that my explanations in the next chapter will shed more light on this matter.

My second point concerns differences in the ratiomorphic apparatus of animals. These differences are due to the variety of the "neuronal outfit" in animals. For example, an earthworm will

Table 5. Behavioral and intellectual capacities in animals and humans

Behavioral-Intellectual Capacity	Animals
Conditioned appetitive behavior	Mollusks, arthropods
Operant acquisition of conditioned responses*	Mollusks, arthropods; vertebrates (fishes, amphibians, reptiles)
Operant acquisition of conditioned actions**	Mollusks, arthropods; vertebrates (fishes, amphibians, reptiles)
Curiosity, play	Some birds, monkeys, and other higher mammals (e. g., dogs)
Insight, observational learning with object; object-dependent tradition	Monkeys and some other higher mammals, some birds
Self-exploration: the "I" becomes an object; planning activities in visualized space; imitation	Apes (dolphins?)
Reflection: one's own thought becomes an object; abstract thought, language (verbal); object-independent tradition; anticipation of consequences of one's own activities and those of the others; wanting; conscience; morality	Humans

Source: After different authors, in accordance with Medicus 1987.

* Operant acquisition of conditioned responses (that is, exploration) is similar to, but more broadly defined than, classical conditioning.

** Operant acquisition of conditioned actions is similar to, but more narrowly defined than, operant conditioning.

never exhibit the same behavioral capacities as a dog or an ape. The earthworm's "world picture" is much more primitive than that of dogs or apes. However, this does not necessarily mean that the earthworm is less fit; it might be that, under certain circumstances, the earthworm is fitter than dogs, apes, or other "higher" animals. But higher animals are capable of individual learning, and they execute actions transgressing the hereditary fixed "instincts"; they explore their environment and they may learn from particular situations (without being conscious of these, past, situations). The information gained about the environment, be it in lower or higher animals, is stored in the genome. "Thus information-processing mechanisms are analogous to learning by trial and error, whereas the storage of information functionally is performed in the same way as memory" (Wuketits 1984a, p. 12; see, furthermore, Lorenz 1974, 1977; Riedl 1984a; Wuketits 1986a). Hence, the ratiomorphic apparatus of an individual organism comprises genetically fixed elements, innate mechanisms of calculating and experiencing the environment (see next chapter). These innate mechanisms are an outcome of evolution by natural selection, the outcome of evolutionary learning processes. Again, the evolution of life is to be regarded as a cognition process. The result of this process is a variety of ratiomorphic mechanisms that serve for the particular organism's survival.

Some readers might suspect a cryptic teleological factor, for I argue using terms like *serve for, for the sake of* (survival), and so on. However, there is no pure teleology in my argument. I use teleological language in the sense of modern evolution-oriented biology, where the concept of teleology is not to be confused with Aristotle's causa finalis, but to make statements about the function of organs, processes of behavior in relations to the whole organism, and so on, biologists frequently speak of a kind of teleology based on the genetic program of the organism. To be sure, this teleology is no longer identical with finality in a strict sense (pure teleology, goal-intended actions). Lorenz (1965, p. 24), for one, writes that, for example, the statement "the cat has crooked, pointed claws 'with which to catch mice'" does not express the biologist's belief in a mystical teleology, but rather the assertion "that catching mice is the function whose selection pressure caused the evolution of that particular form of claws," a function that is genetically programmed in the individual. To describe such quasi-teleological processes biologists and philosophers of biology use the term *teleonomy*, which has replaced the classical notion of teleology (see, e.g., Lorenz 1977; Mayr 1974; Simpson 1963; Wuketits 1978a, 1980). In short, biological functions and processes are goal *directed*, but there is no *intention* underlying the particular function or process. (Goal-intended activities are proper to humans and depend on rational reflections.) This fully applies to the function of an animal's ratiomorphic apparatus: ratiomorphic mechanisms and processes are teleonomic.

Having now explained some concepts that play an important role in evolutionary epistemology, I shall proceed to a more profound analysis of the assertion that evolution actually is a cognition process.

Experience and Expectation

Imagine that you look out of the window one morning and see the street, the trees in your garden, and all the other things around your house colored white. Your conclusion—your almost inevitable conclusion—will be "it snowed." What else could have happened? Should somebody have covered the street with some pulverulent material? This would be hard to believe. For many years you have experienced snow from time to time, when the street and all your surroundings are "colored" white. Thus, whenever you see your surroundings colored white, you conclude that it snowed; and you expect after the next snowfall your surroundings again will be colored white. Your expectation is based on experience, and your experiences lead to your expectation, in this particular case to the expectation of "white colored" surroundings. (And usually your expectation will prove correct.) Generally, there is a connection between experience and expectation. Evolutionary epistemology helps us understand this connection as a result of long-term evolutionary learning processes.

Riedl (1984a, 1985) demonstrated that information, even at the level of lower animals, is gained by an elementary mechanism of trial and error and of experience and expectation, and that certain expectations are programmed, so to speak, by particular experiences. Figure 7 shows the cycle of cognition gaining by experience and expectation. This is a systems model of the dynamics of information processing in animals; the model also covers human preconscious information processing and bears a resemblance to what Campbell (1960) characterizes as increase in knowledge by a process of blind variation and selective retention. The point is that at any level of animal organization, in

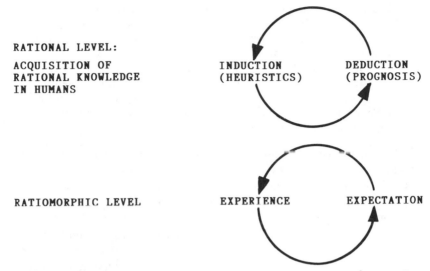

RATIONAL LEVEL:

ACQUISITION OF   INDUCTION   DEDUCTION
RATIONAL KNOWLEDGE   (HEURISTICS)   (PROGNOSIS)
IN HUMANS

RATIOMORPHIC LEVEL   EXPERIENCE   EXPECTATION

Figure 7. A systems model demonstrating the cycle of cognition gaining by experience and expectation.
Source: After Riedl 1984a.

lower animals as well as in higher ones, there is a cyclic arrangement of experience and expectation although the process does not function consciously. "Experiencing its environment and storing the experience (information), the animal is conducted, so to speak, to expect certain events; its expectation bases upon experience gaining by sense-organs" (Wuketits 1987a, p. 322).

An animal's behavior is based on the ratiomorphic(!) expectation that what has been frequently confirmed will probably be true. In other words, organisms "calculate" their particular environment by expecting that experiences from the past will be confirmed now and tomorrow. (Some more details will be given in the next chapter.) Changing experiences, of course, lead to changing expectations. At least, higher animals capable of individual learning are able to learn from new experiences and thus to change their expectations. If, on the contrary, experiences and expectations were unchangeable, learning—both individual and evolutionary learning—would not be possible at all. Riedl has made the following point:

The course is such that the sum . . . of expectations, like that of experiences, always comes together with each new content of perception. In this, the processing operation, the comparison of expectation with the new experience, always meets an alternative. If the expectation is confirmed then the new expectation is reinforced, and the experience is enlarged in that specific area. On the other hand, if the expectation fails, then the subsequent expectation is weakened and the growth in experience is at first nonspecific and therefore remains to be organized only in expectations of another kind. (1984a, p. 166)

The cycle of experience and expectation in the individual, however, is a result of evolution. The members of a population or a species have made the same experiences again and again. In the long run, these experiences will be genetically stabilized so that any member of the species will be equipped with "innate expectations"; that is, a "program" of expectations based on the accumulation of its species' experiences. Thus, evolution can be described as a universal learning process or even a cognition process. Evolution of living systems actually means an overall increase in cognitive abilities. It means that innumerable experiences have been accumulated through the ages and that any individual animal's cognitive behavior is a result of long-term information gaining. To put it in a somewhat metaphorical way, an animal, when confronted with particular situations, *recalls* the experiences made by its ancestors. Thus, we may argue, their evolutionary history has prepared animals to grasp at least some important aspects of the world—those aspects of the world that have been experienced by thousands of individuals during a long line of evolutionary processes. There seems to be some substance to the argument that there is a "phylogenetical memory" in organisms. Animals memorize, as it were, the experiences gained by their phylogenetic ancestors under particular circumstances. How else should one explain, for example, the reactions of young cats which are confronted with a dog for the first time in their life? The cats begin to spit and one can imagine that they "instinctively know" that a dog might be a great danger, although they never before had met a dog; their ancestors, however, must have experienced that danger. This brings us to the idea of "innate teaching mechanisms" that will be discussed in the next chapter.

The process here called *memorizing* or *phylogenetical memorizing* indeed is similar to memory. The individual animal's experiences and expectations are constrained by the cyclic arrangement of experiences and expectations laid down in the species' genome. As stated earlier (p. 55), genetic information itself has not the character of cognitive structures. But such structures can be transmitted genetically. An organism gathers experience through its sense organs and processes experience through the nervous system. (This is true at least to most animal species.) The development of sense organs and the nervous system in an individual animal depends on specific genetical coding. Thus, the peculiarity of experiencing aspects of the world is genetically programmed.

If, now, evolutionary epistemologists argue that evolution is a cognition process, they of course do not believe that evolution itself is a "knowing subject." They lay stress only to the fact that processing information is a particular trait of any living system and that this trait, like other characteristics, has been developed and stabilized by organic evolution. As evolution has provided the animals with sense organs and nervous mechanisms of evergreater complexity, it reveals a process by which cognition serves for survival and, mentioned, increases an organism's fitness. Evolution has "taught," in a sense, the animals (humans included) appropriate responses to different objects and processes, by structuring nervous systems that enable the animals to respond.

Thus, we can establish the thesis that the perceiving (ratiomorphic) apparatus of animals is equipped with experiences acquired over the course of evolution and now the starting point of any animal's individual experience and expectation; furthermore, both experience and expectation rely on ratiomorphic, preconscious mechanisms.

Evolution as a Belief-Gaining Process

One final point is worth mentioning in this chapter. In some readable essays on evolutionary epistemology, Tennant (1983a, 1983b) has suggested that evolution should be regarded as a *belief*-gaining process. He has argued: "For desires and intentions form a teleological pyramid with survival and reproduction at its apex. . . . And the actions a creature undertakes result from its desires and intentions when they engage with its *beliefs* about the world within which it must act, and its fate within which those desires concern" (Tennant 1983a, p. 34). Let me comment briefly on this.

True, in some way or other, an animal's expectation shows the structure of "beliefs." Is it justified, however, to speak of believing in animals, at the level of preconscious cognitive abilities? The term *belief* and its meaning should be expected in a philosophical context; that is, in the context of human rational knowledge. (For a brief philosophical discussion of that term see, e.g., Ayer 1976; Russell 1967.) I see that some philosophers' troubles with evolutionary epistemology actually are troubles with terminology. This concerns the use of concepts like cognition and knowledge, and now it concerns the use of the concept belief. But as cognition, without being identified with (human) rational knowledge, can be found at different levels in the animal kingdom, belief in animals can be found as preconscious expectation based on (preconsciously acquired) experiences. A cat "believes" that a dog would be a danger in that sense that it (preconsciously) expects a dangerous behavior of the dog. And the cat's belief in "dog = dangerous animal" will be confirmed when it is attacked by a dog. Every attack by dogs will be an experience that strengthens the cat's belief, it will be an increase in the belief that dogs are indeed dangerous animals.

Humans have "beliefs" in the literal sense of the word, in a philosophical sense, as it were. But the belief-gaining processes in humans, too, are determined by preconscious, ratiomorphic processes. Remember, once more, the earlier example: when you see the street, the landscape, and so on, colored white, you conclude that it snowed. Actually you *believe* that it snowed last night and you establish your belief preconsciously, without looking for profound rational arguments. Your belief, however, has evolutionary causes: it was established by mechanisms working reliably in the world of our ancestors. To be sure, a child is not born with a notion of snow. But once it has experienced that snow is white it will expect that the snow will remain white, that the snow in winter next year will be white again, and so on. The construction of such expectations—of belief—is based on age-old mechanisms developed in the course of evolution. I return to these arguments in the next chapter. The existence of such age-old mechanisms, however, has important implications for an understanding of humankind. If we are conducted, or even determined, by preconscious mechanisms of the past, then there would be limits to an increase in our knowledge and progress in rational knowledge would be a mere illusion. I do not think that this conclusion is a correct one, but I will argue this in later chapters (particularly in chapter 5).

To summarize briefly, I want to draw the reader's attention to cognition processing as a general character of living beings. The term *cognition* is used in a biological sense and not to be restricted to human rational knowledge.

1. Living systems are information-processing systems. Information processing increases an organism's fitness and can be explained in Darwinian terms.

2. A particular type of organisms (animals) is equipped with sense organs and a nervous system. In the course of evolution these organs and systems have increased in complexity and thus extended the animal's horizon ("world picture").

3. The sum = total of information-gaining and information-processing organs is called the *ratiomorphic apparatus*, which functions in a way similar to a calculation machine; that is, analogous to, but not being identical with, (human) rational knowledge processing.

4. Evolution may be described as a cycle of experience and expectation (both preconscious, ratiomorphic characteristics of the behavior of organisms, including humans). An individual organism's expectations ("beliefs") are based on mechanisms that have been stabilized in the course of evolution by experiences made by many individuals over many generations.

Cognition and Reality

Is there any knowledge in the world which is so certain that no reasonable man could doubt it? This question, which at first sight might not seem difficult, is really one of the most difficult that can be asked.

Bertrand Russell

Is the Eye Attuned to the Sun?

Remember the remarkable fits in the animal eye (Table 4). Obviously, these fits have an advantage (survival value) that also is true to the fits in other (sense) organs. Moreover, there is an obvious link between an animal's perceptors (sense organs) and the animal's particular environment, and this link is useful in a biological (an evolutionary) sense; it has been stabilized in the course of evolution.

Everybody is—or, at least should be—aware of the tremendous *order* in nature, particularly in the living world. From the point of view of evolutionary epistemology this order is *not*, as it has been claimed by idealistic philosophy, a product of human thinking and imagination, but on the contrary, human knowledge itself is a result of nature's order. To put an old metaphor in Goethe's words:

Were the eye not attuned to the Sun,
The Sun could never be seen by it.

Well, *is* the eye attuned to the sun? Many naturalists and

73

philosophers have argued that, generally, there is some correspondence between cognition and nature, between cognitive order and order in the external world, and that cognitive order has been caused, and constrained, by natural laws. (These arguments can be found, e.g., in Campbell 1974a; Lorenz 1941, 1977; Mach 1886; Rensch 1961, 1971, 1985; Riedl 1979, 1984a, 1984b;Spencer 1870; Strombach 1968; Vollmer 1975, 1985, 1986; Wuketits 1978a, 1978b, 1981, 1985a; Ziehen 1913; and others.) The correspondence, or even harmony, between nature and cognition often has been regarded as a result of God's action. "So that," as John Locke said, "the wisdom and goodness of the Maker plainly appear in all the parts of this stupendous fabric, and all the several degrees and ranks of creatures in it" (1854, vol. 1, p. 259). From the evolutionary point of view, however, there is nothing supranatural about the congruence of cognition with nature or, at least, some aspects of nature. This congruence has been developed in the course of evolution by natural selection. Were there no such congruence, an animal could never have survived.

Advocates of evolutionary epistemology have proposed the argument that cognitive structures—be it in animals or in humans—are *adapted* to the external world. Lorenz ([1941] 1982, p. 124) explicitly stated: "Just as the hoof of the horse is adapted to the ground of the steppe which it copes with, so our central nervous apparatus for organizing the image of the world is adapted to the real world with which man has to cope. Just like any organ, this apparatus has attained its expedient species-preserving form through this coping of real with the real during its genealogical evolution, lasting many eons." One should think that, then, the eye is indeed attuned to the sun, because it has been developed and selected to recognize light and because it has been adapted to light. These arguments clearly demonstrate an adaptationist touch. To be sure, evolutionary epistemologists have had a strong inclination to the adaptationist program—and have been criticized for that reason. Lewontin (1982, p. 169) is most explicit on this point: "The fundamental error of evolutionary epistemologies as they now exist is their failure to understand how much of what is "out there" is the product of what is "in here"." Recently, however, Popper (1984, 1987) has argued that organisms, for being *active* systems, have not been molded by their environment and thus are not adapted to a given reality. With respect to the evolution of perception, Wächtershäuser (1987, p. 138) summarizes this view of an "active evolution": "Perception is not a process of passive acquisition of information from the environment by an apparatus which itself is the result of passive adaptation to this same environment. It is rather a process of active foraging within the environment by means of an apparatus which in its major characteristics is shaped by the organism's own foraging activities."

In this chapter I comment on these problems and the proposed solutions. I admit that I, too, had some sympathy for the adaptationist program (Wuketits 1984a). But now I hold this program to be one-sided. I think that a nonadaptationist view does better (Wuketits 1986a, 1987h, 1989), and I shall try to explain this in a later section of this chapter. The starting point in my argument, however, is that organisms gain a "realistic" picture of at least some aspects of their environment and that any individual organisms's perception of "reality" is the outcome of evolution by natural selection. There indeed is a remarkable correspondence between cognitive order and nature; that is, between the "knowing subject" and the external world. But how to explain this correspondence? Adaptation, I trust, is not enough; the adaptationists tell us only the half story. Hence, I shall refer to a systems view of evolution, sketched in Chapter 1, that could give evolutionary epistemology a broader foundation.

Moreover, in this chapter some important philosophical implications should become visible. We are confronted here with a venerable philosophical problem: the problem of *realism*. This problem has challenged both naturalists and philosophers and led to different, sometimes obviously false, theories. Remember the idealist's credo that no material thing could exist unperceived. This is wrong for biological reasons—and it is *obviously* wrong! Imagine that somebody crosses a road and does not perceive a car drawing near. Imagine, furthermore, that except for the person crossing the road and the driver there is nobody to perceive the car. Imagine, finally, that the car runs over the walker, who dies. Now, nobody has perceived the car—is the car, therefore, nonexistent? Is the dead walker nonexistent? Will the walker exist only when somebody has discovered his or her mortal remains? I believe that most people will come to the conclusion that the car is *real*, that the dead walker is *real*, and that the accident was a *real* event, whether or not the walker perceived the car and whether or not the driver was aware of killing a human being. For the moment, we can establish the thesis that it is imperative that we are *realists* in everyday life. Were we not realists, we could never survive in a world of cars. Does this, now, mean that we, or that other living beings, have a "true image" of the world and all its objects? Is reality exactly what we see, hear, smell, taste, and feel? Or, is there also another kind of "reality" beyond the reach of our perception, are there "things-in-themselves" in Kant's sense? Note, by the way, that Kant had firmly stated "that the things which we intuit are not in themselves the same as our representations of them in intuition, nor are their relations in themselves so constituted as they appear to us" (1901, p. 35).

I hasten to say that no advocate of evolutionary epistemology would contend that the thing-in-itself (whatever that might be) is perceivable by us or any other living being; nor would an evolutionary epistemologist argue that we (or other living beings) see, hear, and so on all aspects of reality. But evolutionary epistemologists actually contend that, first, the structures of the external world are real and not just products of our imagination (so that they exist even when they are not perceived), and second, reality is perceivable (knowable) at least in parts. The correspondence between an organism and its external world is a *logical consequence* of the theory of organic evolution (Oeser 1987). But this correspondence does not necessarily mean that an organism's image of (parts of) the world is perfect. Hence, evolutionary epistemologists are not *naive* realists. They—or, better to say, many of them—advocate a kind of realism that has been termed *hypothetic* realism. This term has caused many misunderstandings, so I hope to clear up the matter in this chapter. Lucidity is required because in the problem of reality and realism we encounter one of the central problems of human thinking. I shall try my best.

Why Animals Are Realists

Life in its various aspects (different species, different styles of living) actually shows that it is a reasonable proposition to accept an external world, a world having particular structures that, at least partially, are knowable (knowable to us and knowable to other living creatures). Simpson (1963, p. 98) accurately said: "The monkey who did not have a realistic perception of the tree branch he jumped for was soon a dead monkey—and therefore did not become one of our ancestors." And, to complete the illustration, the person who crosses the road without having a realistic perception of cars, soon will be a dead person—and therefore will never become an ancestor of anybody. In a way, living beings are indeed realists. I am aware that this statement will harm many philosophers. Not long ago, in a lecture on evolutionary epistemology at the University of Bern (Switzerland), I stated that animals are realists and that we humans, too, are equipped, for evolutionary reasons, with a "realistic calculation" of the external world. After the lecture a philosopher turned to me and harshly said: "What's your notion of 'realism'? You are not doing justice to philosophical tradition, you have ignored that tradition." To be sure, I have *not* ignored philosophical tradition, but of course I, like all the other advocates of evolutionary epistemology, have besieged *some* traditional schools of philosophy.

A concern of philosophy has been the problem of showing how we can obtain any knowledge of reality; that is, the world around us. A philosopher might argue that we cannot have any knowledge and no one is able to know something about the world. This position, called *scepticism about the external world* (Stroud 1984), is a serious philosophical problem. But why should I worry about it? The problem of scepticism—and the controversy between realists and scepticists—might be (and actually is) an unended quest; it has no *philosophical* solution. However, it might be that what has no philosophical solution, can be solved by life itself. If you book a flight from New York to Miami or from Boston to Vienna or whatever flight you want—have you any difficulty in believing that your ticket *really* exists? I don't think so. Animals, at the ratiomorphic level, have not solved the philosophical problem of reality, but they "believe," like we humans do in our everyday life, that there is some kind of reality, some kind of external world. One of my favorite examples is a porcupine confronted by a dog, a fox, or any other carnivorous mammal. What will the porcupine do when such an animal comes nearer? "Raise his spines" is the appropriate answer that everybody can observe when porcupines are confronted with certain animals (and humans). Usually this strategy suffices as protective behavior. But it presupposes that the porcupine has a "real" image of an enemy, that the porcupine at least perceives particular traits of dogs and so forth. To put it analogously to Simpson's metaphor, a porcupine without a realistic perception of dogs, foxes, and so on, will soon be a dead porcupine. A thousand and one porcupine have had experience with carnivores and "tested" their protective behavior so that this experience is laid down in their species' genome. This is the (evolutionary) reason for the "porcupine realism." Similarly, the "realism" of other animals (including humans) is to be explained in terms of fitness and survival value. "The prerequisite for evolutionary success, with nervous systems as with any other organ, is survival value" (Olding 1983, p. 1). But to guarantee survival value, it is necessary that the organism is able to cope with its external world—that the organism considers the external world to be real and not just a product of imagination. Animals and also humans in their everyday life have no problem with realism; they solve their immediate problems by being realists. It is true that, in a sense, life is wiser than (philosophical) reason (Riedl 1984a).

This of course does not mean that an animal perceives the world as it "really is." The animal only believes that the structures around are the same as the picture it has gained about them. (Remember what I said about evolution as a belief-gaining process.) In other words, there is not—and need not be—an exact representation of the external world in the animal's brain. The evolutionary epistemologist's notion of realism does not necessarily lead to a correspondence theory of truth; that is, to the assertion that the obvious congruence between cognition and the external world rests upon an exact image of external reality. Rather, it is to be supposed that there is a *coherence*, that reality—and the view of reality—rests on coherence and success in life (Oeser 1987; Riedl 1987a; Ruse 1986; Wagner 1987). Organisms get "a model of a possible world, which enables the nervous system to handle the enormous amount of information it receives and processes" (Jerison 1976, p. 99). Therefore, in a sense, an organism plays an active role in modeling reality, its picture of the external world is not simply molded by influences from the external world (Olding 1983). When evolutionary epistemologists are denounced as naive realists, this is unjustified, because at least modern-day advocates of this epistemology have become aware of the one-sidedness of correspondence theory.

An animal's "realistic perception" of certain aspects of the external world presupposes that the external world is real. This might be a truism to anyone believing in a common-sense realism and dismissing the claims of idealism, according to which "reality" is construed through perception. And, for the evolutionist, it is evident that animals and their perception have evolved, and we have good reason to suppose "that we and these animals have evolved in our diverse ways *while coping with a common environment*" (Bartley 1987, p. 39, my italics). The environment, the external world, cannot be a mere illusion! But, for instance, an antelope that perceives a leopard does not necessarily know that the animal it perceives is *really* a leopard; it suffices to grasp certain traits of the animal, which is called *leopard* by English-speaking humans, and to react adequately. Thus, from the point of view of an antelope it does not matter whether or not the perceived leopard is really a leopard or something else—but it is vital to recognize that there are animals that seek one's life and that the "leopard" is such an animal, so that it is convenient to react adequately, to run away. The antelope's view of the leopard, then, must be coherent, although it need not correspond exactly with the leopard. The only information needed is that "leopards" are predators and a great danger. A thousand and one antelopes have had this experience so that the adequate reaction—running away—is genetically programmed.

Innate "Teaching Mechanisms"

What has been said in the last two sections leads to, at least, three conclusions:

1. An organism's perception of (parts of) the world is conducted to a certain extent by genetically programmed dispositions.

2. These dispositions are the outcome of evolution by natural selection.

3. Although the organism's knowledge about (parts of) the world is never perfect, it is (for survival's sake) coherent.

The point is that there are "innate teaching mechanisms" in any organism's perceiving apparatus that are the result of a vast number of experiences by many individuals of the particular species. Lorenz (1965, p. 16) writes:

> All the teaching mechanisms . . . contain phylogenetically acquired information that tells the organism which of the consequences of its behavior must be repeatedly attained and which ought to be avoided in the interest of survival. This information is preponderantly localized in the perceptual organizations which respond selectively to certain external and/or internal configurations of stimuli and report them, with a plus or minus sign added, to the central mechanisms of learning.

As we shall see, the organisms' ratiomorphic apparatus thus is equipped with inborn "hypotheses" about certain aspects of external reality.

The thesis that there are innate conducts of behavior, so to speak, or innate teaching mechanisms, does not disregard individual learning and modifications of innate capacities by individual experiences. However, through evolution innate teaching mechanisms have been (genetically) stabilized and individual learning has become possible (by the development of nervous systems). The following relations are given:

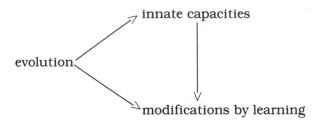

I think that it is common knowledge that the behavior of organisms generally is based on some innate dispositions and the *behaviorist's* credo is desperately defective. The behaviorist's failure is the overestimation of environmental influences upon the individual organism. The behaviorist portrays an organism as a black box or tabula rasa. This cannot be correct because of the evolutionary history of the organisms. I do not want to report here on the old and somewhat fatal nature–nurture controversy. It should be enough to point out that modern ethology amounts to the assertion that heredity and environment play equivalent roles in the development of an individual organism's behavior: "Neither can be said, *in general*, to be more important than the other" (Barnett 1970, p. 212).

From the point of view of evolutionary epistemology it is

clear, however, that innate mechanisms with regard to behavioral capacities in general and cognitive behavior in particular are important determinants. None of the advocates of evolutionary epistemology doubts that, at least in higher animals, there are individual modifications of innate mechanisms and that the environment plays its role. But the tabula-rasa doctrine is absolutely wrong. (Remember Popper's remarks quoted on p. 47.) An individual organism's perception of the external world never starts with nothing—it always starts with some innate capacities that are the result of long-term evolutionary (learning) processes. What we find elaborated in the works of evolutionary epistemologists since Darwin and Spencer is the approach to an (evolutionary) understanding of the preconditions to cognitive capabilities including complex patterns of cognition in humans.

One of the most fascinating phenomena, human *language*, also can be explained with resort to biological evolution. Lenneberg (1967) has given ample evidence that the emergence and development of human language has been constrained by biological factors. Surely, human language "depends upon cultural and social circumstances as well and can be fully understood only in regard to all these components" (Wuketits 1984a, p. 17; Chapters 5 and 6 here). However, I suppose that most advocates of evolutionary epistemology would agree to Hockett's conclusion that "man's own remote ancestors . . . must have come to live in circumstances where a slightly more flexible system of communication, the incipient carrying and shaping of tools, and a slight increase in the capacity for traditional transmission made just the difference between surviving . . . and dying out" (1960, p. 96). Hence, the emergence of a communication system like (human) language would have increased fitness. Similar arguments can be found in Barash (1979), Lumsden and Wilson (1981), Mohr (1987), and Wilson (1978), who have argued from the sociobiologist's point of view. To be sure, every one of these authors would agree that a particular language must be *learned*, which depends upon specific social and cultural conditions, but that its basic potentials are innate, resulting from the processes of organic evolution.

The most important philosophical conclusion established in this context is that the Kantian a priori is to be interpreted as a phylogenetical a posteriori. A priori knowledge in Kant's sense is absolutely independent of experience. Unfortunately, the term a priori, used within and outside of the Kantian tradition, often has been just "a label which philosophers could attach to propositions they favored, without any clear criterion for doing so" (Kitcher 1985, p. 143). However, the question that should be of some interest to everybody interested in the philosophical implications of evolutionary epistemology is whether there is a chance to dismiss or at least to revise the philosophical (Kantian) notion of the a priori with reference to biological findings. Many philosophers (e.g., Haller 1987; Löw 1984; Lütterfelds 1982, 1987) are sceptical about this. Again, the philosophical scepticism is due partly to terminological problems.

Evolutionary epistemologists do not intend to destroy the work of Immanuel Kant. It is true, and fully accepted by evolutionary epistemologists, that Kant's transcendental epistemology from a certain point of view has been the last possible step in the development of an epistemological system. Kant was right to state that our knowledge mediated by the sense organs requires some arrangement that cannot be managed by experience alone but by preexisting patterns of "cognitive order"; that is, the categories and forms of intuition. So far, so good. But where do the categories and forms of intuition come from? The answer of the evolutionists since Spencer has been that they are results of evolution. A priori knowledge remains independent of individual experiences, it preexists in every individual, but it is the result of evolutionary learning processes of the particular species and thus a posteriori knowledge from the point of view of evolution.

Lorenz (1977, p. 89) argues that "one has to postulate the existence of innate teaching mechanisms in order to explain why the majority of learning processes serve to enhance the organisms' fitness for survival"; and he reaches the conclusion that "these mechanisms . . . meet the Kantian definition of the a priori: they were there before all learning and must be there in order for learning to be possible." Riedl (1977, p. 367) summarizes his own view by stating that "the prerequisites of human thinking, though a priori for each individual in the sense of Kant, are a posteriori for the chain of his pedigree." Likewise Mohr (1977, p. 198) says "that the seemingly inexplicable a priori knowledge of the individual is actually a posteriori knowledge about the world, laid down in the peculiar nucleotide sequence of the DNA in our genes." These quotations may suffice to show that the evolutionary interpretation of the a priori is not necessarily at variance with Kant's philosophy. Kant's epistemology is not wrong when viewed through the lenses of evolutionary theory; but, from the point of view of evolution, it is an unfinished system.

Evolutionary epistemology can be regarded as "an attempt to explain *a priori* structures of our knowledge *via* evolution and to 'dynamize' these structures" (Wuketits 1984a, p. 4). Therefore one might argue that evolutionary epistemology does not dismiss Kant's epistemology but is an important supplement to Kantian "a priorism": evolutionary epistemology, as a natural history or biology of cognition, starts where Kant's epistemology ends. This somewhat moderate formulation of the problem of transcendental versus evolutionary epistemology seems to appeal to some philosophers even if they are not to be regarded as advocates of evolutionary epistemology in its strict sense (see, e.g., Engels 1983, 1987; Frey 1987; Krausser 1987). (By the way, as far as I can see, the problem of a possible reconciliation of evolutionary with Kantian epistemology is a target primarily of writers in the German philosophical tradition, whereas English-American writers are less engaged in this problem. This might be explained by the phenomenon that in Germany, and generally in German-speaking countries, philosophy to a certain extent is constrained by its tradition, whereas particularly in America, as I feel, the tradition plays a minor role in philosophy and philosophizing.)

The "Hypotheses" of the Ratiomorphic Apparatus

Having seen that animal (and human) behavior is influenced by innate, genetically stabilized programs, we now turn to a more precise explanation of the innate teaching mechanisms as they relate to cognition. Figure 8 shows the reaction of a paramecium, a unicellular living being, when confronted with a hindrance. This is a most simple feedback mechanism. To put it in a somewhat anthropomorphic manner, the animal operates on the basis of the hypothesis that the hindrance cannot be pushed away, that it (the animal) cannot swim through, and that the object (hindrance) will have limited dimensions so that it would be useful to swim around the barrier. In a sense, the paramecium has a realistic perception of its surrounding—remember the notion of coherence!—and it is able to respond to the presence of a hindrance that hampers its forward locomotion. Now, as Campbell (1960) explains, the external environment is the

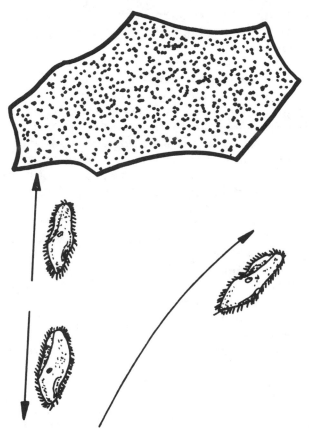

Figure 8. Reaction of a paramecium confronted with a hindrance. The organism and its reaction demonstrate a simple feedback mechanism. Perceiving the hindrance, it goes back and moves forward in another direction.
Source: After Riedl 1984a.

selection agency and the preservation of discovery is embodied in the possibility of persistent, unblocked forward moving; the paramecium has "discovered" that its environment is discontinuous, however, consisting of objects that are penetrable and others that are not, and that impenetrability is a stable characteristic. Hence, the animal responds adequately—it has learned through evolution that, when its locomotion is blocked, it is not reasonable to try to push the object away or to wait until it disappears, but to try to go around it.

Riedl (1984a) has given a full-length exposition of such "hypotheses" of the ratiomorphic apparatus that are the outcome of long-term evolutionary processes and that enable an animal to cope with the environment. (See also the brief overview by Kaspar 1984.) These "hypotheses" are innate teaching mechanisms, ratiomorphic conducts of life, so to speak.

1. *Hypothesis of the seemingly true.* The probability of any event increases with the number of confirmed expectations. Thus, an animal's (cognitive) behavior is based on the expecta tion that what frequently has happened will happen again under similar circumstances, and that what frequently has been confirmed will be probably true. Humans, too, calculate their environment on the basis of this hypothesis. Consider, for instance, a series of numbers, between 1 and 6, that we have cast with a die. Let the series be 3−5−1−2−2−6−4−1−3−5−6−1−2−3. We would call such a sequence of numbers random. If now the same sequence occurred a second time, what would you say? Probably, you would suspect something strange. Mathematically the probability of repetition is very small, extremely small. Every throw of the die has a probability of 1/6, two throws of $(1/6)^2 = 1/36$, three throws of cast $(1/6)^3 = 1/216$, and so on. In short, it seems impossible that the same series will occur a second time. Thus, without any mathematical calculation, we consider a priori this possibility as very small. Our ratiomorphic hypothesis of the seemingly true tells us that the probability of throwing the same series twice is extremely small. On the other hand, speaking more generally, when we have experienced certain events, we expect the same events under the same (or similar) circumstances a second and a third time. Imagine that you have visited Vienna three times and that it has been raining throughout each stay. Now you are planning a fourth visit, and you will think that probably it will be raining again. This is a ratiomorphic conclusion—rationally there is no reason to believe that it rains all the time in Vienna. (And I can tell you that in fact it does not rain all the time.)

2. *Hypothesis of comparison.* With similar objects and events one can disregard their differences and deduce from certain (visible) features to other (not visible) features. An example is given in Figure 9. From the contours you are able to reconstruct the cat; you see some features of the cat and deduce the animal from these features; that is, you deduce its gestalt.

Figure 9. An example for the hypothesis of comparison or gestalt perception. Although you see only different contours, you will be able to "see the cat."
Source: After Riedl 1984a.

This deduction is based on the learning of coincidences, a consequence or application of the hypothesis of the seemingly true. It is called gestalt perception and is as old as the vertebrate lineage (500 million years or so). The mechanism is similar to what Campbell (1966) described as "pattern matching." The ratiomorphic apparatus is able to reckon the essential characteristics of certain objects—those characteristics the perception of which is of a certain survival value—and to reproduce them.

    3. *Hypothesis of the cause.* With increasing confirmation of

consecutive occurrences, the animal expects that the first occurrence is the cause of the second. Remember the experiments of Pavlov. A dog that hears the sound of a bell before being fed finally expects that the sound of the bell is the cause of being fed. Hence, the dog has constructed a causal relations between the bell and the food; the animal considers the latter as an effect of the former. The dog's expectation is based upon an age-old learning program. The dogs have experienced that there are successive occurrences and have established the hypothesis that these occurrences are causally related to each other. Of course, similar experiences and expectations are true of other species including humans.

4. *Hypothesis of purpose.* Relatively late in the evolution of mammals an additional specialization of cognition appeared, which may be characterized as an inverted causality hypothesis. That is to say that the ratiomorphic apparatus expects that two or more things having several features in common will serve the same purpose. This hypothesis appears at the level of primates capable of using tool. I think that the reader is familiar with the classical experiments of Wolfgang Köhler, if not, let me repeat the essential. In the 1920s, Köhler conducted an experiment in which he placed in a chimpanzee's cage, a banana that could be reached only by fastening two poles together into one longer pole (see Köhler 1973). Behold! The chimpanzee succeeded in putting two poles together and reached the banana. Thus, the ape had formed the hypothesis that two poles will serve for one particular purpose. The construction of this hypothesis (expectation) shows that chimpanzees, in a way, are capable of insight and even a kind of intentionality (Rensch 1973), although their actions are not identical with human rational acting and planning.

These hypotheses and their hierarchy may be characterized as "life's innate logic." (Needless to say that the term *hypothesis* is used here in a most general and somewhat metaphorical sense, and it should not be confused with the philosopher's concept of rational, scientific hypotheses.) It is obvious that "every creature has the power to abstract those features that are relevant for its life from all the changes that go on around" (Young 1987, p. 81). This power has been developed through long-term evolutionary learning processes and is now given a priori to living systems; that is, to any individual living system according to the learning process of its species.

We can now formulate the thesis that organisms are realists in a more precise manner: organisms are *hypothetical* realists. They calculate their environment on the basis of innate hypotheses expecting some regularities but not having perfect knowledge or absolute certainty. Campbell elucidates this claim: "An 'external' world is hypothesized in general, and specific entities and processes are hypothesized in particular, and the observable implications of these hypotheses (or hypostatizations or reifications) are sought out for verification" (1959, p. 156). Hypothetical realism as conceived by evolutionary epistemologists therefore is not to be confused with naive realism. It follows from the fact that organisms have developed particular sense organs and nervous systems that allow for processing relevant information about certain structures of reality. Hypothetical realism is *not*, as Vollmer (1975, 1985) suggests, an ontological premise, but a *consequence* of evolutionary epistemology. It follows from the (now well-established) assertion that organisms (including humans) calculate their external world on the basis of innate hypotheses (innate teaching mechanisms) that are the result of experiences accumulated during organic evolution.

I agree with Clark (1984), who argues that evolutionary epistemology is apt to sustain both a *material realism* (i.e., the view that the physical universe exists independently of any knowing subject)[1] and a *conceptual scheme realism* (i.e., the claim that beings other than humans may process information in ways that, some way or other, are different from human information processing). With regard to material realism I do not see any reason to believe that the universe—the planets, stars, and galaxies—and within it the earth with its geophysical and geological phenomena, different species of living systems, and so on, might be dependent on somebody who is able to perceive all these phenomena. Or, could you really believe that, for example, the pyramids of Egypt and the people who built them thousand years ago depend on a contemporary archaeologist's perception? As to the compatibility of evolutionary epistemology with conceptual scheme realism, the following sections might be of some interest. For the moment, let me just stress that different animals have indeed different world pictures for they live in different ecological niches, so that there are various strategies to perceive and process certain aspects of reality.

Facing a World of "Medium Dimensions"

In Chapter 2, I mentioned Uexküll's doctrine, according to which different animals live in "different worlds," each with its own specific ambient (*Umwelt*). Any organism, Uexküll (1928, 1938) argued, has its own "subjective tone." Uexküll was on the right track but unfortunately he failed to see the evolutionary background of life. From the evolutionary point of view it is clear, if not trivial, that the populations and species live in specific ecological niches, that they have evolved under the particular circumstances of the respective niche. According to the ecologist's concept of the niche one can speak of an animal's *cognitive niche*. Vollmer (1975) coined the term *mesocosm* to characterize the particular cognitive niche of humans. Likewise Portmann (1976), without appreciating the approach of evolutionary epistemology, spoke of the "mediocosm" to designate the human way of seeing the world. I shall turn to the human mesocosm later, but first let me give some more general explanations.

Bertalanffy, standing close to evolutionary epistemology, comments on Uexküll's doctrine: "Every animal is surrounded, as by a soap bubble, by its specific ambients, replenished by those characteristics which are amenable to it." And continuing, he presents the following illustration: "Some sea urchins respond to any darkening by striking together their spines. This reaction invariably is applied against a passing cloud or boat, or the real enemy, an approaching fish. Thus, while the environment of the sea urchin contains many different objects, its ambient only contains one characteristic, namely dimming of light" (Bertalanffy 1973, pp. 241–242).

There are many similar examples to show that every animal species lives in its specific ambient, which is not identical with the sum-total of environmental objects but rather constitutes an abstract of these objects. The dolphin's perceptual world, for instance, is strongly influenced by data generated by echolocation (Jerison 1986). Hence, the world picture varies from one species to another. Of course, this has to do with environmental constraints. To give another example, a shark will never have an idea of animals living in the desert or in the jungle. Sharks have evolved, through many millions of years, in an aquatic environment and as the Darwinist would argue, have "adapted" to this environment. Therefore, from the point of view of fitness and survival, it would be useless for the shark to develop organs by which to perceive objects beyond aquatic environment.

The hypotheses of the ratiomorphic apparatus, just presented, were developed, and thus constrained, by specific relations between the organism and its environment. They work reliably only within the specific "life world" of the respective organism, and they stop operating reliably outside of this world. A lion, for instance, when caged, will walk about believing and expecting to find a way out. The animal will not know how to escape, because cages are not elements in a lion's "natural world" and its perception therefore is not programmed by evolutionary experience. Similarly, porcupines are not able to distinguish between their "old enemies"—say, foxes—and cars. They invariably rise their spines even when a car is approaching. This method, however, does not suffice in such a case. We all know this, but how could a porcupine know that such—genetically programmed—protective behavior stops working whenever he meets cars or other technical objects? These objects played no role in the evolution of porcupines, so that the porcupine's perceiving apparatus is not capable of "knowing" them. Only through long-term learning processes would it become possible for the porcupine to distinguish between foxes, dogs, and so on, on the one side, and artificial objects like cars, on the other side.

What is true to the animals' ratiomorphic apparatus also is true to human ratiomorphic capacities. Generally, there are operational limits of sense organs (Autrum 1971). If, for example, phases of light and darkness follow one another too rapidly, we do not recognize the darkness between the phases of light. (The cinema makes use of this effect.) *Visual illusions,* perhaps, are the best illustrations to show the limitations of our perceiving apparatus (see Figure 10). It has been a rather difficult enterprise to explain these illusions. However, the evolutionary view can be of some help. If you accept that humans have evolved through millions of years and that perspective drawing was not invented until recent times, then it should not come as a surprise that humans initially possessed an equipment for handling a three-dimensional world and not its two-dimensional representation (Legge 1975). This would explain, at least, the optico-geometric illusions. Generally, there is some substance to the argument that a "ratiomorphic censor" controls or manipulates visual perception and that we are not consciously aware of this manipulation (Wolf 1985). Rationally, we know that visual illusions are just illusions, but our ratiomorphic apparatus does not know this and, therefore, we get misinformed. We should

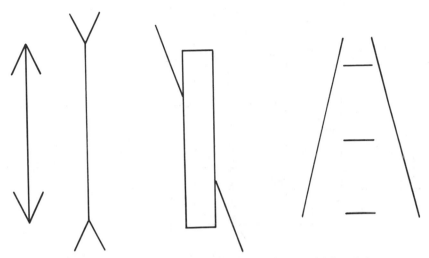

Figure 10. Some common visual illusions. Left: the shafts of the arrows are the same length, although they do not appear to be so. Middle: the diagonal is a straight line, although it does not seem to be. Right: the three short lines are the same length, although they seem to be different in length.

notice that our ratiomorphic apparatus is older than all our rational capacities—no wonder that, therefore, we indeed are able to rationally grasp, but not eliminate, the age-old ratiomorphic teaching mechanisms (Riedl 1984a, 1987b). Like other animals, humans emerged in a particular ecological niche and developed their specific cognitive niche, their mesocosm. Therefore, we can state: "What we experience is indeed a real image of reality—albeit an extremely simple one, only just sufficing for our own practical purposes; we have developed 'organs' only for those aspects of reality of which, in the interest of survival, it was imperative for our species to take account, so that selection pressure produced this partial cognitive apparatus" (Lorenz 1977, p. 7).

Again, our visual perception is an instructive example. The entire electromagnetic spectrum is wide, ranging from less than a billionth(!) of a meter to more than 1000 meters, but the visible spectrum is just a tiny slice of the entire band (Figure 11). "We can see—and most animal vision also occurs—only in that small section between approximately 400 and 700 nanometers" (Bartley 1987, p. 27). Cosmic rays, gamma rays, and so on do not

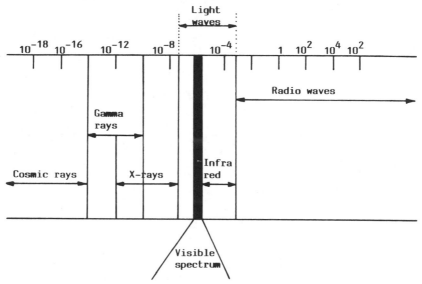

Figure 11. The visible spectrum as a small slice of the entire electromagnetic spectrum.
Source: after Bartley 1976, 1987.

enter our visual organs or any other sense organs. There was no need to take notice of these rays, however, so no organs have evolved to perceive them. This strict evolutionary explanation seems to be most plausible and vindicable.

We humans live in a world of "medium dimensions"; that is, the section of reality that can be measured in meters, years, and kilograms, in short the world of our everyday life. Nobody is able to visualize atoms, a billion years, the speed of light, or any other microcosmic and macrocosmic phenomenon. Evolution has not developed organs for these aspects of reality. However, through our rational capacities we are enabled to reconstruct these entities and to transgress, as it were, our mesocosm (see next chapter). Our ratiomorphic apparatus evolved for practical reasons; that is, it has had to cope with certain aspects of the external world. It seems that we are not free from our innate teaching mechanisms that developed, for the sake of survival, millions of years ago. In my opinion this is well illustrated by our notion of causality. As already mentioned on p. 24, our "classical" conception of causality is that of linear causal chains: we recognize that events succeed one another but we fail to see that cause and effect are mutually related, that an effect can react back upon its own cause(s). Causality seems to be programmed as an one-way cause–effect relation (Riedl 1978; 1984a; Wuketits 1981). This program sufficed in the world of our phylogenetic ancestors and it is sufficient in our everyday life. It is not sufficient, however, if we want to understand complex systems; here we need a concept of feedback causality and must take into account that any effect can react back upon its cause. The conception of feedback causality is a *rational* accomplishment transgressing old evolutionary programs. It goes beyond our world of medium dimensions.

I shall analyze these problems in the next chapter. For the moment, I shall give credit to the thesis that our world view is constrained by processes of evolutionary learning that occurred in the past and which have been essential determinants of our cognitive behavior; and that our mesocosm has been our specific "life world," or *Umwelt*, which is important to recognize if we want to learn something from our own evolution.

The Necessity of a Systems-Theoretical Approach

How can one explain the existence of cognitive niches? How can one explain the human mesocosm? The adaptationist's answer, that any cognitive capacity in organisms is to be understood as a particular reaction of the organism to its environment, looks indeed plausible, but on closer inspection it appears as a weak explanation. Zealous advocates of adaptationism have missed seeing that organisms are not just heaps of molecules to be molded by their environment and that, besides, "many features of organic architecture and developmental pathways have never been adaptations to anything, but arose as by-products or incidental consequences of changes" (Gould 1982, p. 383). Of course, one cannot seriously deny that there actually are adaptations in nature and that certain traits of organisms can be understood only if we look at the specific environmental conditions. But adaptation is not enough! Evolutionary changes seem to imply both adaptation and "construction" (Gagliasso 1984). What we have to consider once more, is, that every organism is an active system engaged in problem solving. True, the environment affects the organism, but also true the organism causes changes in its environment, so that there is no simple causal chain going from the environment to the organism. Living systems and their environments are mutually related.

This has important consequences to evolutionary epistemology. Admittedly, some conceptions of evolutionary epistemology (including Lorenz 1941, 1977) are adaptationistic. Hence, some authors who have criticized the adaptationist program, at the same time have been critical of this epistemology, although they generally have appreciated the evolutionary approach to an understanding of knowledge. (Among these authors are Edlinger, Gutmann, and Weingarten 1989; Gutmann and Bonik 1981; Lewontin 1982, to name but some recent contributors.) We should indeed keep in mind that the interactions between organisms and their environment are very complex, "especially where the active organism partly determines the degree of contact with the world" (Plotkin 1982, p. 5). The problem—one of the most intriguing problems in evolutionary epistemology—is how these organismic abilities to determine, though only to a certain extent, their own contact with the external world, have evolved? Are the well-known mechanisms genetic recombination, mutation, and natural selection—the essentials of evolutionary explanations proper to the synthetic theory (see chapter 1)—sufficient to explain the evolution of cognitive phenomena? These are embarrassing questions. I feel that we have not yet found the satisfactory answers. But what has been established is a theoretical framework providing for a broader approach to understanding evolutionary change and apt to compensate the shortcomings of the adaptationist view. This, the systems theory of evolution, has been outlined in chapter 1 and should be evaluated now as an approach to the explanation of the emergence of cognitive phenomena.

The relevance of the systems-theoretical view of cognition can be summarized as follows:

1. Information processing in organisms presupposes an interaction between organisms and their environment. Information is not something "imprinted" on the organism; the organism itself selects relevant information.

2. The organism's selection of information is constrained by "internal mechanisms"; that is, the organization of the perceiving apparatus, sense organs, and the nervous system.

3. An organism and its environment are linked together by a

feedback principle. This feedback principle is nothing supranatural, but the result of both the requirements of the external world and the organism's construction.

4. Living systems and their environments have not evolved independent of each other. The supposed structural isomorphy between the organism and parts of the external world are the result of rather complex feedback principles. The dichotomy organism–environment is untenable; organisms and their environment constitute a system of interactions.

5. The ability of adaptation is defined not by the environment, but by the living system itself. Cognitive activities, then, are not defined by any environment but by the organism's particular organization.

Thus, in a nutshell, the central claim of a systems view of cognition is that cognition, even at the level of lower (unicellular) organisms, always means action and that to a certain extent the organism selects the (external) stimuli to put them together into a specific world picture (Wuketits 1989).

Cognition or, generally, information gaining presupposes certain activities of the living system; it is the function of hierarchically organized systems whose "self-assemblage" makes the perception of external influences possible. Note that Piaget (1971) developed a similar view by arguing that cognition is a result of constructions and inventions. I am aware that all lacks the characteristics of a fully fledged theory and appears rather as a table of claims. Perhaps, the need for a systems-theoretical approach could be seen if we pose the following problem.

I think that the reader—at least, when familiar with some biology—has no difficulty in agreeing that, first, every organism has innate behavioral capacities and, second, these capacities are transmitted genetically from one generation to another. (Remember what I said on innate teaching mechanisms.) Now, these (innate) capacities are the result of evolutionary learning processes. In other words, the species' particular genome has "learned" something about certain aspects of (external) reality and these experiences, laid down in the genome, are deciphered in the developing individual. But, and this is a rather embarrassing question, how has the evolutionary experience been transported to the genome? There is no answer to this question from the strict Darwinian point of view. On page 22 I argued that there must be a constant flux of information in both directions, from the genotype to the phenotype and back again. If one does not want to adopt a strict Lamarckist view, the only alternative is the systems-theoretical approach. According to this view genotype and phenotype are linked together by feedback loops as the whole organism is interrelated with its environment, so that, theoretically, the flow of information from the external world to the genome of an organism could be understood and does not remain a miracle.

Hence it might be plausible why a systems-theoretical view is needed, even if for the time being it is not fully developed and even if more data from empirical research are required to sustain this view and give it more substance. However, in his comprehensive volume on macroevolutionary phenomena, Riedl (1979) took a decisive step toward an evolutionary theory that prompts us to restate some important problems of life and see those problems from a more "organismic" point of view. Indeed, the organism—its development and its architecture—deserves more attention than the effects of the environment upon it.

A Nonadaptationist View of the Evolution of Cognition

As the reader has recognized, I am not sympathetic with an adaptationist foundation of evolutionary epistemology. Probably, he or she will ask now whether I have developed a theory that does better. Well, I think that the proposed systems view will suffice at least as a framework to the problems in question, even if—as I do not hesitate to admit—it still lacks the status of a theory in a strict sense. My claim is that cognition at every level is a systems process and not just an accumulation of small "information units." Let me outline the argument:

1. Cognition is a function of *active* systems that *actively* interact with their environments.

2. Cognitive capacities are the result of interactions between organisms and their environments, and these interactions have a long (evolutionary) history.

3. Cognition is a process that is not to be described as a chain of adaptations, but rather as a "spiral process."

If it is true that an animal lives in its specific ambient, then we are compelled to ask, What are the building blocks, so to speak, of this ambient? Has the ambient emerged solely through environmental influences upon the organism? Consider, once more, the "life world" of a sea urchin. The sea urchin perceives only darkening and, obviously, is not able to distinguish between a boat and a fish and other objects. Can this be regarded simply as adaptation? I should say rather that the particular style of life, as it were, and that the particular architecture of sea urchins constrains the perceiving apparatus and the capability of perception in this animal. Likewise, if you consider the insect eye—the compound eye with its hundreds of facets, each representing a "little eye"—you will probably agree that this system allows for a mode of calculating the world that is different from, for example, a dog's world view. And indeed there is some substance to the argument that the particular composition of the insect's eye is determined by the requirement of the insect's specific way of life (Horridge 1977). Now, take sea urchins, insects, dogs, or whatever animal—every animal has its own way of living and, thus, its own mode of perceiving reality and coping with the external world. The modes of perception are determined by the different types of organization.

This is not to say that animals construct their external reality. In a way, every animal's architecture is a specific response to environmental conditions but, at the same time, the animal's own requirements constrain its way of coping with the external world. I, of course, do not defend an *anti*adaptationist view. I agree that there are several fits in organisms and that these fits are results of environmental influences. But fitness through adaptation alone does not seem plausible to me, because adaptation already *presupposes* certain regulatory principles in the organism (for similar arguments see Bertalanffy 1973). An organism's realism (discussed earlier) is in fact, at least partly, due to *internal transformations* (Maturana and Varela 1980; Varela 1982) that make the system (the organism) coherent. Through this coherence an organism can survive under certain environmental conditions. The organism's coherence, as seen in its anatomical composition as well as in its functionality (including cognitive abilities), is linked together with the requirements of the external world with which it builds a feedback cycle. Figure 12 attempts to illustrate this view.

As evolutionary epistemology in general, this nonadaptationist view of cognition in particular has some important philosophical implications; namely, for the problem of *subject–object relationship* that has been an issue in epistemological discus-

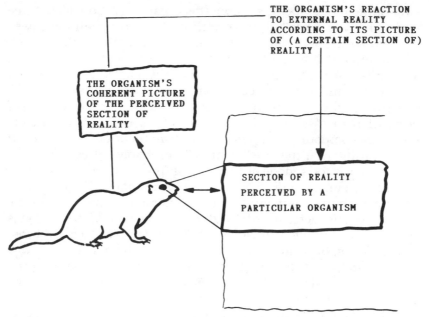

Figure 12. Relation between an organism's coherence and the requirements of the external world. The organism and its environment appear
to be "coadapted."

sions ever since humans recognized their existence vis-à-vis of a
world of objects as a philosophical problem. Despite his attitude
toward adaptationism, Lorenz (1977) correctly claimed that the
knowing subject and the world of objects to be perceived are
closely related and both are part of a more comprehensive reality.
This claim is not to be understood in any metaphysical sense but
almost inevitably follows from the evolutionary perspective.
Knowledge is a result of evolution and hence has been connected
with the physical universe; its emergence and further development is due to an intimate connection with the changing
external world (Oeser 1987). Any knowing subject and the
respective world of objects, therefore, are linked together by their
common history:

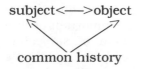

        subject<——>object

This leads to the philosophically relevant claim of a *unity* of subject and perceived object (Götschl 1987): From the point of view of a historical (an evolutionary) reconstruction, subject and object no longer appear to be separate categories.

It should become obvious now that evolutionary epistemology—especially when based on a non-adaptationist, systems-theoretical approach to evolution—has overcome naive realism but, as already pointed out, is in tune with both material realism and so-called conceptual scheme realism, whereas hypothetical realism is its logical consequence. Let me briefly explain this point.

The profusion of life itself may offer most convincing evidence that there has been some physical reality independent of any perceiving organism. How else one should explain the emergence of living systems some billions of years ago? If there were no physical reality, if there were no structures and laws of cosmic and prebiotic (chemical) evolution, what else could have created life on earth? (Perhaps God, somebody might argue, but then He would be the given reality existing independent of a perceiving organism.) How could life have endured on this planet? Needless to stress that living systems, without exception, rely on energy so that the existence of organisms presupposes any kind of energetic resources to be perceived and used. In a way, there is an "economy principle" in living nature, a principle using given resources to render possible certain biofunctions (Radnitzky, 1987a, 1987b). However, in the course of organic evolution, different modes to use the resources—and that means to cope with external reality—have been developed. Organisms are indeed realists, but nobody can teach them how to handle reality in any particular case. They do it by virtue of their particular sense organs and their specific nervous organization, which are the results of a chain of trial-and-error experiences and which, then, are the "inner instructions" laid down in the genome. Let me recall Simpson's metaphor (p. 76). It is true that a monkey without a realistic perception of the tree branch he jumped for was soon a dead monkey. But this does not necessarily mean that the monkey's (realistic) perception of tree branches is the same as ours. And birds probably have their own (realistic) perception of tree branches, which differs from that of monkeys and humans. Who has the "truth"? We, the monkeys, the birds? This is not the question. It is imperative, however, that each of these animals has an adequate "model" of the tree branch, according to which it can react for the sake of survival, whatever the *real* tree branch might be in an ontological or metaphysical sense.

Let me close with Shakespeare's words:

> Upon the earth's increase why should'st thou feed,
> Unless the earth with thy increase be fed?
> By law of nature thou art bound to breed,
> That thine may live when you thyself art dead;
> And so in spite of death thou dost survive,
> In that thy likeness still is left alive.

The main concern of this chapter was to show how evolutionary epistemology can provide for a fresh view of the venerable problem of reality. I continued discussing biological aspects and examples to show that a particular kind of realism, so-called hypothetical realism, follows from the evolutionary view of cognition. This has some implications for understanding humankind. The following claims are of some importance:

1. There is a congruence (or correspondence) between "External" and "internal" reality; that is, between nature and cognition (cognitive order). In a way, organisms are realists—realism is imperative for the sake of survival.

2. The "realism" in animals (including humans), however, does not mean that (external) reality is portrayed in any perfect manner; the world picture of animals is not an exact picture of the world. It is to be supposed that animals develop just an abstract, so to speak, of the real objects with which they are confronted. This abstract, however, must be coherent; organisms must be able to react adequately to certain external objects or events (adequately means for the sake of survival).

3. The organism's perception of certain aspects of reality is conducted by genetically programmed dispositions, which are the results of evolutionary learning processes (experiences). Hence, in every individual living being are innate teaching mechanisms.

4. Kant's a priori is to be interpreted then as evolutionary a posteriori. This is one of the most important philosophical conclusions of evolutionary epistemology.

5. The innate teaching mechanisms can be regarded as (innate) "hypotheses" of the ratiomorphic apparatus. There is a hierarchical system of such hypotheses (hypothesis of the

seemingly true, hypothesis of comparison, hypothesis of causes, and hypothesis of purpose).

6. Every species lives in its own cognitive niche. The human cognitive niche, our mesocosm, is constrained by the experiences of our phylogenetic ancestors, so that we have developed organs only for the perception of those aspects of reality of which it was imperative for our species to take account. We live in a world of "medium dimensions."

7. The adaptationist view, according to which cognition (like any other biofunction)has been just an adaptation to given (external) structures, does not suffice as an explanation of the relations between cognition and reality. This view should be replaced by a systems-theoretical approach that makes clear that organisms are active systems (problem solvers) and that their cognitive capacities are constrained by their own architecture and not just formed by external requirements.

5

The Evolution of Human Knowledge

> What we must recognise is that it is necessary for
> a philosopher to become a scientist, in this sense,
> if he is to make any substantial contribution
> towards the growth of human knowledge.
>
> Alfred J. Ayer

Up to now in this book, I have treated cognition as a universal character of living systems. The contour of a biological theory of the evolution of cognitive capacities in organisms has been drawn, and the reader might have noticed that I lay stress to the claim that evolutionary epistemology is an important aspect of the general biological theory of evolution. From an evolutionary point of view cognition is but one biofunction interrelated with other biofunctions. Any attempt to understand cognition presupposes an understanding of the organization of the living in general, but, vice versa, life generally can be better understood if we realize the elementary principles of cognitive processes. Indeed, "biology has a great deal to say about how knowledge is acquired and organized" (Ghiselin 1981, p. 269).

In this chapter I concentrate on *human* knowledge. Many controversies caused by evolutionary epistemology are centered round the (evolutionists') thesis that human knowledge, too, is an outcome of organic evolution and that at least its preconditions should be studied using biological tools; that, according to the motto of this chapter—taken from Ayer's lucid *Language, Truth and Logic* (1952)—the (biological) sciences can tell the philosopher the most essential things to notice to contribute to an up-to-date approach to an understanding of humans. Humans are animals, most peculiar animals indeed, which, however, cannot be properly understood unless we have recognized their roots in organic evolution. Human knowledge is a special aspect of the processes of information gathering that is essential for all living systems (Young 1987). Particularly, in our *brain* all our knowledge processes, conscious activities, perception, language, and so on are related; in a way, our brain is the center of our life, it controls all our specific manifestations of life (Oeser and Seitelberger 1988). An epistemologist who fails to see this, will not be able to contribute anything to an understanding of (human) knowledge but rather will build castles in the air! In fact, I do not think that any philosopher today would ignore that our brain is the causal substrate of our having knowledge. However, I feel that (many) philosophers believe that epistemology is totally divorced from biology. Indeed, epistemology as a philosophical discipline has its own problems and traditions. And certainly *evolutionary* epistemologists and traditionally oriented philosophers sometimes talk about different things. Therefore, many philosophers even if they are sympathetic to the evolutionary approach would ask, Is it epistemology?

Let me, once more, point out that I see the whole enterprise of epistemology as a comprehensive study of epistemic activities in organisms. As to human knowledge, there might be different possible approaches, and I do not want to cast doubts upon their raison d'être. But, again, we should not forget that humans are organisms having their roots in organic evolution, so that their epistemic activities naturally are constrained by biological factors. By studying these factors, we can learn much about how knowledge has become possible at all. As far as I can see, philosophers qua epistemologists have always been concerned with questions like, What is the very nature of (human) knowledge? How is (human) knowledge possible? What are the origins of (human) knowledge?—questions that now can be answered by the means of (evolutionary) biology or, to tone down this claim, answered better if one looks at the results of (evolutionary) biology. Thus prepared to appreciate the evolutionary approach, we shall now push right up to the evolutionary understanding of humankind with particular reference to the nature of human knowledge.

Transgressing the World of Medium Dimensions

As seen in the last chapter, we humans live in a world of medium dimensions, a mesocosm, that is our cognitive niche and whose perception we have inherited from our phylogenetic ancestors. On the other side, we have been able to delve into spheres beyond the mesocosm, we have been able to *transgress* this mesocosm. (Here and elsewhere in this book I use the term *transgress* in the sense of "go beyond.") We have developed ideas about the structure of the universe (macrocosm) and the smallest compounds of things (microcosm). Although we cannot visualize the dimensions of the macrocosm and the microcosm, we now operate with measures and concepts like elementary particles, nanometer, nanogram, speed of light, and others; we speak of atoms, elementary particles, and entropy, although we cannot see, hear, smell, or taste such entities. Obviously, we have transgressed our world of medium dimensions; and, what is perhaps the most astonishing fact, we have gotten (from the modern sciences) *"finer structures from whose standpoint one can even criticize and evaluate one's own cognitive structures"* (Bartley 1987, p. 39).

Evolutionary epistemologists try to understand the emergence of those 'finer structures' and to reconstruct the preconditions of human rational knowledge, which now makes humans capable of looking behind the mirror. For this reason, evolutionary epistemology frequently is said to be based on a *vicious circle.* This is wrong. As particularly Oeser (1987), Vollmer (1984, 1985), and Wagner (1984, 1987) have argued, science—empirical research—and epistemology are in a continual interplay and support each other. Of course, any reconstruction of the emergence and development of rational knowledge presupposes rationality. But this is true to every epistemology; any epistemologist who wants to contribute something to an understanding of knowledge can do this only as a rational subject. Thus, if our knowledge is studied by the means of empirical research (which already presupposes the existence of rational research strategies), this may be a circle, but it is not necessarily a vicious one. "Instead of claiming any priority to either science or epistemology we propose to look at their interplay as a kind of feedback loop" (Vollmer 1984, p. 77). Investigating the structures and functions of our brain by using the techniques of empirical research leads to results that feed back on our epistemological presuppositions and thus make epistemology a *scientifically* testable enterprise. From this point of view epistemology might even develop into a science; that is, into a discipline that makes use of concepts and methods of empirical research. (This proposition was discussed by Blažek [1979] with respect to Piaget's genetic epistemology.) Anyway, epistemology *without* the sciences, without biological and psychological recourse, will lack substance and be devoid of content.

Now, our question is, What are the basic processes or mechanisms leading to the human capacity to transgress our mesocosm? The prima facie answer of any evolutionary epistemologist is clearly to be put as follows: the processes and mechanisms are rather the same as in the case of any other knowledge acquisition; there are evolutionary processes and mechanisms, particularly natural selection including, as explained in Chapter 1, internal, intraorganismic selective agencies. You may find this answer unsatisfactory. If so, be sure that I understand your doubt. It is, because I do *not* contend that human rational knowledge is *nothing else* but biological information processing. Certainly, rational knowledge and its development is constrained by social and cultural determinants, too. I shall be more explicit on this in the final section of this chapter and throughout in Chapter 7. For the moment, let me draw your attention to the claim that, in first instance, all knowledge processing in humans depends upon an active brain; and if the active brain is a result of organic evolution—it is, in fact!—then its products (including rational knowledge) are due to evolutionary processes. In the previous chapter I spoke of innate teaching mechanisms and argued that these mechanisms, reliefed in the "life world" of our phylogenetical ancestors, influence our behavior even today. On the other side, we must be aware that rational knowledge goes beyond these genetically fixed mechanisms. Generally, our biological make-up has changed little over the past 40,000 years or so (Dobzhansky et al. 1977; Mohr 1987; Young 1971), but our rational knowledge has developed rapidly over a few thousand years. One might suspect that, therefore, organic evolution and the development of rationality are not coupled. Let us examine these problems.

The Emergence of Rational Knowledge

It seems to be of some importance to give, first of all, a definition of what we call *rationality* or *rational knowledge*.

"There is," writes Ayer (1952, p. 100), "no absolute standard of rationality, just as there is no method of constructing hypotheses which is guaranteed to be reliable." This is true. But Bunge (1980, p. 160) comes close to a definition by stating: "Rational thought is thought controlled by certain master thoughts, such as 'Abhor contradictions,' 'Check what follows,' and 'Supply evidence'." More precisely, at least three ideas are linked with the term *rationality* (Agassi 1977):

1. The idea of rational *thinking*.
2. The idea of rational *behavior* (i.e., purposeful behavior).
3. The idea of the rational as the *intelligible*.

Hence, rationality has something to do with thought (especially with the kind of thought that Bunge has in mind in his definition), with teleological action, and with the intellect. Moreover, as will be apparent, there are some other elements in rationality or characters that can be linked with the rational. Let me draw a rather quick (and perhaps incomplete) list of such elements:

1. Verbal communication, that is, language in its strict sense.
2. Use of symbols or symbolization.
3. Self-reflection including reflections upon one's own past and possible future.
4. Awareness of being mortal (awareness of death).
5. Valuing one's own behavior.
6. Freedom of choice (at least to a certain extent).
7. Creation of knowledge, not only for the sake of survival but for its own sake.
8. Construction of theories at an abstract level.
9. Transmission of knowledge by extrasomatic information processing (e.g., writing).
10. Logical examination of one's own thought.
11. Learning from one's own errors.

It seems that these elements or characteristics are peculiar to humans. As mentioned on page 87, our nearest relatives, the chimpanzees, indeed are capable of some insight and purposeful behavior, but even these highly developed animals obviously are not able to reflect upon their past and future, to recognize that they are mortal, to create theoretical knowledge, and so on and so forth.

Having outlined the principles of rationality, we can state that the acquisition of rational knowledge is the youngest achievement in a long chain of the evolution of information processing. It has been an evolutionary novelty. How, I am compelled to ask, had rationality become possible? Lorenz (1977) uses the term *fulguration* to characterize such epoch-making events; and, indeed, the emergence of rationality was a flash, so to speak, it was an event that gave evolution a new direction. "Meanwhile it is true," said Julian Huxley (1947, p. 21), "that the appearance of the human type of mind, the latest step in evolutionary progress, has introduced both new methods and new standards." Because of their rationality, humans are said to be unique among the organisms. And even many of those people who basically agree to evolution, hold that humans are an exception and that our rationality is God's work. From the point of view of evolutionary theory, however, there is nothing supranatural about the *animal rationale*, although its uniqueness in nature is not contestable. The emergence of human rationality—and thus and human "mind" (a term essentially synonymous with *rationality*)—can be explained cybernetically. Lorenz (1977, p. 30) writes that "there is nothing supernatural about a linear causal chain joining up to form a cycle." Continuing, he argues that such a cycle is "producing a system whose functional properties differ fundamentally from those of all preceding systems."

The principle underlying the emergence of rationality is to be compared with the principle that led to the emergence of living systems some billions of years ago. Molecules linked together in a specific manner form new entities having new, specific (systems) properties. A living system is indeed more than a heap of molecules, it exhibits complex patterns of order and is highly organized, "it is an extremely complex integrated entity with a high degree of autonomy in relation to its environment" (Löwenhard 1981, p. 5). Yet, the emergence of life on earth can be explained without resort to any mystical factor. Nucleic acids and proteins linked together built self-regulating, self-reproducing units; that is, living systems in the widest sense. Thus a principle of *integration*, a self-organizing principle inherent in matter, has generated living systems. Similarly, human rationality and its emergence might be ascribed to a principle of integration and self-organization; that is, to a self-organizing brain providing for evermore complex (systems) properties.

Self-organization can be regarded as one of the strands of reality, of the evolving universe (Wuketits 1982); the rational might be traced back to the formation (self-organization) of brain mechanisms.

I admit that many questions remain unanswered in this context. Practical problems are due to the enormous complexity of the (human) brain. Our brain consists of about 10^{10} or 10^{11} (10 or 100 billions) nerve cells (neurons)—estimation of their exact number, as you see, is the first "practical" problem. A typical neuron consists of a cell body and is about 10 micrometers (thousandths of a millimeter) in diameter. Besides, there are synapses, neuronal junctions (i.e., the connections between nerve cells), whose number might be about 10^{14} (100 trillions!). (For more details on this see, e.g., Hubel, 1979; Oeser and Seitelberger 1988; Sagan 1978; see Figure 13 for a quick orientation to the main parts of the brain.) It is important to note that the brain does not depend upon something like a linear program. "It is more like the circuit of a radio or a television set, or perhaps hundreds or thousands of such circuits in series and in parallel, *richly cross linked*" (Hubel 1979, p. 40, my italics).

Perhaps, future research will bring forth many interesting details and astonishing facts and we may have to revise some of our present speculations about the function of our brain. My point, however, is that the brain alone is responsible even for the most sophisticated mental phenomena and that these phenomena, if at all, are to be explained as particular expressions or properties of the brain.

From the evolutionary point of view the human brain is an information processing system that has increased fitness in the human race, as information processing generally has a certain survival value to any organism (see Chapter 3). (One might also suspect the opposite because, through our brain's achievements, we have nuclear weapons that could exterminate humankind—but this is another story.) To put matters in perspective (Table 6), we should take notice of an increasing capacity of cell and brain memory in the course of evolution. Again, organisms can be regarded as problem solvers. The degree of efficiency in problem solving is *intelligence* in a wider sense (Leinfellner 1983, 1987). *Human* intelligence has two great advantages:

1. It helps to *consciously reflect* the problems.

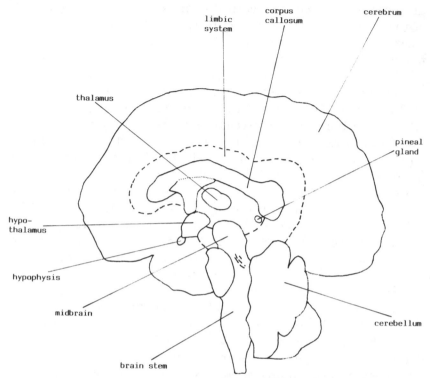

Figure 13. Map of the human brain. The thalamus is the arrangement of grey matter concerned with the relay of sensory information to higher centres. The hypothalamus is the coordinating center for numerous visceral functions. The hypophysis (pituitary gland) is a gland that secretes a number of important proteins and hormones that regulate many body activities, such as growth, reproduction, and metabolism. The cerebellum is the center integrating sensory information relevant to locomotion. The pineal gland is believed to control the onset of puberty. The cerebrum is the dominant region of the brain, the seat of most complex and highest brain functions (including mental capacities). The corpus callosum is a tract of nerve fibers that connects the two cerebral hemispheres. The limbic system consists of structures that control emotions. The brain stem comprises the cerebellum, the whole of the midbrain, and a portion of the hindbrain; it controls voluntary and involuntary muscle activity. The midbrain connects the brain stem with the cerebrum.

Table 6. Evolution towards intelligence.

Time (years ago)	Systems	Capacity of Cell-Brain Memory(bits)		Major Events in Evolution
100,000	*Homo sapiens*	10^{11} $\wedge$	10^{13} $\wedge$	Language, culture
1 million	*Homo erectus*			Increasing brain capacity
150 million	Birds			
180 million	Mammals	10^{11}	10^{11}	Emotions
300 million	Reptiles		10^{10}	Ritualized behavior
400 million	Amphibians	10^{10}	10^{9}	
1 billion	Multicellular organisms			Sexuality
1.5 billion	Eucaryotes	10^{8}		Cell nucleus
2.5 billion	Bacteria	10^{6}		Cell compartments
3 billion	Enzymes	10^{5}		"Cooperation" of proteins and nucleotides
3.5 billion	Hypercycles			Genetic transmission
4 billion	Prenucelotides, proteins			Random assemblage of prenucleotides and amino acids

Source: After : Leinfellner 1987.

2. It makes possible to *construct models* of the problems and their solution at an abstract level.

The point is that humans, in virtue of their intellect, are able to *anticipate* certain situations or problems and to *learn consciously* from their errors. There are game theoretic solutions to problems that are available to humans but not to other animals (Maynard Smith 1984). Therefore, it seems undeniable that the human method of problem solving indeed has increased fitness. The emergence of the rational was a most remarkable event, because it has made possible problem solving by applying games and models. Despite the many still unanswered questions, it seems likely that this new method of problem solving is a result of the increasing brain complexity, a result of the emergence of evermore complex circuits, neurons linked together and interrelated richly.

We are approaching thus a materialist view of the origins of rationality; viz., mind. Such an approach, which, as I trust, will disgust many people for emotional reasons, is part and parcel of evolutionary epistemology, can be learned from some recent publications by its advocates (Lorenz 1977; Mohr 1987; Oeser 1987; Wuketits 1985a). And, as should be expected, this approach is sustained by authors from the sociobiologists' camp. Wilson pronounces "our" view with a characteristic flourish: "We have vastly more to say about nature that is accurate, verifiable and of practical use because this approach has been applied without compromise to very conceivable phenomenon during the past 300 years. It is difficult to believe that the human mind, 'the citadel itself' according to Darwin, will prove a permanent exception" (1987, p. 15). The scientific, materialist approach—the term *materialist* is used here in its widest sense—feeds back on the understanding of our own mental structures and capacities.

We might be tempted to speculate on the dating of the evolution of these capacities. Was *Australopithecus* a rational animal? Was *Homo erectus* capable of rationality? It should be clear that we have great difficulty answering such questions reliably. Of course, we have no fossil record of the emergence and evolution of rationality. However, there are two methods to deal with such questions: one comes from paleoneurology, the other from the study of tools used by prehistoric humans. (For a general account of paleoneurology, see the review of Jerison 1976.) Generally, it is to be supposed that the increasing capacity of tool making in human evolution depends on the increase in brain capacity (p. 27). *Homo sapiens* used and manufactured more complex tools than the members of *Homo erectus*, whose artifacts were more complex than those of *Australopithecus* (Oakley 1972; Young 1971). The really rapid change and progress in tool making did not start until the appearance of modern humankind, some 40,000 years ago. At that time humans already were concerned with an explanation of nature and their place in the universe. This conclusion can be drawn from the cave paintings, statuettes of stone and bone, and engravings on bone, and burials. The existence of these objects is well-documented at the level of the Neanderthals, members of the *sapiens* group (*Homo sapiens neandertalensis*). (For a review see Trinkaus and Howells 1979.) From the fact that the Neanderthals buried their dead and placed offerings with them, like flowers (identified from their pollen), we can conclude that they were aware of their own death, which is an element of rationality (discussed earlier) and presupposes other such elements (e.g., use of symbols, teleological thinking). The true origin of the rational, however, remains obscure. Some authors (Shapiro 1974; Young 1971) have suspected that teleological thinking and acting and even some explanation of the universe might have appeared at the level of *Homo erectus* some 500,000 years ago. But, because of the absence of any evidence, this remains a speculation.

Thus, all things considered, we can conclude that rationality in a narrower sense is not much older than 50,000 years or so, although some features regarded as elements of rationality might have appeared at an earlier stage of human evolution. Ferguson (1988) has argued that we can distinguish five stages of human intellectual evolution (Table 7). His notion of rationality,

Table 7. Stages in human intellectual evolution.

Stage	*Characteristic*
Animistic	Possessing symbolic memory, lack of self-awareness; environmental interpretation: totemism
Magical	Acquisition of "self" and language; claiming miraculous powers; all forces personalized
Normative	Breakdown of dual class societies, rise of craftsmen; awareness of "self" in populace
Rational	Discovery of nature of language, creation of "faculty" of reason, mathematical generalization
Critical	Integration of perceptual and conceptual functions

Source: After Ferguson 1988.

however, is that of *scientific* rationality, which can be dated back to some ancient cultures that appeared only a few thousands of years ago. Despite Ferguson, our thesis that the emergence and development of the rational is to be correlated with increasing brain capacity, seems to have substance. What else would explain the fact that only the species having the most advanced brain, *Homo sapiens*, exhibits such complex mental capacities?

The Meaning of Language

Human rationality is inseparably linked with language. Language is the peculiarly human way to communicate. The term *language*, however, is ambiguous. Sometimes it refers to communication in its widest sense—that is, to communication in animals, too ("language" of bees, dolphins, apes, and so on)—and sometimes it is restricted to human vocal communication. I prefer to use the term to characterize *verbal communication* in humans, being aware that, however, *nonverbal* expression (smiling, laughter, gesticulation, and so on) plays an important role in human communication and social interaction (see, e.g. Argyle 1972; Hinde 1972).

Communication indeed is a widespread phenomenon in the animal kingdom, and animals interact in different ways; for example, by means of optical signals, body movement, and sound. Primates have the most complex communication systems, and there is some substance to the argument that our nearest relatives, for they live in complex social groups, have inherited systems of social signaling that might be viewed as similar to human language (Altmann 1973; Bonner 1980; Hill 1968). Besides, teaching language to apes has shown that chimpanzees indeed are the gifted among all animals. Some of them can learn vocabularies of 200 (English) words and also elementary rules of syntax (see the sympathetic account by Linden 1976). Understandably, there has been enthusiasm for these results among biologists. However, I feel that this enthusiasm has been somewhat exaggerated, because—notwithstanding the chimpanzee's capacities—true linguistic novelty is lacked. As Wilson (1978, p. 27) remarks: "No chimp genius has accomplished the equivalent of joining the sentences 'Mary gives me apple' and 'I like Mary' into the more complex proposition 'Mary's giving me apple why I like her'." Human language, on the contrary, is characterized by inventiveness and also by a king of animism that is testable by the development of language in children (Piaget 1973a) as well as in adults. Examine, for example, the sentence *The wind blows*. It suggests that the wind is like a person and that it can exist independently of blowing. Although we know that this is absurd, we often use such phrases. These peculiarities of human language may be interrelated with the considerable amount of *symbolism* inherent in human communication at the vocal level, as symbolization generally can be regarded as an essential feature of human evolution (Bertalanffy 1968; Ferguson 1988). Furthermore, human language is different from animal communication in its recursive structure; that is, we can have a reflexive understanding of our own communication systems (Tennant 1984).

To stick to the point, in the evolutionary epistemologist's perspective, language depends on biological mechanisms and has evolved alongside anatomical and physiological traits. This has been expounded in a full-length study by Lenneberg (1967; see also his brief account, 1973). A more recent study in German is Müller 1987. Lenneberg, however, has not made any reference to evolutionary epistemology. But recently, Lange (1985) has grasped the evolutionary epistemologist's view and developed it within the framework of linguistics. He adopted "the standpoint that humans are gifted with pre-knowledge items" (Lange 1985, p. 9) which he traditionally calls *categories*: "Nature has gifted the human baby with language, which is a cognitive device more concrete and versatile than anything given to animals. It takes, however, more time to be mastered. Human language has to be developed by the humans themselves, which means that it has to be learnt by the individual, for it is already there as an a priori to him" (p. 12). In chapter 4, I argued that learning a language in the individual is due to innate capacities, although the learning of any *particular* language such as Chinese, Russian, English, or German depends on social and cultural circumstances. The languages now spoken in the world are results of cultural evolution (see next chapter) but the capability of language in general is due to organic evolution. As the anthropologist and ethnographer George A. Dorsey, more than sixty years ago, put it: "Language is part of human adjustment, learned as other actions or habits are learned. Every normal newborn has the potential ability to learn . . . English, Kwakiutl, Chinese, Zulu — any language" (Dorsey 1925, p. 375).

Again, we should be interested in knowing the beginnings of

human language; but, again, we might be disappointed with our knowledge of this fascinating question. We do not know the date of the emergence of language in human evolution. However, for language is linked with other rational capacities, we can derive some conclusions from our findings concerning the "life world" of fossil man. At least, it seems clear that a hominid who was capable of reflecting upon his or her own existence and place in nature was capable of language, too—language in its strict sense of verbal communication. Populations of humans that buried their dead and, obviously, had developed an idea of "life after death" and *the* other world palpably communicated by the means of verbal interaction, because it seems impossible to communicate about such alleged "worlds" by mere gesticulation. Hence, it is highly probable that the Neanderthals were capable of language. Among other authors, Lenneberg (1967) reached this conclusion. Thus, the only acceptable way to date the origins of language seems to be its correlation with other rational capacities, which however, presuppose a kind of language. But this, again, is only an indication of dynamic interactions between different components of the evolution of rationality. Another question concerns the structure of primitive language: its sound and syntax. This question, one of the most vexing questions in the context of human evolution, has not yet found—and probably will never find—an accurate answer. Any attempt to reconstruct the language of primitive people by drawing conclusions from today's existing primitive societies and their communication or from the language of children is desperately defective. Considering, for instance, the language of children we have to take into account "that their situation is quite different from that of our earliest human ancestors, because the child is growing up in an environment where there is already a fully developed language" (Barber 1964, p. 28). The languages of today's primitive societies, too, already are fully developed and result from a long history.

What evolutionary epistemology can contribute to the understanding of human language is little more than explaining the innate disposition of language learning as a product of evolutionary processes. Of course, as rationality in general can be viewed as a motor of increasing fitness, language, too, can be regarded as an action enhancing survival.

Evolutionary Origins of Metaphysical Belief

Once more I want to draw the reader's attention to the burials of Neanderthals and other early representatives of the species *Homo sapiens.* Obviously, these humans were in need of metaphysical belief, which also is documented by the skull cult (see Figure 14). A kind of metaphysics seems to be a general

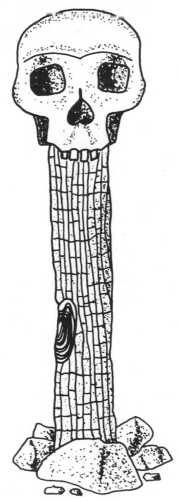

Figure 14. Skull cult of Neanderthals. The human skull has played an important role in the development of metaphysical belief; it demonstrates the existence of a kind of religion.

characteristic of humans who, for that reason, were regarded by Arthur Schopenhauer as an *animal metaphysicum*. Indeed, take any society of modern people and you will recognize metaphysical systems, a notion of life after death, of *the* other world, and so on. This phenomenon has fascinated anthropologists and social scientists for centuries. From the point of view of evolutionary epistemology, there is a clear—and annoying—answer: metaphysical belief is to be explained as the result of particular interactions between early humans and their external world and thus result from specific life conditions (Wuketits 1987b).

Note that I am not speaking of "metaphysics" as a philosophical discipline, but the human requirement for metaphysical belief including religion and, generally, *irrational* world views. True, as rational beings humans, at the same time, are irrational creatures. (For some philosophical reflections on this, see Stich 1985.) But this is somewhat trivial—only a rational being is capable of irrationality and irrationalism. It indeed would be absurd to say, for example, that a cat or a dog is irrational. Ever since the emergence of rationality, humans have invented irrational belief systems and—when they were lacking in rational explanations—projected their own "little universe," their own actions, into imaginary spheres beyond the visible world.[1] This *anthropomorphism* has caused the notion of a teleologically organized universe. Humans cannot imagine that there are processes in the universe without any purpose; hence, they invented the purposeful universe according to their own teleological actions (Lorenz 1976). What has been claimed by some philosophers and now can be substantiated by evolutionary epistemology is that the world picture of humans is often constrained by emotions and illusions reaching back to the living conditions of prehistoric man (Topitsch 1966, 1979).

I feel that many people think of this as a negative chapter in philosophy. Consider the thesis; metaphysical belief does not tell us anything about "first causes" or "last purposes" (God), but rather about our own inclination to such beliefs. And this inclination, therefore we argue from the point of view of evolutionary epistemology, is nothing but the result of specific living conditions of humans. And, as Wilson (1978, p. 183) says, "religion is one of the major categories of behavior"—and nothing else. That means that any kind of religious or metaphysical belief is just an expression of human behavior and therefore constrained by biological (ecological) conditions. (For criticism on this view see, e.g., Austin 1985.) The relativity of metaphysical belief, however, seems to be plausible. Imagine, one of our ancestors observing a flash of lightning and having no idea of physical principles. It is likely that this early human believed in supranatural powers, for the person required an explanation but was far from a physical understanding of the phenomenon in question. The only possibility of explaining this phenomenon was to project a Godlike being having the power to flash. This means that metaphysical belief comes from our own projections, our desires for an explanation of the universe and certain phenomena within it. Metaphysical-religious belief therefore is relative to our own nature including our need to understand external reality.

These claims are not new. They can be traced back to Hume's *Dialogues Concerning Natural Religion* (published posthumously in 1779, quoted in Flew 1978) and can be found in the writings of authors influenced by Darwin's theory in the nineteenth century. Caspari (1877), for instance, argued that religion developed similarly to other expressions of the human mind (e.g., arts) in prehistoric times and that its emergence was due to particular social interactions. Darwin (1871) had established the thesis that metaphysical and religious belief in humans were related to evolutionary processes and thus could be explained like any other mental capacity as a result of (human) evolution. Recently, some authors arguing from the sociobiological point of view, have been most explicit on the evolutionary relativity of religion (Ruse 1985, 1986; Wilson 1978). Their contention is that notions like God, in the last instance, are mere illusions caused by our very nature, which includes a need for comfort and meaning. This contention essentially is in tune with the implications of evolutionary epistemology.

To continue the argument, I should say that our marvelous brain has given rise to creative imagination and that this implies some consequences. "It creates fear or anxiety about the future, fear about our own fancies and imaginations" (Löwenhard 1982, p. 19). These imaginations, of course, transgress our world of medium dimensions but they are the *result* of our commitment to the mesocosm. We project our experiences, actions, and expectations constrained by the mesocosm into spheres beyond this mesocosm. Remember that our vision of supranatural beings reveals figures of humanlike creatures (God as a wise father) or at least of some creatures known to us (animals representing different gods), and that we use symbols to demonstrate or to make visible the action of gods—symbols that we take from our own "life world." (The more complex this "life world," the more abstract are the symbols.)

I am aware that these are very provocative assertions. One might think that the evolutionary explanation of religion explains away religion. This would require a more detailed analysis than the one given here, but I, at least, should stress the fact that evolutionists, when explaining religion by the means of natural sciences, usually do not try to combat religious belief or harm religious people. We, as evolutionists, try only to understand metaphysics-religion and its manifestations on the basis of our knowledge about humans; we accept any religious human being, but we ask *why* humans have developed religious belief and what the sense of such belief might be. When doing so, however, we attain to the conclusion that religion has not been imposed on humans by any *real* supranatural being, but that, on the contrary, this being is the result of human imagination constrained by fear, death awareness, hope, and so on—*ecce homo.* I feel that many people will be taken aback at these conclusions, and I am aware that more empirical data are needed to corroborate our claims. But, on the other side, if one takes evolution seriously, if one agrees that humans have evolved, and if, finally, one is prepared to speculate about the origins of our mind in an evolutionary perspective—then there is no escape from such conclusions. (Sorry for my radical words.) I admit that I myself am much attracted by the possibility of getting rational explanations of irrationalism. There is grandeur in this view of life . . .

Biological Constraints in the Evolution of Knowledge

Humans are the most effective knowledge-producing systems. They not only acquire knowledge about the visible world, but venture to grasp the invisible, too; more than this, they, obviously create pictures of supranatural beings even if these alleged beings are beyond the reach of rational knowledge. Hence, there are at least three types of human knowledge:

1. Knowledge gained through experience in a strict sense;

that is, knowledge gained through sense organs. This knowledge is committed to our mesocosm.

2. Knowledge gained by scientific inference, going beyond the mesocosm.

3. Knowledge gained by mere belief through projection of supranatural beings, again transgressing the mesocosm.

The first type in *ratiomorphic*, the second *rational*, and the third *irrational*. As you see, I use the term *knowledge* in a broad sense. Perhaps, some might wish a clear distinction between *knowledge* and *belief*, and one might argue that knowledge cannot be gained through belief. This, however, is a question of perspective. From a rational point of view God is unknowable; but religious people claim that they actually know God. Hence there is a kind of knowledge, neither empirical nor theoretical (in the sense of scientific theories), but based on certain operations in the human brain and held by many people. This knowledge need not to be true, but it exists and cannot be ignored. Besides, I do not think that it is necessary, for the purpose of the present analysis, to elaborate an exact distinction between rational and irrational knowledge, between knowledge in a narrower sense and (irrational) belief. "Exactly how and where the line is to be drawn is a question which has proved remarkably difficult to answer, one reason for this being that in common speech the distinction is not sharp" (Ayer 1976, p. 55). I content myself with these remarks even at the risk of incompleteness and shortcuts, because I have to make some other points that, in the present context, are more relevant.

First, from an evolutionary point of view, we have good reason to suppose that the *experience of living* is the basis of knowledge (Young, 1987). It indeed is the immediate experience of every human being that he or she lives, has some desires, hope, fear, and so on and so forth. What we know and what we believe to know comes from our living conditions. Thus, our knowledge is constrained by life and our experience of living. Societies living in the desert particularly will develop some knowledge about how and where to get water; people living in the arctic region will generate knowledge about how to keep alive under the extreme cold. There would be many examples of this kind, showing that human knowledge processing is determined by elementary living conditions and needs and that particular ecological constraints require particular knowledge. But also emotions are influenced by such constraints. Hence, we can state that the biological factors of human knowledge processing include both internal needs (elementary drives that cannot be controlled rationally, like hunger) and external (ecological) conditions.

My second point concerns, again, brain mechanisms. Everything and anything perceived by humans must be processed in the brain in order to get a model that allows for life-preserving reactions. (Remember what has been said about realism and coherence in the last chapter.) Our active brain produces models of internal and external reality, it generates rational knowledge as well as irrational belief. In short, that brain mechanisms are responsible for even the "highest" intellectual capacities, like creative imagination, should be a commonplace—and *is* a commonplace accepted even by authors like Eccles (1970) despite their inclination to a kind of mysticism (see also Popper and Eccles 1977). But, if we agree to the important role that our brain plays in our life, then we should agree to the assertion that our knowledge is constrained by brain activities and thus depends upon biological processes. Moreover, we can argue that the brain plays a major role with regard to the *motivation* to acquire knowledge, be it rational or irrational. Roederer (1979, p. 103) has made the claim that "even 'objective' science cannot be dissociated from human brain functions in an absolute way." And Oeser (1987) has defined scientific knowledge as a particular brain power. (I shall deal with scientific knowledge from the point of view of evolutionary epistemology in Chapter 7. To be sure, science does not depend solely on biological factors; but, for the moment, let me draw your attention to just these factors.)

The third point, following on the second, is that our brain gives us the capacity for problem solving. It has been argued that to live means to solve problems (see p. 62). This seems to be obvious, and we humans indeed are constantly engaged in problem solving, not only in our everyday life but also with regard to problems beyond our mesocosm (concerning the structure of the universe, the atomical compounds of things, etc.). It is worth mentioning, however, that our brain not only solves problems but also *creates* problems (which are not easy to handle). "*Homo sapiens,*" writes Hofman (1988, p. 443), "despite its impressive intellectual capacities, might in the end become the victim of its own mind by, paradoxically, creating problems that it is then unable to solve." I am not sure whether one should say "*despite* its intellectual capacities"; I rather suspect that this is *because of* these capacities. We should bear in mind that the human is the only one living creature known in this universe able to invent Utopia, create ideologies that in themselves are most problematic and continue to harm humankind. At least, it seems that our intellect is janus faced. And again, this is due to our brain, which has produced rational as well as irrational knowledge but, at the same time, has not the power to control this knowledge.

It might become apparent that evolutionary epistemology, by studying the biological conditions of human knowledge, has most relevant anthropological implications. However, our knowledge is constrained by social and cultural factors, too. A biological theory of the evolution of cognitive capacities can yield important aspects explaining the (biological) preconditions of human knowledge, but it does not suffice to describe and reconstruct the particular paths in the development of this knowledge from primitive world pictures of prehistoric peoples to the most sophisticated explanations by modern science, transgressing not only our mesocosm but also irrational belief. Note, for the moment, that indeed our brain—and thus a biological system—produces ideas, but that the manifestation, the "materialization" of these ideas in cultural and technological objects shows a certain *Eigendynamik* that ontologically is not to be reduced to organic entities. A more detailed analysis of culture and its evolution will be given in the next chapter. I shall try to show that evolutionary epistemology applies to cultural evolution but that it has to do justice to the peculiarity of cultural systems. One might wonder how this can be managed. Please be patient.

Cultural Constraints in the Evolution of Knowledge

It is customary to separate culture from nature and, as I believe, most people intuitively know when a certain object is to be characterized as "natural" and when as "cultural." Now, what is *culture*? And what is *nature*? A most cursory answer to these questions is this: culture is the sum-total of constructed objects, whereas nature comprises all structures and processes that exist and occur independent of any human action. This definition of culture requires some further elaboration. I shall be more explicit on this in the next chapter. For the moment it may suffice to state that culture is "an extrasomatic, temporal continuum of things and events dependent upon symboling," and that its constituents are "tools, implements, utensils, clothing, ornaments, customs, institutions, beliefs, rituals, games, works of art, language, etc." (White 1959, p. 3). True, many animals produce *extrasomatic* structures—for instance, the beaver's huts and the birds' nests—so that one is tempted to speak of evolution of culture in animals (Bonner 1980), but human culture (i.e., culture in a strict sense) always depends on teleological actions induced by a conscious brain and not simply programmed by innate teaching (and learning) mechanisms. Because consciousness is peculiar to humans, humans are the only living creatures capable of culture, which then, vice verse, points to the uniqueness of humans in the living world.

In this section I want to call the reader's attention to the fact that the evolution of (human) knowledge is strongly influenced by social and cultural determinants. This might be a truism; however, the question of how social and cultural constraints affect the growth of knowledge is less trivial. The problem with this question appropriately arises from some not yet clarified interactions. On the one side, the existence of societies and cultural systems depends on the existence of some knowledge, be it rational or irrational knowledge; on the other side, there seems to be substance to the argument that sociocultural factors strongly influence the development of knowledge. Sociocultural systems imply *meaning;* knowledge requires a certain horizon of meaning or, as Shaner (1987) puts it, a *contextual relief.* Particular observations, theories, and so on remain meaningless, if they are in no way comparable to at least some elements in the existing corpus of knowledge:

> The object of perception or thought requires a horizon, or backdrop, or stage that serves as the condition for the possibility of its having discernable borders; it must be so limited in order to have any meaningful conceptual content or be perceptually distinguishable. Even an idea like infinity requires some understanding of its antithesis in order to be understood. Some notion of finitude must be implicitly dormant or explicitly brought "to mind" within the person's greater horizon or meanings (Shaner '987,m pp. 38–39).

Again, to put it in a terminology that by now might be familiar to the reader, our perception of objects or events should be *coherent*, now with respect to sociocultural contexts. To be sure, the sun is the *sun*, but in order to make it plausible as a physical object, we require some physical knowledge as background; it would be difficult to explain it as a physical object to a person who is "imprisoned" by the myth that the sun is a god.

From the point of view of evolutionary epistemology it is trivial to say that sociocultural systems—and sociocultural constraints upon the development of (human) knowledge—have evolved. Another question—a most important question—however, is whether the evolution of sociocultural systems (including the growth of *scientific* knowledge) has been determined by mechanisms explainable in biological terms; that is, whether models of organic evolution can be applied to sociocultural evolution. Up to now I have been concerned with evolutionary epistemology as a biological theory or with the first of two evolutionary epistemology programs (remember the Prospectus, Table 1). Many authors consider evolutionary epistemology a biological theory that helps us understand the (biological) *preconditions* of the acquisition of knowledge in humans, but has to say nothing about the particular paths of the evolution of human knowledge and the mechanisms underlying this knowledge processing. For this reason, evolutionary epistemology has been regarded as a mere descriptive theory or discipline that rests on biological data (evolutionary biology, physiology, neurobiology, ethology) or, as Stegmüller (1985) has argued, as an *explanatory* theory concerned with the *dispositions* of knowledge and not with knowledge itself, so that one might object that evolutionary epistemology is *epistemology* in name only (Hull 1982). However, another research program is running under the title *evolutionary epistemology*, and the advocates of this program indeed are interested in the evolution of human knowledge (particularly scientific knowledge) and its possible explanation. This program has become an area of controversies and will be target in the next two chapters.

Let me present an illustration of the interactions between biological and sociocultural constraints in the evolution of human knowledge and between the two research programs of evolutionary epistemology (Figure 15). By means of this illustration I want to emphasize the following:

1. Human knowledge is constrained, in the first instance,

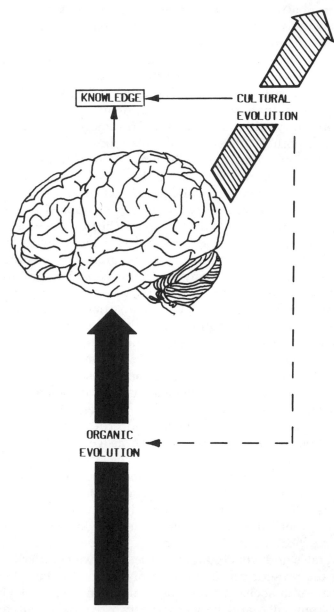

Figure 15. Interaction between organic and cultural evolution and between organic and cultural constraints in the development of (human) knowledge. The brain is to be considered as the "first instance" of knowledge gaining, however, the development of knowledge is constrained by cultural forces, too. Cultural evolution shows a particular direction, and it even acts back upon organic evolution.

by the brain or the CNS (which is the organ that produces knowledge and which is clearly a result of organic evolution).

2. The human brain has produced cultural systems that have developed characteristics that transgress their producer, so to speak; that is, characteristics that cannot be sufficiently explained by their producer's evolution.

3. Cultural systems build constraints on the particular development of knowledge.

4. Cultural evolution (including the evolution of scientific ideas) even feeds back upon organic evolution.

As the reader will recognize, it is my intention to link the two programs of evolutionary epistemology. The crucial problem, however, is to show that, although cultural evolution depends on organic evolution (and the emergence of culture is due to brain functions), the mechanisms underlying organic evolution, on the one hand, and cultural evolution, on the other hand, are different. Is it justified, then, to speak of cultural *evolution*? I think it is not only justified but necessary, because there is one common trait: both organic and cultural evolution can be regarded as learning processes. Evolutionary epistemology has offered some evidence that evolution is a universal learning and cognition process and that there is a hierarchy of such processes from unicellular organisms to humans. Culture can be understood as the most sophisticated learning process requiring particular modes of explanation and a particular type of evolutionary epistemology. This type of evolutionary epistemology, too, requires a view of (cultural) evolution that goes beyond strict Darwinism and is to be characterized as a systems view.

I am afraid that in this chapter I have gone too fast through an enormous aggregate of problems. The aim of this chapter has been to sketch just some relevant aspects of human knowledge and hint at the evolutionary approach that might be apt to explain some enigmas of (human) knowledge. Evolutionary epistemology has some lessons to teach us about our own knowledge processing.

1. By means of rational knowledge humans are able to transgress their own ratiomorphic apparatus and the medium-sized dimensions to which this apparatus has been related.

2. Rational knowledge emerged late in evolution; it is typical of humans and can be characterized by elements such as verba

communication, symbols, and self-reflection. The evolutionary epistemologists' claim is that rationality, its peculiar characters notwithstanding, is a result of brain evolution, which has been a complex process of integration.

3. Language is inseparably linked with the emergence of rational knowledge. However, language, too, is a product of organic evolution. The capability of learning language is inborn, the development and learning of any particular language is constrained by sociocultural evolution.

4. Knowledge generally depends on both biological and sociocultural factors. The human capacity for knowledge—that is, rational knowledge—is due to biological structures and mechanisms, but the particular paths of the development of (rational) knowledge are constrained by sociocultural factors.

5. Rationality implies, in a way, the irrational; irrational belief has been a product of the human aspiration for an understanding of ourselves and our place in nature. Metaphysical belief (religion), therefore, can be explained as the result of certain living conditions.

6

Evolutionary Epistemology and Culture

Man is both a biological being and a social
individual. Among his responses to external or
internal stimuli, some are wholly dependent upon
his nature, others upon his social environment.

Claude Lévi-Strauss

Culture: A Break with Organic Evolution?

The problem of how to define culture in relation to or in
distinction from organic evolution absorbs much of the interest
of social scientists, anthropologists, and biologists. Before
discussing the relationship between organic and cultural
evolution and inspecting these relations from the point of view of
evolutionary epistemology, we should focus on a possible
definition of *culture.* In the last chapter I approached a definition
by stating that culture is an extrasomatic continuum of things
and events and that it depends on teleological actions. Also, I
stressed the uniqueness of human culture and distinguished it
from the animals' production of extrasomatic structures. Finally,
it has become apparent that cognition in humans is partly
determined or constrained by culture.

It is true that "cognition in man depends upon the existence
of objective, external symbolic models of reality in a way no ape's
does" (Geertz 1965, p. 47); that is, it depends upon culture. We
should realize, however, that *culture* is made up of many *cultures*
(Linton 1955), an enormous variety of tools, customs, and so on.

Cultural evolution has not produced species and genetic programs, but a variety of extrasomatic structures depending upon the capacity of one single species. (I shall be more explicit on this in the next section.) The concept of culture, then, can be used as descriptive concept covering the sum-total of extrasomatic structures produced by humans; but it can also be used as an explanatory concept explaining the historic processes that have channeled humankind's particular way of living (Kluckhohn and Kelly 1983).

Speaking of culture in an abstract sense, one might be tempted to think of a "superorganic" entity. Such an entity has indeed been suggested by Popper's concept of World 3, which comprises knowledge in an objective sense (cultural heritage coded on material, extrasomatic structures, and scientific ideas) and contrasts with World 1 (physical objects and states) and World 2 (states of consciousness) (see Popper 1972a; Popper and Eccles 1977). I should say that this view does not much comfort an evolutionist (and in spite of my admiration of Popper's philosophy as a whole, I have not much sympathy for the concept of World 3). If culture were a "world" per se, then it indeed would be a break with organic evolution. How about a more biologically founded concept of culture? Count (1958, p. 1049) argued that "culture is man's peculiarly elaborated way of expressing the vertebrate biogram." (The concept of the *biogram* characterizes the specific "way of living" in any animal group. According to Count's view in vertebrate phylogeny the specific, vertebrate, biogram has been elaborated without being radically modified.) This view implies that culture in humans is just a special case of behavior, a special expression of behavioral patterns in vertebrates.

As the reader will have recognized, there is disagreement with respect to a definition of *culture*, although everybody has an intuition of what culture, in its broadest sense, means: human-made objects that, some way or other, contrast natural objects. This intuition, however, has tempted even many anthropologists to separate culture from nature, to believe that culture has developed independent of nature, of organic evolution. Kroeber (quoted in Geertz, 1964) speculated along these lines. For Kroeber culture was a sudden event, an all-or-none occurrence in the evolution of the primates. Culture, "once begun, set upon its own course so as to grow wholly independently of the further organic evolution of man" (Geertz

1964, p. 38). This contrast of nature and culture is *not* a primeval fact—it is a result of our speculations about culture, a creation of culture itself, "a protective rampart thrown up around it because it only felt able to assert its existence and uniqueness by destroying all the links that lead back to its original association with the other manifestations of life" (Lévi-Strauss 1969, p. xxix). But once we have separated culture from the other manifestations of (human) life, it becomes more and more difficult to understand it.

I want to define *culture*, therefore, as a particular manifestation of human life, dependent upon the working brain and constrained, at least to a certain extent, by human biological evolution. However, as indicated in Chapter 1, this does not mean that culture is reducible to organic evolution and that it is nothing else but an "organic event." Special events in cultural evolution cannot be sufficiently explained in biological terms. The pyramids of Egypt and the myths around them have no adequate biological explanation; the same is true, for example, of the rise and fall of ancient Rome, World War II, Picasso's paintings, and so forth. Is cultural evolution, then, a break with organic evolution?

Julian Huxley (1957, p. 70) wrote that culture "appears *sub specie evolutionis* as a self-maintaining system or organization of intercommunicating human beings and their products." Huxley, a biologist, thus did not neglect the peculiarity of culture and its capacity of self-maintenance. The same is true to many other biologists. It is not true that, as might be suspected, a biological or, in a broader sense, an evolutionary approach to an understanding of culture inevitably leads to a reductionistic view. Evolutionary epistemology—basing on the tenet that humans, like other organisms, are information-processing systems—does not disregard culture and the peculiarity of cultural evolution. Advocates of this epistemology do not claim that the evolution of cultural systems obeys the same principles as organic evolution, or that cultural evolution is just an extension of organic evolution (see, e.g., Vollmer 1984). They are interested in possible connections between organic and cultural evolution, however; and, as we shall see, such connections can indeed be found and explained by an approach based on a view of information processing.

The evolutionary approach can yield an explanatory definition of culture. Culture indeed means a break with organic evolution, in the sense that its evolution exhibits its own principles; but its emergence cannot be properly explained independent of organic evolution—which should be somewhat trivial, because humankind, as a biological species and at the same time the "carrier" of cultural evolution, has been shaped by the principles of organic evolution. Hence, *natural history* is the broader framework to which *cultural history* can be related (Oeser 1987) without being reduced to it in an ontological sense. The point is to find connections between nature and culture, historic connections, as it were, without denying the *Eigendynamik* of cultural evolution. To draw parallels or show analogies between organic and cultural evolution without knowing a mechanism by which these parallels, if there are any, come into existence is not enough. Therefore, analogizing cultural evolution to biological evolution, as many evolutionists like Haeckel (1905) did, has not much substance.

Now, if we look for an explanatory, a "historic" definition of culture, we are prompted to ask on which primary factors the emergence of culture depended. Two factors are most obvious: communication and social learning (remember the definition of culture by Lumsden and Wilson quoted on p. 30). Social learning, *sociality*, presupposes communication (Baylis and Tang Halpin 1982); communication makes social learning most efficient. Higher primates have highly complex social systems due to their capability of communication; even at the subhuman level, we have efficient strategies of social learning and thus something similar to what we call tradition in human systems. Hence, it can be said that socialization, based on communication systems, has been the precondition of culture. Humans have attained culture "in part by means of teaching conducted during the socialization of the young" (Lumsden and Wilson 1981, p. 4). Social evolution, therefore, was the antecedent of cultural evolution in the history of humankind; social and cultural evolution cannot be separated from each other, because culture always occurs as an affair between many individuals (even if only a few individuals really advance the process of culture).

To summarize briefly to this point, I argue that cultural history depends upon specific biological processes, that the emergence of culture is part of the grandiose universal natural history, but that cultural evolution, once started, obeyed its own principles and gave human evolution an entirely new direction, even acting back upon organic evolution. Surely, the emergence of culture was a recent event in the great chain of universal evolution, it was, as Riedl (1987d) puts it, a "retarded ignition" (*Spätzündung*) in evolution. Before entering a discussion of the close relationship between organic and cultural evolution, however, I concentrate on these differences.

Organic and Cultural Evolution: Striking Differences

If we compare cultural changes to processes of organic evolution, we realize a few more or less profound differences (see Table 8). (For further details see, e.g., Dobzhansky 1962; Dobzhansky et al. 1977; Hull 1982; Osche 1987; Wuketits 1984c.)

1. There is a difference with regard to tempo and rapidity. The evolution of life started more than 3 billion years ago and has been a rather slow process. Since the emergence of modern humans (*Homo sapiens sapiens*), some 40,000 years ago, the biological character of humans has changed little. But it was apparently within this period that humans evolved exceptionally

Table 8. Differences between organic and cultural evolution.

Organic Evolution	*Cultural Evolution*
Slow processes	Rapid processes
Goal-directed processes without any goal intention	Goal-intending processes
No direct inheritance of acquired characteristics	"Inheritance" of acquired characteristics
Type of information: genetic	Type of information: intellectual
Endosomatic continuum of information processing (genetic transmission)	Exosomatic continuum of information processing (intellectual transmission)
Producing a variety of species	One species produces a variety of cultures
No cross-lineage borrowing	Cross-lineage borrowing

rapidly through culture and that there was an explosive growth of cultural systems, including a variety of artefacts, institutions, languages, ideas, and so on. Furthermore, if we consider the evolution of technology in a narrower sense, we become aware of an even more explosive—and formidable—development in the last four or five decades.

2. Cultural evolution differs from organic evolution with regard to the mechanisms giving the processes their direction. At the level of organic evolution no intention underlies the evolutionary process. Organic evolution exhibits goal-directed changes without any intention—there is nobody to consciously anticipated any goal. Cultural evolution, on the contrary, always depends on a director—it depends on human conscious activities that tend toward certain goals. Thus, cultural evolution not only occurs at a rapid pace, but also "in an entirely new direction from that which any species population has previously taken" (Stebbins 1971, p. 177). Culture is the expression of a really creative organism, cultural evolution is directed by this organism. Consequently, the human appears to be the only species that has changed its evolution to its own purpose. It is true that other animals also act upon their environments, but they do not really *control* them (Ayala 1974). For this reasons humans also might have the chance to escape becoming extinct. No other species has had this chance, simply because no other species has been able to manage its own evolution. "Hence, if mankind were to become extinct, it would be the first instance of *evolutionary suicide* of a biological species" (Dobzhansky et al. 1977, p. 441, my italics)!

3. In organic evolution there is no direct inheritance of acquired characteristics, whereas acquired cultural characteristics are transmitted directly from one generation to the other. This is due to the type of information and the mechanisms of information processing.

4. Biological information is genetic information, laid down in the DNA. Cultural information is intellectual information, stored in the brain.

5. Biological (genetic) information can be transmitted to the next generation only by way of reproduction and inheritance, so that organic evolution is to be characterized as an endosomatic continuum of information processing. Cultural evolution, on the other side, is an extrasomatic continuum of transmitting information; intellectual information is transmitted by the

means of language and symbols, particularly writing, and represents a certain state of consciousness (see p. 55) that manifests itself in exosomatic structures and thus can be processed at a rapid pace.

6. Organic evolution produces a variety of species, whereas cultural evolution is to be characterized as the development of a variety of cultures depending on one single species (see Figure 16).

7. Finally, cultural evolution permits cross-lineage borrowing, whereas organic evolution does not. This is to say that members of one particular culture can adopt elements of other cultures by learning ("multiple parenting," see Boyd and Richerson 1985).

The most central difference between organic and cultural evolution is in information processing. This difference explains the tempo in cultural evolution. To process and transmit intellectual information does not require biological reproduction and heredity. One can lay down an idea by means of writings that can be spread directly, transmitted to many people. Hence, a person who has died can transmit intellectual information if this information is laid down in exosomatic structures, like books. (Whereas, as a matter of biological fact, a dead person no longer can transmit genetic information.)

In a way, cultural evolution indeed is a break with organic evolution; at least, it is a new *quality* in the long chain of evolutionary processes since the origin of our universe some 20 billion years ago, and it has given us newer and more sophisticated methods to cope with our environment, methods unknown to the other species. However, this is only the half of the story. As already mentioned, cultural evolution can be regarded as a particular case of the universal natural history.

Organic and Cultural Evolution: Intimate Connections

The argument that there are connections and a close relationship between organic and cultural evolution is as old as the claim that, because of the obvious differences between these types of evolutionary change, the study of organic evolution is of no use to the study of culture. True, many authors who have argued that the development of society and culture depends on

Figure 16. A striking difference between organic and cultural evolution is that organic evolution produces a variety of species, cultural evolution, however, depends on one single species that produces a variety of cultures that can be seen in different tools, architecture, writings, ornaments, and so on.

biological evolution often have misused biological concepts; and many of them have sustained Social Darwinism—a really bad ideology. This ideology, however, is not due to Darwin's own reflections, because "Darwin himself was always careful to dissociate his theory from any social implications" (Ruse 1987, p. 25). Other evolutionists, particularly Spencer and Haeckel, were not so careful with regard to this point. Therefore, I hasten to say that today's evolutionary epistemology is not to be confused with ideologies like Social Darwinism. None of the contemporary advocates of evolutionary epistemology has ever argued along the lines of Social Darwinism; and none of them has ever claimed that society and culture can be reduced to organic evolution. So, in which way are evolutionary epistemologists concerned with the relationship between organic and cultural evolution?

Recently, these relations, and the epistemological as well as the anthropological problems they pose, have been discussed extensively by authors advocating the view of evolutionary epistemology (see Callebaut 1987; Campbell 1975a, 1975b; Lorenz 1977; Mohr 1987; Oeser 1987, 1988; Riedl 1985, 1987d; Somenzi 1987; Stanzione 1984; Wuketits 1984c). If I am right, most of the advocates of evolutionary epistemology, as far as they are concerned with cultural evolution, would agree with Hull (1982, p. 322) that "one negative effect which the analogy between biological and sociocultural evolution has had is a tendency to misconstrue the units of sociocultural evolution." Hull himself dislikes being called an evolutionary epistemologist, which he has made clear in one of his most recent papers (Hull 1988), but this is not the point. The point is—or should be—that drawing parallels between organic and cultural evolution is not sufficient if we really want to understand the mechanisms of cultural evolution and its "units." How things could be done better? In what follows, I shall epitomize an evolutionary epistemologist's attitude toward cultural evolution and its relations to organic evolution.

Let me, first, recall that advocates of evolutionary epistemology indeed are prepared to appreciate the peculiarity of cultural evolution but that, second, they are not prepared to disconnect cultural and organic evolution. Evolutionary epistemologists neither claim that cultural evolution obeys the same laws of principles as organic evolution nor do they contend that cultural evolution is unimportant in the attempt to explain (human) knowledge (see the last section of the previous chapter).

From the point of view of evolutionary epistemology, one of the most striking connections between organic and cultural evolution is that both represent information systems or, better to say, evolving systems capable of information processing. As already mentioned, information processing at the cultural level cannot dispense with biological preconditions, because cultural evolution is possible only as a result of an active brain. Why, the reader might ask, am I arguing then that cultural evolution is not to be reduced to organic evolution? This question has a clear answer. Let me give a simple illustration. Human walking is undoubtedly constrained by biological structures and functions; it is constrained by muscles, bones, and so on, in short, by the biology of our locomotive apparatus. But where to move in any special case is *not* determined by the function of this apparatus. We have "room to move," in the literal sense of the word. If, for example, I want to walk in a park, I of course need by legs, but the *decision* to go there (or elsewhere) comes from my mind and not from my legs. Analogously, the creation of culture depends on a most complex biological apparatus, but the structure of this apparatus does not prescribe any goal to cultural evolution. The evolution of culture and the transmission of cultural systems has been favored by a wide range of *phenotypic plasticity* in humans (Brandon 1985). This means that only a species, which is highly plastic with regard to its biological nature, can be capable of culture. Hence, culture is a consequence of biological *preadaptations;* though these are necessary conditions to the acquisition of cultural behavior, they do not prescribe the particular pathways of cultural evolution. The pathways of cultural evolution are channeled by the human creative brain. The evolutionary flexibility and range of the brain's capacities provide humans with new experiences going beyond genetic determination (see the next two sections). Obviously, our brain is not an inflexible lump, but rather an "instrument manifesting its most fascinating potentiality as an *open system*" (Löwenhard 1982, p. 6, my italics) and allowing for loopholes. Therefore, even if culture depends on brain activities and even if cultural evolution, then, is closely related to brain evolution (and hence to organic evolution), it is not necessarily predetermined by the principles of organic change.

What I mean is that the producer does not determine the development of his products. A concern producing cars does not anticipate or determine the street traffic and its effects (for example, traffic accidents) although the traffic depends on companies that produce cars; were there no such companies, there would be no cars. Similarly, all cultural products depend, in the first instance, on the brain, but there are no laws fixed in the brain according to which cultural systems have to develop. Young states:

The properties of the brain may provide the basis for religion and culture but they do not dictate its detailed forms. The plasticity of the brain is one of its most characteristic features yet the brain of the newborn child certainly does not represent a *tabula rasa*. It has definite tendencies to attend to human characteristics and to acquire language. It also seems to be very ready to adopt a culture, since all societies have one. But the particular form of that culture is a product of the influences of the environment and the history of the group in the recent past. (1907, p. 204)

Hence, the very connection between nature and culture, between organic and cultural evolution is defined by the brain and its functions. If one day humankind were to become extinct, this would be the end of cultural evolution; only material objects, for example books, works of art, and buildings would exist, as "fossils" as it were. Popper's World 3, if you prefer this terminology, cannot develop without a working brain; hence, if all human brains were to become extinct, this would also mean the "death" of culture (in the literal sense of the word). Even Eccles (1979), in spite of his proneness to a kind of mysticism, agrees that it was the evolution of the brain that made the origin of culture possible.

Many authors like to speak of culture as a supraworld. From the point of view of evolutionary epistemology this is alright as long as one agrees that "this supraworld, however, is produced in the brain. It is mediated in symbolic form by means of words, writing and artefacts. It is absorbed by the individual person through learning processes for his own personal use, and is thus once again at his disposal, fixated in the brain in material form. By this complex system of relations this gigantic learning process takes place as the history of the human race" (Seitelberger 1984, p. 138; see also Oeser and Seitelberger 1988). I think that through these remarks the connections between organic and cultural evolution are made clear enough. The crucial point, however, is a more profound explanation of the connections, the more so because we should strive for an explanatory definition of culture.

A Case of Sociobiology?

Before I continue to discuss the evolutionary epistemologists' argument with respect to cultural evolution, I shall briefly present the sociobiologists' argument. Sociobiology starts with the same claim as evolutionary epistemology: that, because humans are a result of organic evolution, the emergence of culture was due to the evolution of brain mechanisms. We shall see whether the approaches of sociobiologists can be of some help with regard to the evolutionary understanding of culture.

In the present context, *Genes, Mind, and Culture* by Lumsden and Wilson (1981) is of particular interest. This book presents an exhaustive attempt to establish a theory of *gene-culture coevolution* and thus to demonstrate the intimate connection between organic evolution and culture (see also Lumsden and Gushurst 1985; Lumsden and Wilson 1985). The theory has caused many controversies and there has been both resistance against it and sympathy for it. Generally, as the reader will have noticed, sociobiology has met with fierce resistance from different corners. In this book, I will not comment on the various aspects of the sociobiology debate, but focus on the question of whether the sociobiologists' theory of the gene-culture coevolution is in tune with evolutionary epistemology.[1]

Let me start with a passage from Lumsden and Wilson: "The uniqueness of the human mind is due to the specific cognitive mechanisms that create culture through self-awareness. The evidence shows that the mechanisms are genetically based, that is, they are grounded in programs of neural development and operate in a consistent manner across a wider range of environments. They are also robust, in the sense of being less sensitive to the environment than the cultural products they create" (1985, p. 356). As this quotation shows, the authors have made, at least, two claims:

1. Culture (cultural evolution) depends on specific cognitive mechanisms that are unique in humans.
2. These mechanisms, and hence the creation of culture, are constrained, if not determined, genetically.

Introducing the notion of *epigenetic rules*, Lumsden and Wilson (1981) have argued that there is a close relationship between genes and external influences on the organism (see also Markl 1982; Ruse 1985, 1986). By definition, an epigenetic rule is any regularity that channels the development of anatomical, physiological, behavioral, and cognitive characteristics in a certain direction. The epigenetic rule is genetic in basis, its nature depends on the DNA. (Note, by the way, that the concept of the epigenetic rule and Riedl's notion of the epigenetic system, mentioned on p. 21, partly overlap, but do not express the same intention.)

To stick to the point, according to Lumsden and Wilson (1981) the array of transmissible behaviors, mental structures, and artefacts, called *culturgens,* and thus accessible for learning and teaching is processed through a sequence of epigenetic rules. These rules are regarded as "the genetically determined procedures that direct the assembly of the mind, including the screening of stimuli by peripheral sensory filters, the internuncial cellular organizing processes, and the deeper processes of directed cognition" (Lumsden and Wilson 1981, p. 7). Moreover, these rules constitute the restraints placed by genes on development.

From this point of view, culture is to be regarded as a genetically based system. This is not to say that sociobiologists simply mean that particular genes determine any particular cultural activity. They rather assert that there is a fundamental mechanism of gene-culture coevolution that, however, is constrained by biological principles. Lumsden and Wilson (1985, p. 356) write: "Within the thrust and pattern of cultural diversity, the pathways of transmission are themselves subject to biological evolution." Hence, the authors would argue, the epigenetic rules responsible for the human capacity for culture were stabilized by the means of organic evolution and imposed on any cultural activity of present humans. As Ruse (1985, p. 255) puts it: "Cave-man and physicist are linked by the same epigenetic rules."

As far as I can see, none of the sociobiologists has neglected the peculiarity of culture and the uniqueness of humans in nature. But, if I am right, every sociobiologist claims that culture, some way of other, is genetically based and that the peculiar pathways of cultural evolution have been channeled, in a way, by biological mechanisms. The theory of gene-culture coevolution is perhaps the strongest, and certainly the most provocative, account concerning the issue of biology and culture. The theory, based on the concept of epigenetic rules regarded as innate propensities necessary to perform any cultural activity, displays a bias toward a kind of geneticism. Undoubtedly, human behavior depends on genetically stabilized factors, but the question is whether a genetic "everything explanation" really does justice to the complexity of culture. Dawkins (1976) argued that human behavior, including cultural behavior even in its most complex aspects (morality), depends on *selfish genes*. I am aware that Dawkins has used a metaphorical language, but one might be tempted to see a genetic determinism in his arguments, the more so because he describes organisms (including humans) as genetically directed "survival machines."

So, has sociobiology important things to say about culture and cultural evolution? It *has*, indeed, because it is difficult to deny that culture, although it soars beyond organic evolution, has its roots within human natural history. However, I am not sure about the sociobiologist's advantage when I compare sociobiological explanations with those of evolutionary epistemology. Ruse (1985, 1986) has tried to establish an evolutionary theory of cognitive phenomena through the concept of epigenetic rules. But, as Wagner (1988) critically remarks, this concept, and thus a sociobiological version of evolutionary epistemology, does not contribute more to an understanding of cognition than already is contained in the concepts of the ratiomorophic apparatus and its four hypotheses (remember chapter 4).

Let us now, first, pay attention to genetic determinism and its fallacies and, second, look at a nonreductionist view of cultural evolution as proposed by evolutionary epistemologists.

The Fallacy of Genetic Determinism

Years ago, Lewontin (1976) attacked some biological concepts concerning human nature and argued that any attempt to establish universal biological principles guiding human behavior is due to nothing but an ideology; namely, that of biological determinism. Lewontin has continued to criticize mercilessly the conceptions of human ethology and in particular sociobiology. This is not the place to discuss his arguments, or the arguments of other "environmentalists," in detail. I want only to hint at the paradox that some evolutionists—and Lewontin has indeed contributed much to our understanding of evolution—stop arguing in terms of biology when the questions concern *human* behavior. On the other side, social scientists have noticed the importance of biological studies and tried to link sociology to biology without any inclination to biological (genetic) determinism (Meyer 1982, 1987). It is true that speaking of human behavior in biological terms does not necessarily mean adopting a determinist view.

Sociobiology often is regarded as a biological (genetic) determinism sustaining ideological claims. I do not want to discuss here the ideological debate surrounding the sociobiologist's conceptions. It is worth mentioning, however, that even some authors from East Germany, influenced by a Marxist point of view, have paid attention to sociobiology as a fruitful theory concerning human nature (Hörz and Wessel 1983). These authors argue that it is important to know the biological basis of human action, but that one has to consider the interrelations between biological and social (cultural) factors.

No serious biologist concerning with the study of human evolution would neglect the peculiar pathways of cultural evolution; and no serious social scientist should ignore the biological basis of human behavior even in its most complex aspects including sociality and culture. We should focus on the mutual relations between organic evolution and culture and establish a nonreductionist view; that is, a systems view of cultural evolution (see next section). The question is *not* whether heredity or culture alone determines the specifity of human behavior, but in which way biological and social-cultural factors work together. Unfortunately, many people still think that any biological contribution to an understanding of humankind ends up with ideologies like that of Social Darwinism. This is wrong even if one must admit that there have been tendencies among biologists to sustain such ideologies. The great majority of today's biologists, however, stand beyond such claims. Every serious biologist would agree that one has to take into account this *fact*: "Man's personality, as well as his physical traits, results from a process of development in which both heredity and environment play important parts" (Dunn and Dobzhansky 1952, p. 38). Most sociobiologists indeed are prepared to appreciate this connection. Therefore, I would not say that the whole corpus of sociobiological theorizing simply is to be regarded as biological (genetic) determinism. However, by the extension of the Darwinian survival parameter to cultural processes they tend toward a geneticism. I am not going to criticize this tendency for ideological reasons, but concentrate on some objections that can be drawn from an "organismic" view of evolution.

Looking at genes as replicators (and at organisms as their

vehicles or carriers), Dawkins states: "Replicators began not merely to exist, but to construct for themselves containers, vehicles for their continued existence. The replicators which survived were the ones which built *survival machines* for themselves to live in. The first survival machines probably consisted of nothing more than a protective coat. But making a living got steadily harder as new rivals arose with better and more effective survival machines" (1976, p. 21).

What's wrong with these arguments? Remember, please, what I have said in Chapter 1 about the relation between the genotype and the phenotype: I argued that there is a flux of cause and effect in both directions and that the genotype (DNA) does not simply determine the phenotype (organism). Thus, the fallacy of genetic determinism—the fallacy of Dawkins' argument that replicators construct vehicles (organisms)—is that it disregards the complexity of the relationship between the organism and its genes. Replicators do not just build organisms "for themselves," but the organism actually constrains the activities of its own replicators. I think that this proposition allows for a deeper understanding of the complex processes of evolution and development in the living world. Gould (1980, p. 92), another indefatigable critic of sociobiology, has made his point by saying:

> Organisms are much more than amalgamations of genes. They have a history that matters; their parts interact in complex ways. Organisms are built by genes acting in concert, influenced by environments, translated into parts that selection sees and parts invisible to selection. Molecules that determine the properties of water are poor analogues for genes and bodies. I may not be the master of my fate, but my intuition of wholeness probably reflects a biological truth.

Turning to culture, sociobiologists have tried to establish the view that cultural evolution constitutes the peculiar *adaptive* patterns of modern humans. Because my own view of evolution, biological and cultural, is not that of the adaptationists, I have objections against this claim. This is not to say that I generally would dismiss "the idea that we can give a naturalistic account of the evolution of culture in hominids" (Smillie 1985, p. 93). I mean only that adaptation is not sufficient to explain evolution in general and cultural evolution in particular. What I said in Chapter 4, that there are feedback principles linking together the organism and its environment, seems to be even more relevant to cultural evolution. Humans did not create culture to be better adapted to their environment and to be better and more efficient vehicles for their genes; culture, as an extrasomatic product of human systems, does not serve only for survival in a strict biological sense. The fallacy of genetic determinism, in this context, is that speaking of "selfish genes," biological survival, and Darwinian fitness cannot explain any outstanding cultural creativity. We cannot properly understand the great works of Goethe and Shakespeare or the paintings of Leonardo da Vinci by reducing the efforts of these geniuses to a drive toward gene replication (Wuketits 1984c)!

To avoid any misunderstanding, let me state once more that, of course, I am in agreement with the sociobiologists' claim that culture has its roots within organic evolution, that it is constrained by biological factors, and so on. The shortcomings of at least some arguments of sociobiologists, however, come from the commitment to reductionism. The genetic reductionism inherent in works of many sociobiologists should be "supplemented by considerations from evolutionary epistemology and other perspectives whereby the role of 'downward causation' and cognitions in integrating organism's behaviours may be more adequately understood" (Meyer 1987, p. 21). In fact, cultural activities seem to be influenced by certain genetic propensities, but one should also consider that culture acts back upon its own biological fundament. Culture represents, in a way, new constraints to human organic evolution. I do not think that "it is obvious that culture influences our behavior to a much greater extent than our genetic endowment does" (Morris 1983, p. 163). As already mentioned, the question is not that of greater influence, but of the interrelationships between biology and culture. However, as to the transmission of cultural information, we should be aware once more that this transmission occurs "through purely social modes . . . rather than in the genes" (Campbell 1975a, p. 1104).

In sum, I think that sociobiologists have done important work, but that a broader approach is still needed if we really want to understand the evolution of culture. Up to now, most sociobiologists have developed their conceptions independent of evolutionary epistemology. I think that a dialogue between sociobiologists and evolutionary epistemologists would be useful. Perhaps, this book will start such discussion—I would be pleased if it did.

A Nonreductionist View of Culture and Cultural Evolution

Clearly, what is needed is a nonreductionist view, a multilevel approach that helps us realize the relations between levels rather than structures defined by single elements (Jantsch 1979). Just to make the demand, however, is not enough. We should see, how to fulfill it. Let us see in which way evolutionary epistemology can help.

Even Dawkins (1976) admits that besides the gene, the basic replicator in the organic world, there is a "new kind of replicator," to be called *meme,* which would be the unit of cultural transmission; that is, the transmission of cultural (intellectual) information. The point is not to give this unit a name—call it *meme* or take whatever concept you like—but to explain its emergence and its way of working. Clearly the emergence of culture and the development of cultural replicators is due to the evolution of complex cognition processes. The sociobiologists' argument would remain a skeleton unless supplemented by a theory of cognitive behavior. Lumsden and Wilson (1981) have realized the importance of studying cognitive mechanisms. Perhaps, they are prepared to appreciate the evolutionary epistemologist's view that has been elaborated explicitly as an evolutionary view of cognition.

There can be no doubt that cognitive mechanisms, because they are properties of organic systems (brain, CNS), are genetically based. Some of these mechanisms in animals are robust and hardly variable. However, the greater the plasticity of the nervous system, the higher is the probability that cognitive mechanisms will change if necessary for the sake of survival. Plasticity of the nervous system presupposes a certain genetic plasticity. Hence, my point is that the most recently developed cognitive mechanisms, particularly human (rational) knowledge mechanisms, are not—and cannot yet be—genetically fixed. The genetic stabilization of cognitive mechanisms, as of any other brain function, seems to be a rather long process, a long-term enterprise, so to speak. True, there must be a genetic propensity toward certain modes of behavior; but this propensity does not predetermine any particular route of behavior and its possible modifications by individual learning. Human knowledge appears to be the most plastic cognitive system among all the cognitive systems in the animal kingdom. Churchland's intention might be located within this context for we find expressed "that what an adequate epistemology must begin by acknowledging is the thoroughgoing *plasticity* of human understanding, and among the things it must be able to account for is the rationality not just of minor but of wholesale changes in the form that understanding assumes" (Churchland 1979, p. 88). The plasticity of human understanding would mean a plasticity in cultural systems, that these systems are flexible to a great extent and that their flexibility is not restricted to genetical changes.

To underscore the nonreductionist argument, I wish to make two points:

1. Changes in social or cultural history do not find an appropriate biological explanation. There are no biological concepts to describe or even to explain, for example, the transition from monarchic to democratic systems. Such changes have their roots within society and can be properly explained only by studying the particular social-cultural situations and their constraints.

2. People indeed always act as biological systems, but their particular actions can be motivated by social-cultural forces. Certain social situations can cause aggressive behavior, for example. Aggression is a biological phenomenon and thus explained in biological terms. But its proximate causes can lie in social conditions, and they are not amenable to biological explanations.

From the second point follows that we have to adopt a multilevel approach to explaining culture and society. Such an approach is in tune with evolutionary epistemology. Evolutionary epistemologists agree that society and culture, although indeed produced by biological systems, are irreducible entities. They are linked, as mentioned earlier, to the human brain, but they cannot be *reduced* to the brain in an ontological sense. Hence, from the point of view of evolutionary epistemology, the question for an evolutionary description and explanation of culture has a clear answer: culture has indeed *evolved*, but the principles of cultural evolution are not the same as in the case of organic evolution. Moreover, the units of cultural evolution—ideas—though linked to brain states and mechanisms, are processed and transmitted by language and writing, so that cultural information processing rests on a mechanism different to biological information processing. Is this the opinion of all advocates of evolutionary epistemology? I should think so. Let me give a few examples.

Campbell, having much sympathy for the natural-selection approach to an understanding of the development of ideas, concludes:

> Urban humanity is a product of both biological and social evolution. Evolutionary genetics shows that when there is genetic competition among the cooperators (as for humans but not for the social insects), great limitations are placed upon the degree of socially useful, individually self-sacrificial altruism that biological evolution can produce. Human urban social complexity is a product of social evolution and has had to counter with inhibitory moral norms the biological selfishness which genetic competition has continually selected. (1975a, p. 1123)

As you can see here, it is argued that our social-cultural evolution is not based on biological egoism, but rather to be conceived to compensate this selfishness and create cooperative behavior. (For game-theoretical reflections on these and similar arguments, see Leinfellner 1984.)

Likewise Mohr (1987) defines *culture* as a particular activity of humans capable of teleological actions (remember p. 124). He pays special attention to ethical demands that would *cultivate* human life (in a literal sense of the word). However, he argues that the limits to our capacity of culture lie in our organic evolution, that organic evolution has set bounds to our cultural evolution—and thus to the acquisition of morality (see chapter 8, last section).

An interesting point has been made by Oeser (1987). He says that sociocultural evolution in humans has changed the way of organic evolution in the following sense: organic evolution has progressed toward more complex individuals showing an ever-greater autonomy (compare an insect society with a group of primates, like baboons, that represent highly individualized animals cooperating in a group); this progression has culminated in the human species, which—because of its complex brain—represents the highest level of individuality among its members. The turning point, however, has been human sociocultural evolution showing a progression toward more complex societies, beginning with small groups (twenty individuals or so) and ending up in anonymous urban societies consisting of millions of members (see Figure 17). In short,

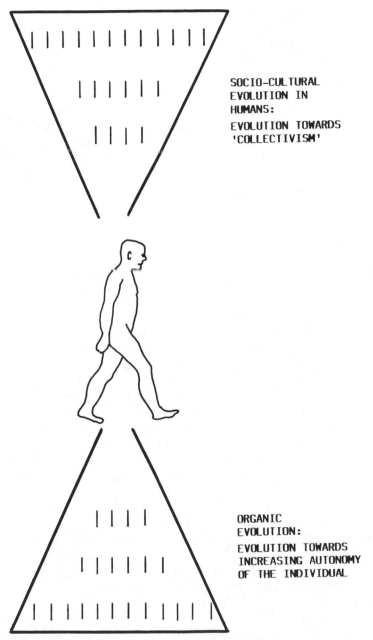

Figure 17. Organic evolution as a process toward increasing autonomy of the individual, and sociocultural evolution as a process toward increasing complexity of social systems and "collectivism."

sociocultural evolution means a development toward "collectiv-ism" (a term which in the present context of course is *not* to be used in any ideological or political sense). Thus, the essential characteristic of human sociocultural evolution, according to Oeser (1987), is the constant invention of goals, not just for the sake of survival in a strict biological sense; it is the creation of knowledge (science) for its own sake (!) without respect to any survival value. Like other advocates of evolutionary epistemology, Oeser (1987) sees a major feature of sociocultural evolution in the change from biological selfishness (competition) to cooperative behavior that, in a way, displays an abstract mechanism: ideas are transmitted through exosomatic structures, a person may be confronted with the ideas of other persons who are not *personally known* to him or her.

These few hints may show the evolutionary epistemologists do not try to reduce cultural evolution to organic evolution, but rather seek appropriate concepts and models to characterize cultural evolution, to show its specifity and its links to the evolution of organic entities. It is important to note that today's evolutionary epistemologists are not so much looking for mere analogies between organic and cultural evolution, but the mechanisms underlying this "type of evolution" and different from the mechanisms of organic change. Hence, we are fully aware that, as Skagestad (1978, p. 620) puts it, "man has generated a novel mode of evolution . . . which proceeds by means of mechanisms differing from that of natural selection." And indeed it is a crucial question of evolutionary epistemology, how this type of evolution was generated by *organic* evolution. The answer to this question, however, might have become visible from the foregoing sections: we see the (organic) evolution of the human brain as the very process that made possible the emergence of culture. In this field much work is still to be done. Integrating knowledge coming from neurobiology within the theoretical framework of evolutionary epistemology remains a desideratum. One decisive step, however, most recently has been taken by Oeser and Seitelberger (1988), who linked modern neurobiological research with epistemological questions and attained to a kind of neuroepistemology.

My concern here is to underscore the nonreductionist argument inherent in works of evolutionary epistemologists as far as they are explicitly interested in cultural evolution (and most of them are indeed interested in this enterprise). I cannot speak in behalf of all advocates of evolutionary epistemology, but I think that most would agree that their view is nonreductionist in two different senses:

1. Ontologically, because they do not argue that culture is nothing else but an organic entity or just an extension of organic evolution.

2. Epistemologically, because they do not see their case in translating statements about cultural history into the language of biology.

Moreover, I suppose that most evolutionary epistemologists would agree that cultural evolution is an open program, by no means predetermined by the principles of organic evolution. Hence, evolutionary epistemology is at variance with determinism and (the ideology of) *historicism*, which already was subject to Popper's critique thirty years ago (see Popper 1960).

Two Levels of Evolutionary Epistemology

Grant now that there are two types of evolution in the living world: organic evolution as an endosomatic continuum of information processing; and cultural evolution characterized by the generation of exosomatic structures and exosomatic information processing. Life, I argued (Chapter 3), means information processing, it means that an organism—be it a bacterium or *Homo sapiens*—has to be informed, for survival's sake, about certain properties of reality (without knowing anything about reality in itself). Hence, information processing is a character of living beings. Humans are no exception; rather, they are the most sophisticated information-processing systems and their particular mode of processing information is culture. What I want to say is that there is a common feature in organic and cultural evolution: information processing. But, as has been said, cultural evolution is to be characterized by a novel mode of information processing (language, writing) that has no predecessors in organic evolution.

Evolutionary epistemology is concerned with both information processing at the organic level and information processing at the cultural level. Again, we have to envisage two programs of evolutionary epistemology, one concerning information gathering in animals by the means of their ratiomorphic apparatus (see

Chapter 3), the other concerning the same phenomenon in humans by the means of rational knowledge acquisition. The latter includes the study of scientific knowledge processing (see the next chapter). I have learned that many critics of evolutionary epistemology refer to evolutionary models of human rational (scientific) knowledge (see, e.g., Cohen 1973), as if evolutionary epistemology were mainly an attempt to develop evolutionary explanations of this type of knowledge. This is not true. I should say—and by saying this I agree with Campbell (1988)—that the majority of evolutionary epistemologists are concerned with the organic evolution of cognition processes beginning with information and learning processes at the level of unicellular organisms and going on to ratiomorphic cognition in humans. Thus, an evolutionary theory of cognition in animals is now well established, as can be seen particularly from the works by Lorenz (1977) and Riedl (1984a). For these authors, and many others whose primary concern has been the *natural history* of cognition, the study of cultural evolution (including the evolution of scientific ideas) is not the main task of evolutionary epistemology. However, they have drawn consequences from their biological views, consequences with regard to cultural evolution including the evolution of moral systems, scientific knowledge, and so on (see, e.g., Mohr 1984, 1987; Riedl 1985, 1987d). Other advocates of evolutionary epistemology, particularly Oeser (1987, 1988), Popper (1972a, 1972b), and Toulmin (1972), have tried to establish an evolutionary theory of cultural evolution with special reference to the evolution of scientific knowledge. This group of authors, however, is to be characterized as biologically oriented philosophers of science (which also is true, for example, of Hull 1982, 1988), asking questions like these: To what extent is the acquisition of intellectual information constrained by organic evolution? To what extent can biology, the study of organic evolution, help understand cultural information processing? What can we learn from biological constraints on our species in studying cultural evolution?

As mentioned in the Prospectus, both programs of evolutionary epistemology have a long tradition. In the nineteenth century Darwin was an advocate of the first, Spencer an advocate of the second program (remember Chapter 2). But, of course, both programs are linked by their advocates' conviction that evolution is to be taken as a basis for cognition processes of all kinds. However, from the point of view presented in this chapter, that cultural evolution is characterized neither by mere analogy to nor as a mere extension of organic evolution, it follows that evolutionary epistemology at the second level must account for the particular mechanisms of cultural evolution. I want briefly to address to the mechanisms that the two programs of evolutionary epistemology have to take into account.

At the first level, evolutionary epistemologists must pay attention to the fact that organisms and their environments are mutually related, so that an organism cannot be just adapted to, and molded by, the environment. Considering the internal constraints on evolution, cognitive structures appear not only as structures corresponding to a given external reality, but as the "producers" of a coherent scheme of reactions to external phenomena (remember p. 78). Hence, the classical Darwinian and adaptationist view inherent in conceptions of evolutionary epistemology should be replaced by a more organism-oriented view, a nonadaptationist and systems view of the evolution of cognitive phenomena (remember chapter 4). The evolution of these phenomena, like organic evolution in general, appears to be a process controlled by an interrelationship between external and internal (intraorganismic) selection. Thus, our view is still that inherent in the natural-selection paradigm, but this paradigm is presented in a more organismic fashion and transgresses Darwin's concept of selection as well as the synthetic theory of evolution.

At the second level, evolutionary epistemologists should concentrate on the fact that humans, when producing culture, act teleologically, that the "active component" in evolution plays the major role. This component is that of *construction;* that is, a particularly interpretation of reality through the lenses of human rationality and irrationality (see Diettrich 1989). Without having much sympathy for the argument that (human) knowledge means just the socially constrained construction of reality, I agree that our everyday knowledge as well as our scientific knowledge is filtered, to a certain extent, by social-cultural conventions, norms, goals, and so forth (Berger and Luckmann 1966). These constraints operate in a way similar to selection, but they are not to be identified with *natural* selection working as "directive" principle in organic evolution. So, at the second level of evolutionary epistemology what is to be considered is this construction of a type of reality visible in conventions, norms, and so on.

Bradie (1986) argued that the first program of evolutionary

epistemology is genuine, but that the second is not. True, drawing analogies between organic and cultural evolution is not enough. But because we have realized the particular mechanisms of cultural evolution, information processing through exosomatic systems, the second program of evolutionary epistemology might be genuine, too. I admit, however, that many of the older conceptions of this second type of evolutionary epistemology suffer from misconstruing social and cultural evolution. On the other hand, evolutionary conceptions of society and culture have had the advantage of noticing biological constraints on sociocultural evolution and have been genuine in this sense. If such conceptions do not rest on mere analogies to organic evolution, they may be taken as an important endorsement of the first level of evolutionary epistemology.

What has been presented up to now as the second level of evolutionary epistemology of course is not a monolith. There are rather different approaches and concepts developed in a vast number of works whose authors do not always refer to each other. In the next chapter I summarize some of the most important views with regard to the "evolution of science" and present some critical comments on these views. For the moment, it seems important to note that (most) evolutionary epistemologists pay attention to the role of *emergence* in knowledge and, as we have seen, reject reductionism. The notion of emergence is closely related to both programs of evolutionary epistemology, and its analysis therefore should be connected with an examination of the respective evolutionary model (Egidi, 1987). If the emergence of human rational knowledge was an evolutionary novelty—and of course it was—then the evolutionary analysis of the development of scientific knowledge cannot rest with the analysis of the factors of organic evolution.

I close Chapter 5 by stating that evolutionary epistemology has some lessons to teach us about our own knowledge processing; this, as the present chapter might have shown, also is true of the study of culture and cultural evolution. In this chapter the evolutionary epistemologist's attitude toward culture has been outlined.

1. Cultural evolution cannot be sufficiently explained in biological terms; it is not to be reduced to the mechanisms of organic evolution.

2. There are some striking differences between organic and cultural evolution. The most important of these differences is that the units of cultural evolution, ideas, are transmitted extragenetically, through exosomatic structures, so that cultural evolution differs from organic evolution with respect to tempo and rapidity.

3. Moreover, in organic evolution there is no "creative factor," whereas cultural evolution is based on human intentionality. Therefore, the component of "construction" plays an important role in cultural evolution.

4. The necessary condition of the emergence of culture, however, was biological evolution, particularly the evolution of the human brain. Cultural evolution has channeled the human creative brain. This brain is the producer of all culture, but this is not to say that the particular pathways of cultural evolution are prescribed by any single brain mechanism. Hence, cultural evolution has its own dynamics, going beyond the dynamics of organic change.

5. Sociobiologists have established a theory of gene-culture coevolution that might demonstrate and explain the close connections between organic evolution and culture. Whenever the sociobiological theory amounts to a genetic determinism, it becomes at variance with evolutionary epistemology. Evolutionary epistemologists indeed argue that culture is linked to biology, but that the processes of cultural evolution are not determined genetically.

6. The evolutionary epistemologist's view of cultural evolution is nonreductionistic and nondeterministic.

7. Evolutionary epistemology at its first level offers an understanding of the necessary biological preconditions of culture and cultural evolution. The second-level approach of evolutionary epistemology is an attempt to reconstruct and explain the mechanisms of cultural evolution. At this second level, however, we have to consider that the development of culture indeed is evolutionary, but that it does not obey the same principles and mechanisms as biological evolution.

7

Evolutionary Epistemology and the Evolution of Science

Science is simply common sense at its best; that is, rigidly accurate in observation, and merciless to fallacy in logic.

Thomas H. Huxley

Evolution and Science: Analogies and Metaphors

To continue our discussion of cultural evolution, we now come to an analysis of the evolution of science that is to be regarded as a particular aspect of cultural evolution. Many philosophers of science have been greatly attracted by the possibility of applying the paradigm of evolution to the study of the growth of (scientific) knowledge. Toulmin (1967), for one, established an evolutionary view of the development of natural science and argued that in this context *evolution* does not mean only a mere *façon de parler,* an analogy or a metaphor, but that the evolutionary paradigm should be taken seriously. Other authors, too, have taken this paradigm seriously with respect to an explanation of the growth of scientific ideas (Campbell 1960, 1974a, 1984; Oeser 1976, 1984, 1987, 1988; Popper 1959, 1972a, 1972b; Radnitzky 1987a, 1987b). Some have explicitly formulated a selection theory of the evolution of science, based on the conviction that there is a selection of ideas similar to natural selection of organisms. In particular Popper (1972a), as quoted in Chapter 2, has claimed that there is a natural selection of hypotheses and theories and that the growth of human knowledge is the result of a process that resembles selection in organic evolution.

It seems that such natural-selection epistemologies have a mere *metaphorical* character. Do not think negatively of metaphors in science and philosophy of science. Metaphors, to a certain extent, play an important cognitive role in the articulation and justification of theories (Bradie 1984). They may help to better illuminate both some complex processes in nature and the structure of the theory conceived to explain the processes in question. Darwin's struggle for existence, for instance, is a metaphor that illuminates some characteristics in the living world although it is not meant to describe just a struggle in the literal sense of the word. Some notions inherent in the biological theory of evolution may be used to illuminate the process of the growth of scientific knowledge. One might argue that there are "mutations" in scientific research: ideas produced accidentally by a scientist's brain. Also, one could argue that there is a process of "selection" in science: "good theories"; that is, theories that explain much, will be favored, other theories will be rejected. Consequently, one might even speak of the survival of the fittest (i.e., the "best") theory.

With respect to analogies between organic evolution and the evolution of scientific ideas, there would be a great number of characteristics underlying both processes. As the whole process of cognition in animals can be described as a trial-and-error process, we might say that scientists also advance by trial and error; problem solving is an essential feature not only of organic evolution but also of the evolution of science (every animal is a more or less effective problem solver, the scientist, too, tries to solve problems and does it more or less effectively); furthermore, all knowledge is hypothetical knowledge, and this is true to cognition at the ratiomorphic level (remember chapter 3) as well as to scientific knowledge. There are many other such similarities or analogies. Does this mean, however, that the mechanisms underlying the evolution of organisms and the evolution of scientific theories are the same? The answer is *no*.

Let us, once more, take up the two-level approach of evolutionary epistemology. Consider the following differences between the two levels (here the second level is restricted to the evolution of scientific knowledge and means an evolutionary theory of science) (see Vollmer 1987):

1. At its first level evolutionary epistemology deals with the evolution of cognitive capacities from unicellular animals to human ratiomorphic operations and is part of the biological theory of evolution. Evolution, therefore, is an aspect of organic evolution caused by mutations, genetic recombination, and selection. We have to encounter processes that have occurred over millions of years.

2. At its second level, as an evolutionary theory of science, evolutionary epistemology refers to a specific type of knowledge, (human) scientific knowledge. The term *evolution* is used in a broader sense. At the same time, however, we must be aware that the evolution of science is part of cultural evolution. The period to be considered is one of some thousands of years or, thinking of modern science, only a few centuries.

Hence, drawing analogies between organic evolution and the evolution of scientific ideas cannot be sufficient if we really want to understand scientific theories and their development. But Campbell (1988, p. 171) already said: "The valuable core *for a theory of science* is not the biological analogy to evolution *per se*, but a more abstract *selection theory*." Such a selection theory, however, would have to take into account that the development of scientific theories starts with biological operations in the human brain but is constrained by sociocultural factors; that there is a teleological factor in scientific research, because scientists *consciously* perceive problems and try to solve them; that scientists are able to *consciously* reflect upon their errors and correct them.

Taking these problems seriously, an evolutionary epistemologist dealing with the development of scientific ideas has to ask whether he or she is able to make some substantial contributions to a theory of science—or whether such a view will remain a mere construction of analogies. The main question posed by philosophers to the advocates of an evolutionary theory of scientific knowledge is, Does an evolutionary view help to illuminate the notion of *scientific rationality*? This question was posed by Tennant (1988), who, as a philosopher, strongly advocates the evolutionary view of knowledge. It will be, I suppose, a touchstone of the second-level approach in evolutionary epistemology. In detail, Tennant (1988) divides this question into some subquestions, for example:

1. How does an evolutionary theory of science help us gain an understanding of normative forces of our methodological ideas?

2. Does this theory account for necessities in our thought?

3. Does it help better understand the idea of scientific progress?

4. Does it help to justify our inductive or deductive reasoning?

I do think that an evolutionary approach to the growth of scientific knowledge can throw some light on the concept of scientific rationality. Perhaps, this chapter will be of some help. Let us, first, look at some conceptions of an evolutionary theory of science as they have been developed in the last decades. In, "The Evolutionary Development of Natural Science," Toulmin wrote: "Science develops . . . as the outcome of a double process: at each stage, a pool of competing intellectual variants is in circulation, and in each generation a selection process is going on, by which certain of these variants are accepted and incorporated into the science concerned, to be passed on to the next generation of workers as integral elements of the tradition" (1967, p. 465). Some years later, in a more exhaustive treatment, he puts forward the following argument: "The disciplinary selection process picks out for 'accreditation' those of the 'competing' novelties which nest meet the specific 'demands' of the local 'intellectual environment.' These 'demands' comprise both the immediate issues that each conceptual variant is designed to deal with and also the other entrenched concepts with which it must co-exist" (Toulmin 1972, p. 140).

It is worth noting that Toulmin makes a distinction between his view of scientific change and the Darwinian program regarding organic evolution. For him Darwin's theory of organic change refers to "one special case of a more general pattern of historical change" (Toulmin 1972, p. 320). In a way, Toulmin's claim resembles what Campbell has in mind when he postulates a "more abstract selection theory", that is, a more general principle of evolution. Here I am not going into full detail concerning Toulmin's approach. However, I should mention that this approach has been criticized mercilessly by Cohen (1973), who has argued that Toulmin's analysis is nothing more than a metaphor and that it fails to explain changing in science. "The ultimate argument against Toulmin", says Cohen (1973, p. 53), "is that such an analysis will still leave a gap that needs to be filled by some other type of theory—which will do for an intellectual discipline . . . what physiology does for an organism." (For discussion, also see Ruse 1986.)

Indeed, it seems that Toulmin's approach to scientific change does not offer the same understanding of scientific theories as physiology in case of organisms. However that might be, I think that Toulmin's quasi-Darwinian approach is a good example of an evolutionary account for science soaring beyond mere description of theories to justification. But, is Toulmin's enterprise really no more than a metaphor or an analogy? I should say that it is more. But, even if it were just an analogy, it is not as bad as Cohen's criticism suggests. More than once in this volume I have argued that drawing analogies between organic evolution and cultural evolution—here in the concrete case: evolution of scientific ideas—is not enough. On the other hand, I do think that seeing analogies might have—and actually has had—at least, some stimulating heuristic effects (see also Blažek 1978). Therefore, we should take evolutionary models of science seriously—be it only to reject them. In case of rejection, however, we should try to do things better. Perhaps, some evolutionary epistemologists are on the right track. I, as an adherent of evolutionary epistemology, believe that the approach to scientific change coming from this epistemology has been most fruitful because it has gone beyond mere reconstructions of the history of the sciences and because it includes attempts to show how science really works.

Let me draw your attention to a serious objection against evolutionary models of science, however. This objection is that organic variation is blind whereas epistemic variation is not and that theories have people trying to make them better (Thagard 1980). True, as we have seen in the last chapter with regard to cultural evolution in general, there is a teleological factor in the production of theories depending on human consciousness, and according to our present understanding of evolution, there is no such factor in biological processes. Hence, there seems to be much substance to the claim of a fundamental disanalogy between organic evolution and the evolution of ideas.

However, the weakness of such claims is that they rest on a particular view of organic evolution based on the assumption that evolutionary change is nothing more than blind variation. If we take a systems view of evolution (see Chapter 1), then it should be clear that evolutionary change is constrained by organismic factors, so that organic variation is not just blind. Most recently Stein and Lipton have argued along these lines, reaching the following conclusion: "In biological evolution, complex organs evolve from other organs. The earlier preadaptations make complex organs possible. They also effectively restrict biological variation, since the form that a complex organ can take is strongly influenced by the particular preadaptations available. Similarly, we have argued that epistemic variation is often restricted by preadaptations in the form of heuristics" (Stein and Lipton 1989, p. 54). Hence, the objection often raised against evolutionary models of the development of science is not as strong as it might appear to be. However, this is not to say that the development of (scientific) ideas is nothing more than a development comparable to organic evolution. But perhaps this analogy can have some heuristic effects on discussing the evolution of science.

Popper Retried

Another of these attempts to describe and explain science in evolutionary terms is due to Popper's work. Unlike Toulmin, Popper was more interested in establishing a Darwinian model of science. As we have seen, Popper took up the model of natural selection and transferred it to scientific ideas. In chapter 2 we saw that Popper's view of science is similar to some older conceptions and his starting point, to analyze science in an evolutionary perspective—namely, the assertion that science is an evolutionary phenomenon like any other human activity—can be found in some authors of the nineteenth century. Popper's message, however, has gone beyond a mere (evolutionary) reconstruction of the history of ideas. His claim has been that there is no "perfect knowledge," that our knowledge is conjectural and must be amenable to criticism. Thus, there grew up, and has endured as an influential school of contemporary philosophy, what is called *critical rationalism*. (Discussions include Albert 1977; Bartley 1982; Radnitzky and Andersson 1978; Salamun 1989). From this point of view, not only scientific ideas, but ideas in general (including political ideas) must be freed from any totalitarianism, as Popper has been an indefatigable critic of all totalitarian and authoritarian ideologies. Popper's view, and that of the advocates of critical rationalism, is in tune with the idea of an "open evolution," with the idea that the evolution of life (including human evolution) is not determined by eternal laws and that we, in some way or other, are the masters of our own fate (see also Wuketits 1987e).

Hence, Popper's philosophy, as a whole, has important social implications and indicates a kind of humanism. However, here we are concerned with Popper's philosophy of science and his attempt to establish an evolutionary model of the growth of scientific knowledge. For Popper science means problem solving as every organism's life means solving (at least) some problems. Thus, science does not start simply with observations but with certain problems. Like organisms, operating in virtue of their ratiomorphic (innate) hypotheses (chapter 4), we humans start with some inborn knowledge that, according to Popper (1972a, p. 259), "will . . . create *our first problems.*" Therefore, Popper continues, "the ensuing growth of our knowledge may . . . be described as consisting throughout of corrections and modifications of previous knowledge." All human knowledge, including scientific knowledge, is to be regarded, then, as the (preliminary) result of the step-by-step process of trial and error (conjecture and refutation).

The analogy between the evolution of science and organic evolution is most obvious. According to Popper, hypotheses or theories are established to solve problems, and the problem situations vary; developing experimental situations will tolerate a number of rival hypotheses or theories (see Watkins 1974). Now, the aim of science is not—or, should not be—the preeminence of *one* theory over any other theories; but every theory should be criticized, each should be falsifiable. This imperative includes an ethical demand in scientific research, Mohr (1984, p. 195) puts it: "Be ready, any time, to modify or replace a theory in view of inner inconsistencies or experimental refutation." All things considered, scientific research is an open program, many solutions of problems are possible—the focal question is whether a scientist will be ready to tolerate ideas (theories) developed by rivals instead of insisting dogmatically on his or her own "truth" (or the "truth" of somebody else). Again, the analogy to organic evolution is the production of different competing *species*—in the case of science, however, competing *theories.* (Fortunately, this analogy ceases at one important point: whereas members of competing species struggle, sometimes in the literal sense of the word, using their teeth and claws, scientists usually do not try to hurt or kill rival colleagues.)

Campbell (1974a), who commented on Popper's view and

elaborated his own perspective of the evolution of science similar to Popper's account, presented a model that contains blind variation and selective retention as mechanisms of the development of scientific ideas (see also Campbell 1960). Briefly, scientists create ideas as "blind variations" or "mutations," they generate an idea intuitively, they arrive at an idea through a brain wave, and so on. True, there is no absolute method to arrive at a successful hypothesis. Also true, some "selection processes" (in the widest sense of the term) constrain (or eliminate) a theory. However, in some cases scientists may solve a problem by *trying* to solve it in virtue of *rationally* conceived methods and by working *systematically*, so that in such cases the factor "blind variation" does not play an important role.

Consider the following proposition: scientists arrive at their hypotheses by a wild zig-zag (see Koestler 1959 for similar arguments). If you look at the history of scientific ideas, you will recognize that scientists sometimes arrive at a theory rather incidentally, Kepler, for instance, arrived at his laws of planetary motion by trying to solve another problem; namely, the mathematical significance for the number of planets and their (relative) distances from the sun. Hence, yet another factor seems to play an important role in scientific research, *serendipity* (Kantorovich 1988; Kantorovich and Ne'eman Forthcoming), which in a way completes Campbell's notion of blind variations.

The gist of the attempts by Popper and Campbell to explain the growth of scientific knowledge is that evolutionary processes similar to those inherent in organic evolution have directed the construction, validitation, and falsification of theories. Such an evolutionary account, however, might—and actually has—caused misunderstandings. Explaining the scientist's creation of ideas does not necessarily lead to statements concerning the validity of a particular theory. Critics of evolutionary epistemology, like Holzhey (1983), have stated (correctly) that a distinction must be made between *genesis* and *validity*. (This problem is closely related to the distinction between the context of discovery and the context of justification; a recent account for this is Hoyningen-Huene 1987.) What the critics have failed to see is that evolutionary epistemologists actually take notice of the importance of that distinction. Popper clearly states:

> The question of the sources of our knowledge, like so many authoritarian questions, is a *genetic* one. It asks for the origin

of our knowledge, in the belief that knowledge may legitimize itself by its pedigree. The nobility of the racially pure knowledge, the untainted knowledge, the knowledge which derives from the highest authority, if possible from God: these are the (often unconscious) metaphysical ideas behind the question. My modified question, "How can we hope to detect error?" may be said to derive from the view that such pure, untainted and certain sources do not exist, and that questions of origin or of purity should not be confounded with questions of validity, or of truth. (1972b, p. 25)

Unpacking this passage, one cannot simply say that, as Hookway (1984) seems to believe, for the evolutionary epistemologist 'true theories' are survivors. Remember the notion of coherence (p. 78). I have argued that any organism's perception of reality does not offer a true image of the world-in-itself, but rather has to yield a coherent scheme of certain aspects of reality allowing for the organism's survival. Likewise, a scientific theory cannot be regarded as an approach to the absolute truth or something like that. "The intelligible goal of science", says Clark (1986, p. 157), ". . . is *not* the description of the world-in-itself but the production of more and more highly tolerated models of the world we find around us." Hence, evolutionary epistemologists argue that those theories are the survivors that provide us with the most useful arrangement of information. And "just *what* arrangements of information we find useful will depend on our human needs and capacities and the particular cognitive orientation we happen to possess" (Clark 1986, p. 157).

To pay more attention to the problem of selection in evolutionary models of science, let us consider the type of selection theory inherent to such models. Popper seems to think of something strongly analogous to natural selection. Campbell, however, as said earlier, makes the claim that a more universal principle of selection, a more abstract principle is needed. most recently, Hull (1988) has made a similar point by arguing that a selection theory is needed that would sufficiently encompass different realms, social and conceptual (scientific) change as well as organic evolution. Hull sees selection processes generally based on "replicators" and "interactors." In scientific research the (conceptual) replicators include all the elements that build up science and are known as *problem solutions, methods, beliefs about goals and norms of science,* and so on; and the scientists are the interactors, recognizing problems, trying to solve them, and transmitting information about their ideas to other scientists. This concern places Hull within the tradition of evolutionary epistemology (whether or not he likes it). And, like any other of the advocates of this epistemology, he is confronted with several objections; as one of Hull's commentators, Stokes (1988, p. 223), argues, that where Hull's "model may be applicable to natural selection, it is not able to give more than a schematic description of conceptual change."

To conclude this section, it is obvious that the efforts to establish evolutionary models of science, though criticized (for good and bad reasons), have found some sympathy among both scientists and philosophers. The argument *for* evolutionary models of science may be summarized as follows: "A good understanding of the genesis and development of the conditions that make science possible yields a better understanding of the nature of science, and this in turn permits a more appropriate framing of questions about what science ought to be" (Munévar 1988, p. 213; see also Munévar 1987).

Evolution of Science as an Information Process

The models discussed so far have only one conviction in common: that the growth of scientific knowledge is an evolutionary process and that a kind of selection plays a major role in this process. As for cultural evolution in general, particularly for the evolution of science, the transmission of information via exosomatic structures must be regarded as an important aspect, so that there are limits to analogizing scientific change to organic evolution. Concentrating on this aspect might be more fruitful than trying to explain the evolution of science with respect to any kind of selection. This does not mean that I disregard the selection-theoretical models. I have argued that such models, even if they were conceived as mere analogies, have their heuristic relevance. But science is a cognition process—a trivial remark, I see—so that one should try to find the peculiarities of this process by studying the specifity of information processing. By doing so, one should be able to understand that science—generating scientific knowledge—is nothing more than one particular level within the hierarchy of information processing in the living world; that it is, in the first instance, constrained by the faculties of our brain. This approach is not at variance with selection-theoretical models; such models would be parts of the approach. Besides, the aim of this is to show the link between the two levels of evolutionary epistemology.

Table 9 presents a tentative list of elements inherent in scientific knowledge processing and compares these elements to the ingredients of ratiomorphic cognition processes. Note that the four hypotheses of the ratiomorphic apparatus, discussed in chapter 4, find their parallels in some operations at the rational

Table 9. Parallels of scientific and ratiomorphic operations.

Scientific	*Ratiomorphic*
Information gaining:	Information gaining:
Empirical research	Learning, experience
Useful experiences, discoveries etc. made in history	Evolutionary learning, innate teaching mechanisms
Rational observation	Perception
Inductive inference	Ratiomorphic expectation
Deduction	Experience
Rational belief	Ratiomorphic belief
Hypotheses	"Hypotheses" of the ratiomorphic apparatus
Theories	Associations
Explanation:	
Causal	Hypothesis of the causes
Teleological	Hypothesis of purpose
Prognosis	Hypothesis of the seemingly true.
Concept formation	Hypothesis of comparison, gestalt perception, gestalt abstraction

level, the level of scientific information gaining. Now, you might object that I am simply showing nice analogies. In fact, what I want to show goes beyond the construction of mere analogies. Note that scientists are living organisms, that they, like other human beings, not only act rationally, but that ratiomorphic information processing is part and parcel of their brains' activities. In the case of inductive inference, for example, the innate disposition to generalize (i.e., the ratiomorphic expectation) seems to play an important role. The scientist's conjectures seem to be strongly determined by innate "generalizing feelings" (Stemmer 1978).

The process of scientific knowledge gaining corresponds to the basic patterns of preconsciously gained information, although it transgresses the phylogenetically stabilized information processing by the means of rational learning and (rational) error elimination. "It is only that scientific information processing is more complex, more differentiated than the phylogenetic, biological acquisition of cognition" (Wuketits 1987a, p. 322). Another important point is that our innate cognitive apparatus, as a result of evolution, like the perceiving apparatus of any other living being, can be transcended only with the aid of the apparatus itself; that is, the repetition and, where necessary, the correction of the original procedure. Hence, the creation of knowledge can be characterized as a process of *self-regulation*.

Paying particular attention to self-regulating principles in knowledge gaining, Oeser (1976, 1984, 1988) has developed an *information-theoretical model* of science and rational knowledge gaining in general. Also, he has regarded "concentration of information" (*Informationsverdichtung*) as a universal "economy principle" of evolution (Oeser 1985). But consider Darwin's reference to Goethe: "In order to spend on one side, nature is forced to economise on the other side" (Darwin [1859] 1958, p. 142). According to Oeser, the scientific method has rather the same structure as the elementary mechanism of trial and error elimination; that is, a *cyclic* structure or a structure showing elements mutually related one to the other. Of course this mechanism of scientific knowledge gaining transcends the principles of trial and error elimination at the ratiomorphic level by being a consciously developed "supraindividual" mechanism for *self-correction*. This mechanism of self-correction not only eliminates incorrect information but also stores corroborated knowledge: it concentrates information in an abstract manner.

Oeser's model of scientific knowledge gaining and the growth of scientific knowledge is a *systems model*, showing a functional relationship between methods of acquisition, systematization, and justification of scientific knowledge. In detail, this model, as presented in Figure 18, demonstrates that the growth of scientific knowledge resembles a spiral. Elementary information gained by empirical research (I_1) allows for building a hypothesis (H_1) and, subsequently, a "stronger" hypothesis—that is, a theory (T_1)—which, then, leads to a prognosis (P_1). Reducing the prognosis to more information, comparing it with new data, increases the theoretical content of science: new and more comprehensive hypotheses and theories (H_2, T_2) are built. This forms the basis of prognosis, a new, and perhaps better, prognosis (P_2) can be made—and so forth. Moreover, the model makes clear the following:

1. Science does not work exclusively by induction or by deduction, but is based on both induction and deduction at the same time and to the same extent.

2. Science is neither a mere gathering of data ("facts") nor mere hypothesizing and theorizing, rather hypotheses and theories are as important as empirical data.

3. Scientific research is a process that never ends but that

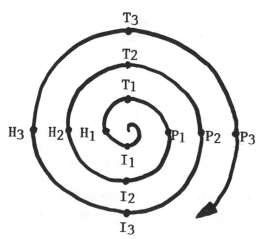

Figure 18. Systems model of the growth of scientific knowledge, showing the structure of a spiral.
Source: After Oeser 1979.

in itself is a process of stabilization and systematization of rational knowledge.

4. There is no optimal starting point, but there are many and different ways possible to solve a certain problem.

What is *evolutionary* about this model? Oeser (1984, p. 176) says that "in the model . . . the separate sectors of the quasi-circular process form not only a logical systematical sequence, but also a historical, genetic one." He argues that the *evolution of scientific method* can be reconstructed with respect to the history (of science) and would, then, show three phases:

1. A pretheoretical phase, characterized by the development of the inductive method in its most simple, enumerative, form. An example of science in this phase is the ancient *historia naturalis,* a comprehensive corpus of observations made to get an overview of minerals, plants, animals, and other natural things. But even at this pretheoretical level there is a general hypothesis; namely, the homogeneity of the world and the permanent repetition of events; even at this level it is possible to make prognoses or, at least, predictions about future effects by extrapolating a homogenous series of observations into the future.

2. The phase of theory construction; that is, a period characterized by the decisive step from inductively gained statements to general statements or laws (theories) that allow the (theoretical) explanation of more general and complex phenomena. At this theoretical level, science succeeds by the discovery of general principles such as, for example, the laws of motion of planets. Terrestrial mechanics, then, is revealed to be a special case of a more general mechanics. Science in this phase is embarking in a period of integrative growth. "The more abstract and comprehensive a law, the more complex and ample its context, because it integrates previous regularities as structural conditions" (Oeser 1984, p. 178). Newton's theory of gravitation is a classical example: it contains both the laws of terrestrial and celestial mechanics.

3. The phase and systematic perfection allowing for prognosis and explanation of any individual phenomenon within a certain area in the sense of an algorithmic method. At this level, the formal, analytical method of deduction is well developed. Hence, there is a shift from the procedure of observing, measuring, and experimenting to a theoretical calculation of

phenomena. An example, perhaps the best example, is the analytical mechanics of Lagrange and Laplace, developing Newton's theory into a formal axiomatic (deductive) system.

These three phases in the development of science show that, as there is a "concentration of information," more and more complex theories develop. In other words, science has become a more and more abstract system, a great variety of (separate) observations can be integrated within abstract theories, and a great variety of single phenomena can be deduced from comprehensive theoretical systems. Therefore, one evolutionary principle in the growth of scientific knowledge seems to be the process toward theoretical intricacy. It should be clear, however, that this has not been a linear process, but rather a process of interaction among different methods, between analysis and synthesis, observing, measuring, theorizing, and so on. As Sir Peter Medawar said, there is indeed no such thing as *the* scientific method (Medawar 1971, 1974).

As far as I can see, Oeser's approach has the advantage of not operating on the basis of a selection theory in a strict Darwinian sense—nor by applying Darwin's theory of natural selection to the evolution of science—but that the actual selective mechanism is regarded as constituted by *science itself.* Oeser (1984, p. 181) puts it bluntly: "This selective mechanism treats the individual mercilessly but with absolute justice. In science, no structure of order is ever lost." In fact, any discovery made too early and thus forgotten (or ignored) for a while, was (and will be) rediscovered later (Mendel's laws of heredity are a good example). And continuing, Oeser writes:

> For the individual, however, this justice is usually administered too late, as the selective forces are not attuned to the individual person. On the contrary, they cut right through personal ideas and scientific efforts, where truth and errors, sense and nonsense constitute a uniform system.
>
> This selective agency, for example, separates Galileo who founded physics from Galileo who established abstruse theories on high and low tide; it separates Newton who founded a uniform astronomical physical . . . theory from Newton who dabbled in pyramids, theology, and alchemy. (1984, pp. 181–182)

Yet, another point should be mentioned. This model of the

evolution of science is apt to link the two levels of evolutionary epistemology. The quasi-circular fundamental structure of cognition-gaining processes—the mutual relationship between experience and expectation, trial and error elimination—is given at the ratiomorphic as well as at the rational level. It is given in all scientific disciplines; in the field of the humanities it is the so-called hermeneutical circle of understanding that becomes the action circle in applied sciences. "The difference," writes Oeser (1984, p. 181), "lies not in the structure of the cognitive mechanism, but in the peculiarity of the object-area which contains different kinds of order." (See also Riedl 1985 for similar arguments.)

Let us now, for a moment, return to the question posed by Tennant (1988): whether the evolutionary view helps to illuminate the notion of scientific rationality. I think that it is indeed of some help. If we not only draw analogies but are prepared to see that every scientist, in the first instance, is a living organism and that the intimate connection between ratiomorphic and rational operations is given in the scientist's brain, then we also might be prepared to accept a flood of prerational elements in the scientist's way of problem solving. If, furthermore, we are prepared to accept rationality transcending the ratiomorphic operations, then we will—or, at least, should—be ready to look at selective mechanisms constituted by rationality itself, not only by the individual scientist's rationality but by what Toulmin (1972) has termed *collective reason*. So, what does scientific rationality, in an evolutionary perspective, mean? A tentative answer might run as follows: scientific rationality is a particular aspect of the *evolving human rationality* that is constrained by the (human) brain capacities but that, as it produces knowledge at a great pace, works as a selective mechanism; it selects its ratiomorphic predecessors *and* its own results; it is a selective principle at an abstract level, so that we have difficulty keeping abreast of it. Moreover, scientific rationality is the way some people (scientists) act to understand the principles underlying this universe. They build theories that not only should meet the facts, but have to be consistent in themselves. This theory construction has turned out to be a process displaying evolutionary principles, again, at an abstract level. From the point of view of evolutionary epistemology theories are not species or populations that evolve, but mental constructions that, certainly, evolve, too, but not by the means of natural selection. They evolve by the means of their consistency and inconsistency, by the means of the prognoses deduced from them.

I am aware that from this explanation you cannot see a sharp criterion of scientific rationality. Perhaps, it will not be possible to give this criterion on an evolutionary ground. The question, however, was only to illuminate scientific rationality. And as soon as you are ready to see that this rationality, like rationality in general, has its roots in organic evolution (i.e., in a long sequence of evolutionary learning processes), you will see that "pure rationalism" in science is science fiction.

Evolutionary Epistemology and the Idea of Scientific Progress

The poet and philosopher Ralph Waldo Emerson once said: "All science has one aim, namely, to find a theory of nature" (Emerson, 1894, p. 10). To find *the* theory of nature has been I feel, an important motive for what is commonly known as "scientific progress." Indeed, a widely spread opinion seems to be that there actually is progress in scientific research; because, as one might argue, our knowledge about nature is "better" than the knowledge available, say, from ancient Greek philosophy. Even if this were true, even if our knowledge about nature were better than the knowledge before us, this is not a good argument for the notion of progress in science. So, what does scientific progress really mean? Let us, first, get some answers from recently published literature.

To begin with, Popper, clearly, has linked the notion of scientific progress with progress towards the truth admitting that the search of *verisimilitude* is a more realistic aim in science than the search for truth. More precisely, Popper (1972a, p. 58) argued that making progress towards truth means "that the theory T_2 is preferable to its predecessor T_1, at least in the light of all known rational arguments." This would be in tune with the point made by Hull (1982, p. 321) on progressive science: "Scientists do not leap from total ignorance to final theories. They work their way painfully from theory to theory." And the effect of this procedure might be, as Hull continues, "coming closer and closer to an evermore accurate portrayal of the regularities which characterize the empirical world."

Another example for defining—and defending—the notion of

scientific progress is Mohr's claim that theories and laws are becoming "better." "This implies," says Mohr (1977, p. 136), "higher accuracy of prediction and explanation, wider scope, increase of simplicity, and esthetic appeal." Besides, according to Mohr, scientific progress is not so much related to *scientific revolutions* (in the sense of Kuhn 1962) as to an increasing *consolidation* of given paradigms.

These claims, particularly the demand that science advances toward accuracy of prediction, resembles what Lakatos (1970) has characterized as "mature science," in contrast to pedestrian trial-and-error gambling. For Lakatos mature science consists of "research programs" in which novel auxiliary theories and novel facts are *anticipated,* so that mature science has "heuristic power."

Of course, we also can see scientific progress within the broader context of cultural progress. Consider, for example, the following passage: "Progress is possible because there are images of knowledge to which we have stuck for many centuries, and these determine some criteria of progress. Such are utilization of natural resources, overcoming disease, fighting famine in *Western culture* . . ., religious tolerance, literacy, etc. According to these criteria we have made enormous advances" (Elkana 1981, p. 54). But, on the contrary, "there are other images of knowledge, like the image that knowledge must serve for more people to live and to restrain human aggression; these images persist too, but measured against these, we have failed, and even regression is noted by some observers" (Elkana 1981, p. 54). This brings us close to the demand that "measuring" progress in culture depends on the criteria by which we measure.

With regard to scientific progress, however, there seems to be one good criterion. That is, as these quotations have given to understand, the increase in the "explanatory power" of theories. Scientific progress thus means that theories of evergreater generality are built, theories that explain evermore observations and allow for everbetter prognoses. This progress of science is a consequence of what has been discussed as the "concentration of information" in the last paragraph. To be sure, scientific progress is not just an increase in the number of observations, of "facts." Rather, progress is given by our capacity to draw general lines, so to speak, to integrate many single observations in one comprehensive, general theory. In short, scientific progress means an expansion of explanations on the ground of extended theories.

I do not want to stop here. Yet we have to consider the dangers of what is commonly called *scientific progress;* namely, the application of scientific knowledge in the domain of technology. The problem here is that the tempo of technological production is extremely fast; our technology, particularly during the last decades, has developed at a breakneck speed. This is a consequence of the acceleration in cultural evolution (Chapter 6). True, modern technologies have helped us in many respects, like in the field of medicine; but technology also creates new problems and thus exposes humankind of danger. Today it is most obvious that by the means of modern technology humankind has the capacity to commit collective suicide. This is not just due to science and technology *per se*—it is because the development of humans does not (cannot) keep pace up with the evolution of technology. Remember that our biological make-up and our mental capacities have changed little in 40,000 years or so. It is one of the most important anthropological implications of an evolutionary theory of knowledge to notice this discrepancy.

Hence, it might be that the progress that we are ready to ascribe to the development of Western civilization will soon turn out to be a *regression;* that cultural evolution (including scientific progress) will change its way toward the decline of humankind. Can evolutionary epistemology here be of some "practical" help? Can we use this epistemology to rescue something of the future? To be modest, I do not want to claim that evolutionary epistemology will be enough to rescue humankind and to keep humankind from the collapse that might be caused in the future by expanding technology. But I do think that evolutionary epistemology can be regarded as a framework to which basic anthropological design may be related. Once we have recognized that humans are animals, that their knowledge is constrained by mechanisms of organic evolution, and that rational knowledge production (including applied knowledge in technology) may "overtax" our evolutionary make-up, we should be able to direct the processes *rationally* toward survival. I shall return again to these aspects in the Epilogue; for the moment, these few hints may suffice.

Anyway, it would be naive to believe that we can manage our problems irrespective of science. Scientific research—scientific progress in the sense of gaining everbetter explanations and prognoses—is (and will remain) indispensable for planning our future.

Limits to Scientific Knowledge?

Emil Du Bois-Reymond closed his lectures on the limits of our knowledge about nature by saying that, with respect to the enigma of matter and force, the naturalist must confess that "we will never know"—*ignorabimus* (Du Bois-Reymond 1907). The representatives of the Age of Enlightenment, some 200 years ago, were more optimistic. Thus, the French philosopher and advocate of educational reform, Condorcet, contended "that no bounds have been fixed to the improvement of the human faculties, . . . the perfectibility of man is absolutely indefinite" (quoted by Levinson 1982, pp. 490–491). Or, consider Darwin's claim that those who know little, and not those knowing much, assert that some problems will never be solved by science (so that, if we know much, we would not have a good reason to believe that some problems can never be solved) (see Darwin 1871).

Now, we have seen that science has indeed made progress, that we have been able to conceive theories and explanations of evergreater power; that science has helped us to solve many problems, problems of nature and life; and that, despite some regressive tendencies in recent times and despite its obvious danger, applied science has allowed for a somewhat pleasant life at least to people living within Western civilization. Our question, however, is whether there are limits to the advance of scientific knowledge on principle grounds. Is there good reason to believe that problems, which have not been solved up to now, will be solved in the future? Or, are there actually "natural" bounds, "natural" limits to our knowledge? Let us look for a possible answer from the point of view of evolutionary epistemology.

At first glance it might seem plausible that there are indeed limits to knowledge, limits to (human) knowledge acquisition, limits to approaching the ultimate truth. We have seen that our cognitive apparatus has evolved by biological selective mechanisms and that, like the cognitive apparatus of other species, it is capable of perceiving only particular aspects of the world. Hence, for any human being's perception is constrained by its biological outfit, which had evolved for the sake of survival, the growth of knowledge may be limited. Lorenz ([1941] 1982, p. 134) states that "there are limitations in the image of the universe traced out by our sense organs and cognitive apparatus." Thus there emerged, and endured, a "limitation hypothesis" of knowledge that seems to fit well with evolutionary epistemology. Regarding such complex structures as our own brain, some authors have exposed their believe in the *ignorabimus*: "It must be impossible for us to ever explain the functioning of the brain in any detail" (Popper and Eccles 1977, p. 30).

But how about the following proposal: "New methods bring new results and new results foster new ideas, and so we should not be too easily discouraged" (Crick 1979, p. 188). For all that, Lorenz ([1941] 1982, p. 140) admits that, for example, "from the palpable and sensible phenomenon of light, the impalpable, unvisualizable concept of wave phenomena has developed." He notes, furthermore, that "the self-evident comprehension of causality is replaced by considerations of probability and arithmetic calculations." For this reason, we should be sceptical of limits in science. Nobody could imagine, say, 400 years ago, that we would be able to know the molecular basis of heredity; and some 100 years ago, it was impossible to imagine our present knowledge about the universe, its possible origin 20 billion years ago, its structure and its expansion; and a scholar in the sixteenth century would have considered the findings of today's anthropology regarding fossil man as blasphemy, incredible, unimaginable; and so forth. Undoubtedly, our knowledge about nature (including our own) has increased; in many cases the *ignorabimus* has turned out to be a confession, a mere dogma, but not a useful advice.

Therefore, the limitation hypothesis of knowledge has been rejected by some authors pursuing evolutionary epistemology. In particular, Levinson (1982) proposed an evolutionary epistemology *without limits*, arguing that *evolution* means a continual growth of our intellectual powers. Moreover, Levinson (1982, p. 492) says that "technology amplifies the evolutionary flexibility and range of our cognitive capacities by providing us with new sensory experience, speeding our powers of calculation and organization." Likewise Radnitzky (1980), ensuing Popper's methodology—and of course, sceptical of "final answers"—argues that our capacity for conjecturing creatively would be, at least, a condition of the possibility of cognitive progress.

From my own point of view, the limitation hypothesis of knowledge is untenable, at least in its strict sense. It is true—and it seems to be most evident—that "man's innate teaching mechanisms . . . have set bounds to his development as a biological species" (Wuketits 1984a, p. 23). But it is also true that by the means of rational learning, by the means of scientific theorizing and reasoning, we humans have amplified our biologically given world view. Note that already the insight into our biological, innate capacities, an insight to which we have attained through the acquisition of rational knowledge, signifies a remarkable advance leading to a better self-conception of humans. Hence, I do not hesitate to say that evolutionary epistemology, as the understanding of our cognitive capacities and their possible improvement, signifies a cornerstone in the history of our intellectual development.

This is not to say that we humans can hope for "perfect knowledge." It would bc naive to believe that *everything* unknown to us will be known to future generations. But simply to say *ignorabimus*—we *shall* be ignorant—is bad advice for the scientist. Don't be too modest! Evolution is an "open program." This does not mean that *everything* is possible, but that does mean that it entails evernewer possibilities; some of them we cannot imagine today, but perhaps in the near future.

We have regarded science as produced by the activities of the human brain, insofar scientific research is constrained by biological factors. However, like cultural evolution in general, the evolution of science in particular displays a certain *Eigendynamik* that is not prescribed by organic evolution. The arguments presented in this chapter can be summarized as follows.

1. Analogies have been drawn between organic evolution and the growth of scientific ideas. Particularly, it has been argued that in the evolution of science a mechanism is working analogously to natural selection. However, such analogies, though heuristically useful, do not really characterize the mechanisms of the evolution of science.

2. The evolution of science can be understood as an information process. In the hierarchy of information-processing activities science is the most sophisticated information-processing system. Scientific knowledge gathering amounts to a "concentration of information" and represents a cyclic structure. In this way it closely resembles information processing at the ratiomorphic level, but it transcends this level by being a consciously developed "supraindividual" system of self-correction, eliminating errors and,

at the same time, storing corroborated knowledge and concentrating it in an abstract manner.

3. From the point of view of evolutionary epistemology, there is progress in science. This progress means the construction of evermore comprehensive theories and explanations allowing for everbetter prognoses. Despite this progress, the growth of scientific knowledge, undoubtedly, entails difficult problems, nay dangers for humankind. These dangers, however, are not due to scientific knowledge itself, but to applications of this knowledge. It seems that our brain, evolved in a world completely different from our today's world, has been "run over" by its own products.

4. There are no principle limits to (scientific) knowledge, because evolution—the evolution of our brain and, also, the evolution of scientific techniques and methods—is an "open process." From the evolutionary point of view there is no reason to believe in a definite *ignorabimus*, even if we cannot imagine the solutions to many problems. Besides, for the sake of our own survival, we need science; many problems afflicting humankind will not be solved without scientific research.

8

The Challenge to Philosophy

> We all have our philosophies, whether or not we
> are aware of this fact, and our philosophies are
> not worth very much. But the impact of our
> philosophies upon our actions and our lives is
> often devastating. This makes it necessary to try
> to improve our philosophies by criticism.
>
> Karl R. Popper

It is now time to discuss the philosophical implications of
evolutionary epistemology. In previous chapters I approached some
of these implications, but it is important now to see in which way
evolutionary epistemology starts to influence the whole corpus of
philosophical thinking—and to note that some of the old philosophical schools are in conflict with our evolutionary view. If philosophy is to make any progress, however, then philosophers are
compelled to meet the concepts and theories of the sciences and
not to stick to obsolete positions. Otherwise, they will not be taken
seriously by (natural) scientists. As Alfred N. Whitehead said in
his Lowell Lectures: "Philosophy is not one among the sciences
with its own little scheme of abstractions which it works away at
perfecting and improving. It is the survey of sciences, with the
special objects of their harmony, and of their completion. It brings
to this task, not only the evidence of the separate sciences, but
also its own appeal to concrete experience. It confronts the sciences with concrete fact" (Whitehead [1926] 1975, p. 109). Hence
philosophy, in a way, means to penetrate into the sciences; on the
basis of obsolete categories, however, such a penetration will remain without any effect. Evolutionary epistemology means a great

challenge to philosophy. Philosophical criticism is welcome, but, on the other side, philosophers have to put up with the onslaught on some of their conceptions.

A New Copernican Revolution?

Undoubtedly, evolutionary epistemology has carried some important innovations. Some advocates of this epistemology have argued that it has signified a new Copernican revolution. Let me give a few examples.

Riedl (1984a) has hinted at a third Copernican revolution, having in mind Copernicus and Darwin as the inaugurators of the first and second revolutions in the history of the sciences. Likewise Vollmer (1975) has claimed that evolutionary epistemology takes humans from the center of the world, making them mere spectators of cosmic processes (which include them). The parallel drawn by Vollmer between the Copernican turn and the evolutionary epistemologists' view expresses the fact that Copernicus displaced humankind from the world's center *cosmologically*, whereas the evolutionary view of knowledge displaced us from this center *epistemologically*. With regard to Popper's (evolutionary) epistemology, Radnitzky (1980, p. 96) has made the same argument: "Popper's work signified a Copernican revolution both in methodology and in epistemology: he produced the first worked-out non-foundationalist view of human knowledge." Allow me, finally, to refer to one of my own publications (Wuketits 1981) where I, too, stated that evolutionary epistemology announces a new Copernican turn (however, I avoided the term *revolution*).

Is it indeed justified to speak of a *Copernican revolution* in the context of evolutionary epistemology? I am not sure (see also my reserved answer in Wuketits 1984b). Let us examine the notion of Copernican revolution.

Since Kuhn's celebrated *Structure of Scientific Revolutions* (1962), the term *revolution* has been frequently discussed, and sometimes it appears as a mere *façon de parler* (which is often the case with frequently used terms). I do not want to revitalize Kuhn's view (and the view of his critics) here, but only draw the reader's attention to the point that not every event said to be a *revolution* in science was a "revolution" in a strict sense. Take the Copernican turn. To be sure, Copernicus led us into the new world, so to speak, but this "new world" was not the result of one single brain wave; it had forerunners, reaching back before modern times. Copernicus's primary intention was just a restoration of astronomy, and his work signified not so much a revolution as an innovation in science (and philosophy); it was a great synthesis. Copernicus had recourse to older conceptions. There is, worth noting, the "Egyptian Hypothesis" showing that, some way or other, the heliocentric world view was approached by Egyptian astronomers some thousand years ago (see Oeser 1979). In short, the Copernican turn was just a *turn* and not a revolution in its strict sense—although its *effects* upon human thinking have been revolutionary in a sense.

The same is true to Darwin's theory. As any historian of biology knows, Darwin had eminent forerunners; he was not the first to conceive the idea of evolution, his work is rather the result of a genuine synthesis (Mayr 1982). But, as it has been the case with the Copernican view, the effect of Darwin's theory was somewhat revolutionary.

As to evolutionary epistemology there is a similar situation. Therefore, I do not think that it is justified to speak of a revolution in a literal sense of the word. Remember that today's evolutionary epistemology had forerunners in the nineteenth century (Chapter 2) so that it was not established abruptly. It emerged rather in such a way that certain findings in different areas of scientific research, all based on the fact that humans result from (organic) evolution, now are combined (see Figure 19). However, it is clear that this epistemology, being a particular way of seeing and solving some problems in science and philosophy, has an enormous impact on human thinking.[1] In the following sections we shall examine this impact.

Evolutionary Epistemology and Transcendental Philosophy

As pointed out in chapter 4 evolutionary epistemologists have gone beyond Kant's philosophy (epistemology). Recall that Kant argued that our mind orders our sensations, so to speak, that we possess some knowledge a priori (independent of any perception); but Kant did not tell us why our sensations are ordered by our mind as they are and not otherwise; nor did he tell us anything about the origins of this mental order. From the point of view of evolutionary epistemology any a priori knowledge is the result of evolutionary experiences, of evolutionary learning,

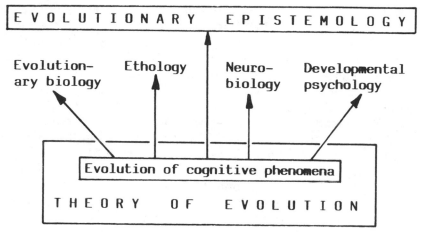

Figure 19. Evolutionary epistemology integrating the results of different fields of research, and the evolution of cognitive phenomena as an aspect of the (biological) theory of evolution.

as it were, so that the individual's a priori appears as an evolutionary a posteriori. Hence, a controversy emerged between evolutionary epistemology and what is called *transcendental philosophy;* that is, Kant's claim that our sensations are synthesized according to the categories of our minds. I can be brief here, because the problem already was examined in Chapter 4. However, a few remarks should be made on the controversy between evolutionary epistemology and transcendentalism.

The evolutionary point of view means the "dynamization" and the "historization" of the (Kantian) categories. In this way, evolutionary epistemology goes beyond Kant's philosophy, which has had a great impact on philosophy during the last two centuries, at least on the European continent. Has Kant's transcendentalism become obsolete under the influence of evolutionary epistemology? No, I do not think so; but I do think that by now we are able to answer questions that remained unanswered from a strict Kantian point of view or that were irrelevant within the framework of Kant's philosophy. I know that it is mere speculation, but let me suggest that Kant, had he lived in Darwin's century, would have accepted the theory of evolution and perhaps converted to evolutionary epistemology.

However, it is possible to accept both transcendental epistemology and evolutionary epistemology (Titze 1983), if we are ready to see that the former was established 200 years ago without any knowledge about evolution. That is, Kant's transcendentalism has been one particular approach to understanding (human) knowledge generated on the particular intellectual basis of the eighteenth century. Cassirer (1950), standing in the Kantian tradition, said that for Kant the theory of knowledge was a closely organized whole, and that within this whole every part has its own definite place. In a way, Kant's epistemology is a rigid system lacking the dynamic aspect that is of greatest importance for the understanding of the nature of (human) knowledge. One who takes evolution seriously may admire Kant, the architect of pure reason. But having realized the evolutionary origins of humans, one will be prepared to see that there is biological grounding for the architecture of pure reason.

Cogito, ergo sum — Sum, ergo cogito

Another philosophical position is challenged by evolutionary epistemology: Descartes's subjectivism. The French philosopher and mathematician René Descartes established the famous axiom: *Cogito, ergo sum* (I think, therefore I am). From the point of view of evolutionary epistemology, just the opposite is true: *Sum, ergo cogito* (I am, therefore I think) (Riedl 1984a).

Consider, once more, the following claims made by evolutionary epistemologists:

1. The evolution of life is a cognition process or, better, a cognition-gaining process (chapter 3).

2. Any organism is confronted with some kind of reality, with an external world to which it must refer for the sake of survival (chapter 4).

3. Human knowledge, some way or other, is constrained by experiences made through evolutionary processes by the antecedents of *Homo sapiens* while coping with external reality (chapter 5).

Hence it follows that one's own existence is not just created through thinking, but that one's thinking already presupposes one's existence as a material, physical (i.e., biological) being. If, for example, you drink a lot of wine, say, Bordeaux, you will have difficulty in shaping clear thoughts. The reason for your difficulty is obvious: a certain quantity of wine influences your brain activities in such a way that your thinking is hampered. This does not come as a surprise to anybody who agrees that (human) thinking has a material basis (the brain) and that it can be influenced by material processes, such as drinking wine. If Descartes's axiom were true, one could not explain the effect of material objects and processes on our thinking—and one could never explain where our thinking comes from. In an evolutionary perspective our thinking is a result of brain mechanisms, so that human beings do not exist because they think, but they are able to think because of their active brains. Of course, Descartes is right that our existence is mediated to us through our thinking in a particular way, but this mediation itself depends on complex brain mechanisms that, then, have priority in a genetical sense.

Descartes's view has constrained philosophies of mind to today. As we shall see later in this chapter, Descartes founded a mind–body interactionism, according to which body and mind are separate categories that interact, however. This position has been held by Popper and Eccles (1977). For the moment, I wish to point to Gilbert Ryle's brilliant exposition of Descartes's myth in *The Concept of Mind* (1966). Yes, it is a myth (and nothing else) to believe that mind is not something in space and that mental operations are something independent of biological processes. According to this myth, reaching back to Plato's philosophy, many philosophers insist "that our most distinctive characteristics cannot belong to creatures of flesh and blood: the true me and the true you must be things essentially incorporeal" (Flew 1978, p. 123). Such claims are at variance with evolutionary epistemology. Evolutionary epistemologists try to understand the origins of mental phenomena with respect to organic evolution; and when doing so, they discard any mythology of the mind. It is not easy to object successfully to an official doctrine. However, it is not suitable to a philosopher to live with mythologies.

Beyond Rationalism and Empiricism

In Western philosophy since the sixteenth century or so it has been a matter of controversy, whether (human) knowledge is due to sensations or to reason; that is, whether our knowledge is mediated through sense organs or through reasoning. Hence, there were established, and have endured, two main lines in epistemology: *empiricism* or *sensualism* and *rationalism*. (For a more detailed historical and systematical overview, see, e.g., Flew 1971.) The empiricists (including such figures as Francis Bacon, David Hume, and John Locke) have maintained that knowledge rests on experience—and only on experience—so that it is gained exclusively by sense organs. Consider Locke's thesis: *Nihil est in intellectu, quod non prius fuerit in sensu* (Nothing is in the intellect unless it was in the senses before). The rationalists, for example, René Descartes, Gottfried W. Leibniz, and Benedictus de Spinoza, on the other hand, have claimed that reason is the source of knowledge. Descartes's axiom that I am because I (rationally) think and know might be regarded as a typical rationalist claim. Then came Immanuel Kant, whose position, in a way, is an attempt to overcome both empiricism and rationalism in a strict sense. Recall that Kant accepted the importance of experiences but, at the same time, he regarded the mental ordering of perceived data as an a priori prerequisite for all knowledge. Many philosophers have supposed that Kant's epistemology is the last word. That it is not is clear to everybody who has adopted an evolutionary view.

Now, it might seem that evolutionary epistemology is a more empiricist approach to knowledge, because the advocates of this epistemology lay stress to (evolutionary) learning and experiencing the world and because they have regarded even Kant's a priori as (evolutionary) a posteriori. However, it would not be correct to identify evolutionary epistemology with the age-old empiricist view. At least, at the level of the individual, there is, as we maintain, a priori knowledge or, to put it in a less philosophical way, *innate* "knowledge" resulting from our evolution; that is, from the accumulation of relevant information over millions of years. Locke (1854, vol. 1, p. 261) said that perception is "the first step and degree towards knowledge, and the inlet of all the materials of it." In opposition to such claims an evolutionary epistemologist like Popper (1972a, p. 36) would argue "that there is nothing direct or immediate in our experience," but that "we have to *learn* that we have a self, extended in time and continuing to exist even during sleep and total unconsciousness." And, to complete the argument, our capacity of learning, of perceiving and experiencing the world (or, at least, parts of it), is due to a complex organic apparatus, the brain, which has evolved over millions of years and, therefore, contains an array of experiences made in the past.

Appreciating the evolutionary view, we can hardly agree to

the rationalist's credo that all knowledge stems from the intellect, from our reason. Our intellect is the result of evolutionary processes, it has developed alongside anatomical structures and physiological mechanisms by which information is gained about (parts of) the external world. The intellect is a brain capacity, and its existence presupposes a long chain of evolutionary experiences, at it were.

The evolutionary approach leads us beyond rationalism and empiricism, because it is neither the individual's intellect alone nor mere sensation that allows for knowledge, but rather a specific connection of both sensational data and the individual's a priori given in the intellect. Furthermore, it leads us beyond "subjectivism" and "objectivism," because the claim is neither that the knowing subject generates the world of objects nor that these objects, impressed upon the subject, create the subject's knowledge of them.

In the context of the rationalism–empiricism debate there has been the often-discussed problem of innate ideas. Many philosophers and scientists have held that there are certain dispositions in humans, which are "self-evident," so to speak, and which exist before, and independent of, any individual learning (see Table 10). Evolutionary epistemology offers amply evidence that there are indeed innate capacities in any individual (see chapter 4) and that these capacities are the starting point of any individual organism's learning. However, from the points of view of this epistemology, the innate ideas are results of evolution; they are not immutable categories, but might be changed through evolution over long periods. Hence, speaking of innate dispositions in the context of evolutionary epistemology does not mean any testimony of invariable "ideas" in the sense of Plato. Just on the contrary, Plato's idealism is incompatible with evolution and evolutionary epistemology.[2]

A New Realism

To continue this discussion of age-old philosophical problems in an evolutionary perspective, we now return to the problem of reality and realism, on which there has been discourse in different sections, particularly in chapter 4. In chapter 4 I tried to illuminate the evolutionary epistemologist's attitude toward the problem. Recall that I started with the

Table 10. The notion of innate ideas in philosophy and science.

Plato	Abstract ideas
Aristotle	Axioms of logic
Francis Bacon	*Idola tribus* (e.g., perception of form)
David Hume	Instincts
René Descartes	First principles (e.g., man's own existence)
Gottfried W. Leibniz	Essential truths of mathematics and logic; intellectual ideas (e.g., substance)
Immanuel Kant	The "causes" of the "forms of intuition" and categories
Hermann von Helmholtz	Ideation of space (three dimensionality of space)
Konrad Lorenz	Elementary patterns of behavior, forms of intuition, and categories
Jean Piaget	Norms of reaction, elementary structures of perception
Carl G. Jung	Archetypes (e.g., *anima*)
Claude Lévi-Strauss	(Ethnical) "structures" (e.g., marriage types, structures of kinship)
Noam Chomsky	Generative grammar

Source: After Vollmer 1975.

somewhat provocative thesis that animals (including humans) are realists, and that they would not survive without a realistic picture of (parts of) the world. Remember, furthermore, that from the point of view of evolutionary epistemology I presuppose the existence of some kind of reality independent of any organism's perception. Hence, evolutionary epistemology rests on what has been widely discussed under the term *common-sense realism* (Popper 1972a; Putnam 1987; Rescher 1986; Ruse 1986). Whether this realism meets the standards of certain philosophies, it is the best we have when trying to solve some problems of everyday life, it is the best for *biological* reasons. If it were a bad advice, we would hardly survive. (I believe that even a philosopher, however sceptical of "reality," masters the more or less trivial problems of everyday life rather by his or her common sense instead of by a retreat to Plato's idealism or similar philosophies.)

Evolutionary epistemologists have challenged many philosophers by the argument that our image of the world cannot be completely wrong, because up to now we humans have survived with it, even if it is no more than a *hypothetical* image. Hence, the problem of reality–realism has been discussed at the biological level (which some philosophers, obviously, dislike). However, the lesson that biology has to teach us in this context is that the question whether reality is "real"—an old philosophical question—does not matter, neither to humans nor to other animals. Any organism lives under the condition that there actually are certain objects and processes to be perceived, that there actually is an external world and coping with it is an imperative of survival. But let me point out again that this stance is not to be confused with the view of a naive realist who believes that he or she is perceiving the world *as it really is,* the world-in-itself. We have seen that there are different ways of perceiving the world, its objects and processes, that the dolphin's world picture differs from the world picture of a porcupine, that the world picture of a lion is different from that of a sea urchin, and so on. The only serious problem in the life of the organisms is how to survive. Philosophers are the only species allowed to ask questions like, Is there any real world outside my (the philosopher's!) imagination?

Scientists usually do not doubt that there *is* an external world. They are common-sense realists, in the first instance, believing that the objects or processes they are going to study are *real,* so that the evolutionary view might be of some substance to a "realistic philosophy of science" (Kanitscheider 1981). What would you think of a scientist who doubts that an object to be studied is a real object? But don't worry about this; a biologist interested in, say, the anatomy of a shark's fins, and who wants to study these organs, indeed is convinced that sharks and their fins are *real.* But this, I believe, is not the problem. The problem is—or arises from—the conviction that, as Rescher (1983, p. 229) puts it, "the world actually is as science takes it to be and that its furnishings are as science envisages them to be." This conviction is problematical. Remember that modern science is concerned with many theoretical entities, like quarks and spin, entities that are unobservable by human sense organs. Science can reconstruct such entities, this is true; it can deduce them from existing theories and from some observations made within the sphere of the visible world. But such reconstructions do not mean that science possesses an image of the world-in-itself. In this I agree with Rescher's argument that "a viable scientific realism must . . . turn not on what *our* science takes the world to be like, but on what *ideal or perfected* science takes the world to be like" (Rescher 1983, p. 231).

Certainly, every scientist will be interested in coming nearer to the truth, to contribute as much as possible to the understanding of the world. But at the same time the "good" scientist will welcome the critical method, will be aware that there might be better solutions (theories) of each problem and thus be open to criticism. Scientific realism, therefore, does not, and cannot, mean that a scientists possesses the image of the "last reality" (whatever that might be); but it does mean, that science does well by starting with the assumption that there is a real world, having different structures that are, at least partly, knowable.

The reader will wish to know what I understand under the "new realism," the concept I have placed as the title of this section. By the *new realism*—I am not sure that it is really new—I mean at least two claims:

1. We humans should recognize the fact, and it is a fact beyond any dogmatism, that we are animals and that our world picture has developed through the course of evolution, that this world picture is nothing invariable, that it can be corrected and accomplished at every (new) stage of our evolutionary development. There indeed are *facts* in scientific research, which cannot be unhinged, but,at the same time, there are hypotheses, models, conjectures—yes, and myths. The new realism discards particularly the myths and replaces them by the postulate to change any belief if it is not suitable to the relevant findings. Hence the claim is to eliminate mythology from studying ourselves and the world around us.

2. Having recognized our evolutionary past and the evolutionary constraints upon our behavior and having taken notice of

our mutability as organisms and "cultural beings," we should be prepared to eliminate illusory styles of thinking. Our history often has been guided by illusions, and ideological and political doctrines based on such illusions—for example, that humankind was created in the image of God or is "a mixture of the divine and the devil, or . . . devilish" (Agassi 1977, p. 318)—and these doctrines have hampered the progress of knowledge. To put it bluntly, it's time to be more "realistic", that is, to notice that our self-conception is just a *self*-conception constrained by our own evolutionary development, biological and cultural.

Evolutionary epistemology can help to fulfill these demands.

Evolutionary Epistemology and the Notion of Truth

" 'What is Truth?' said jesting Pilate; and would not stay for an answer" (Bacon [1626] 1904, p. 13). *Truth* is an ambiguous concept. Christians, for instance, claim that they posses the "truth," but actually they only have their belief. In our everyday life we often speak of the truth without reflecting upon whether what we call *truth* corresponds to something real. If somebody says that, for example, today the weather is fine and if I have the same feeling, then I will admit that the person is right, has spoken the truth.

What does the notion of truth mean in science and philosophy? It is not the task of this book to discuss the different approaches to this problematic concept. My concern, again, is to see what evolutionary epistemology can tell us about truth. (Please recall what has been said in chapter 4 on coherence.)

Ayer writes: "It is easy to see that the purpose of a 'theory of truth' is simply to describe the criteria by which the validity of the various kinds or propositions is determined" (1952, p. 87). This brings us close to the evolutionary epistemologist's attitude toward truth. To be sure, evolutionary epistemologists, particularly at the first level of their approach, are not concerned with testing validity. But being concerned with the organism's picture of (certain aspects of) reality and with the creation of this picture, they assume that any living being has developed this picture as valuable for the sake of survival. Hence, evolutionary epistemologists are going to describe the particular conditions under which an organism believes to have the truth, so to speak.

For the sake of survival it is not necessary to possess the "absolute truth," whatever that might be, but only to develop certain strategies to cope with what is assumed to be true.

Thus, we reach a *coherence theory* of truth that replaces the correspondence theory, according to which human knowledge, if it were to be considered as *true* knowledge, should be thought of as a correspondence to a prestructured reality. Advocating a coherence theory we do not claim that sense data always correspond to something real; that is, what is mediated through our sense organs is not necessarily an "exact picture" of what is perceived. Remember, for example, the phenomenon of mirages. In such cases we perceive something real, but the way we perceive it does not give us a true image of the physical causes of the phenomenon, which lies beyond the reach of our sense organs. From a strict biological (evolutionary) point of view the only important aspect is that we (like other living beings) are able to cope with the phenomena by developing adequate "schemes of reaction." In this Vollmer (1987) is right in saying that survival is to be regarded as a test or a criterion of what we call truth, but he is not right in arguing that evolutionary epistemology operates on the basis of a correspondence theory of truth. Whoever is prepared to see the different world pictures in animals will find that there are many different ways to cope with the external world and that the only imperative is to create a coherent view; that is, a view that allows for survival.

However, one might suspect that this leads us to *relativism*. From an evolutionary point of view there indeed is no reason to believe in an "absolute truth." But this does not necessarily mean that there is no such truth; and it does not mean that everything is possible. Certainly, we can survive even if we do not believe that the earth is a sphere. Before Copernicus people believed that the earth is a disk, and survived without knowing the truth. Trying to explore the universe or at least parts of it by the means of spaceships *presupposes* the knowledge about the spherical structure of the earth; otherwise astronautics would not be possible at all. What I mean is that survival depends on particular "true knowledge" about (parts of) the external world but that the importance of possessing such knowledge is relative to particular situations. In the everyday life one might succeed without having a true image of the earth's structure, an astronaut *has* to have precise knowledge about this structure. It should be obvious, however, that an astronaut's knowledge counts for nothing if one has to survive, say, in a tropical forest. You see, knowledge or its importance is constrained by the particular conditions of living, it depends on what one wants to achieve, it depends on particular intentions. There might be *the* truth, but for an organism's survival it is imperative to have but *one* truth.

Mind and Body: Against Dualism

Having now established the view that there is a naturalistic, biological approach to certain age-old philosophical problems, I analyze the most puzzling of these problems: the *mind–body problem*. Traditionally there have been two main views of this problem, *monism* and *dualism*, which can be found in different versions (see Table 11).

According to Bunge (1980) it is possible to take one of the following stands with regard to the problem:

1. The problem is a pseudoproblem and therefore it is not worthwhile to deal with it.
2. It is a genuine problem, but it is insoluble.
3. It is a genuine problem, but it is soluble.

I think that the mind–body problem *is* a genuine problem and not just a pseudoproblem; and I believe that it is soluble. But let me immediately say that dualism, the claim that body and mind (brain and consciousness) are separate categories, is untenable. Since Descartes many philosophers and even some neurobiologists (particularly Eccles, to name but the most prominent contemporary dualist among neurobiologists) have tried to substantiate the view of brain–mind *interactionism* (see Popper and Eccles 1977). They separated mind from material entities and discussed possible interactions between mind and brain. This reminds me of separating locomotion from the locomotory apparatus and discussing their interactions. Doing so would be a scientific anomaly.

In the light of evolutionary epistemology, the dualist view is to be replaced by a monistic view that, too, has a long tradition. As you can see in Table 11, monism has had many faces, so that it will be important to explain *monism* in the context of evolutionary epistemology. For the moment I want to draw the reader's attention to what Ryle (1966) has called a *category-mistake*. Consider the following illustration:

Table 11. Main views of the mind–body problem and some of their advocates.

Monism	Dualism
Idealism, spiritualism: Everything is mental (G. Berkeley, G. W. F. Hegel, P. Teilhard de Chardin)	*Autonomism:* Mind and body are mutually independent (L. Wittgenstein)
Neutral monism: Mind and body different manifestations of a single (unknowable) substance (B. de Spinoza, B. Russell)	*Parallelism:* Mind and body are parallel or synchronous (G. W. Leibniz)
Eliminative materialism: There is no mind at all (J. B. Watson, B. F. Skinner)*	*Epiphenomenalism:* The body produces (causes) the mind, which does not react back upon (T. H. Huxley)
Physicalist materialism: Mental states are body (brain) states (Epicurus, J. O. de Lamettrie)	*Animism.* The mind animates (controls, causes, or effects) the body, which does not react upon it (Plato, St. Augustine)
Emergentism: The mind is a special biofunction (D. Diderot, S. Ramón y Cayal, K. Lorenz)	*Interactionism:* Mind and body interact, the body (brain) being only the "material basis" of mind (R. Descartes, J. C. Eccles).

Source: In accordance with Bunge 1980; Bunge and Ardila 1987.
Note: This is a rough systematization; some of the positions overlap; also sometimes, one philosopher has advocated more than one of these positions during his lifetime.

* I am not sure whether Watson and Skinner actually used the term *eliminative materialism*. However, their conclusion can be so named.

A foreigner visiting Oxford or Cambridge for the first time is shown a number of colleges, libraries, playing fields, museums, scientific departments and administrative offices. He then asks "But where is the University? I have seen where the members of the Colleges live, where the Registrar works, where the scientists experiment and the rest. But I have not yet seen the University." It has then to be explained to him that the University is not another collateral institution. . . . The University is just the way in which all that he has already seen is organized. (Ryle 1966, p. 17–18)

The mind–body debate often has suffered from such a category-mistake. People often think that mind or that consciousness is "another institution" to be separated from brain states. This can be seen even in the title of the book by Popper and Eccles (1977), *The Self and Its Brain*. One might suspect that "the self" is a category per se having a brain. What we should have learned from modern neurobiology, however, is that just the opposite is true; that "the self" is a *functional reality* of the brain (Oeser and Seitelberger 1988).

The biological approach to the mind–body problem leading to the thesis that mind is not an autonomous category but depends on an active brain has been discussed by many authors standing close to or advocating an evolutionary theory of knowledge (Bunge 1979, 1980; Bunge and Ardila 1987; Churchland 1979; Cooney 1978; Creutzfeldt 1979; Hofman 1988; Jerison 1976; Leinfellner 1984, 1985; Lorenz 1977; Löwenhard 1981; Oeser and Seitelberger 1988; Riedl 1984a; Vollmer 1986; Wilson 1987; Wuketits 1985a; Young 1987).

The advocates of evolutionary epistemology had made a stand against dualism. From the evolutionary point of view the mind is not a category per se nor does it interact with material phenomena (brain), but rather is to be regarded as a *systems property* of brain mechanisms; that is, the brain produces mental activities. The evolutionary epistemologists' view of the mind–body problem is to be characterized as *emergentism*. Hence, we agree that mind is an evolutionary novelty and that it is not to be reduced to the brain in an ontological sense (no one has ever seen the mind or parts of it in single neurons) but that it has emerged as a result of particular interactions between the elements of the brain. This view can be summarized as follows:

1. Mental phenomena depend on material structures and mechanisms. These phenomena are biofunctions comparable with other such functions; for example, locomotion and digestion. However, they are the most complex functions in a living system and proper to humans. Despite many "open questions" due to their complexity, contemporary neurobiological research has corroborated the thesis "that every mental process is the specific function of some subsystem of the brain" (Bunge and Ardila 1987, p. 218). This view contradicts the dualist's claim.

2. The mind is a result of the emerging complexity of the (human) brain, its evolution is a result of brain evolution.

Remember that over some 4 or 5 million years the brain of hominids increased in size and capacity (Chapter 1). Through these processes of increasing complexity, mental capacities emerged as systems properties of the active brain. Therefore, we have no reason to believe that mind had to be imposed by a deity.

3. When did mind emerge? Elsewhere in this book (chapter 5) I paid attention to the Neanderthal's burials, which offer convincing evidence that humans were capable of death-awareness and language (as a precondition to communicate metaphysical belief) some 50,000 years ago. Since that time the human brain has produced, so to speak, more and more complex mental phenomena.[3]

4. The mind emerged not as a category but as a property; that is, a property of material elements and their interactions. According to Ryle's illustration we can say that mind is the particular way in which the most sophisticated interactions between neurons are expressed.

5. The question is not, How came the mind into the brain? because it is not in the brain. (Likewise locomotion is not in the feet, so that it would be absurd to localize it there.) Nor is it useful to ask, How do the brain and mind (body and mind) interact? There can be no interaction between something material and something immaterial; but the mind is neither a material nor an immaterial entity, for it is, to say it again, to be regarded as a property. Properties can develop only alongside material objects, so that, in an evolutionary perspective, the evolution of brain has been the precondition to the emergence and evolution of mind.

In short, our (evolutionary) view is a restatement of the old mind–body problem by the means of modern biology. Some philosophers might become angered and disappointed and they will insist that the mind–body problem is something different from what has been presented here. The "real" mind–body problem in philosophy consists of the dilemma that body and mind have been separated—this at least is my interpretation of most philosophical approaches to the problem. In fact, dualism has hampered the solution of the problem. More than this, it has led to many problems that appear unsolvable. Evolutionary epistemologists may not have solved *the* mind–body problem—if the problem actually consists of the duality of body and mind, then, perhaps, there indeed is no solution. But evolutionary epistemology makes clear that there is a different way of formulating the problem. This way is a way out of the dilemma. To be sure, formulating a problem does not mean a solution. But you can formulate a problem in a way that it remains unsolvable forever. So, science and philosophy indeed has to do with the "art of the soluble" (Medawar 1971); the *art*, in this context, is a particular way of looking at the mind–body problem.

Please note that I am not speaking here for the entire "community" of evolutionary epistemologists. As you can see from Popper's approach to the problem (Popper and Eccles 1977), even the advocates of this epistemology have not always been monists. From my own point of view, however, an evolutionary epistemologist should hold a monist view. This view indeed is a materialist one, but it must not be confused with the somewhat naive materialist claim that the mind does not exist or that it is nothing else but a heap of neurons. It *is* something else in the same way as locomotion is not just an assemblage of muscles and bones. But as locomotion is constrained by the (material) locomotory apparatus, mind is constrained by the (material) machinery of the brain. Such a view has far reaching consequences that may affect many people's religious beliefs.

The Decline of Metaphysics

Thomas Aquinas (1939, p. 200) said that man, "as regards the things he receives from God, . . . needs *prayer: I called upon God, and the spirit of wisdom came upon me.*" There is no doubt that metaphysical belief is a character of "mindful living systems," that humans, as soon as they began to reflect upon their own existence and their place in the world, developed more or less sophisticated metaphysical belief systems. Such belief systems have been useful in a biological—and, consequently, in a psychological—sense. To believe that we are the favored creation of a benevolent God and not just the result of nature's chance and necessity (Monod 1971) might be comfortable, as is the belief that, even if we are mortal as physical objects, our mind would persist and "live" after death. Hence, metaphysical belief is, as I said previously (chapter 5), to be understood as relative to human nature; it is to be understood as a particular trait of human nature. My heresy, which, of course, has a long tradition, is that religious belief is not imposed upon us by God, but follows from our very nature. It follows from our existential needs, from our hopes and desires, from our fear and awareness of death. Therefore, there is substance to the argument that humans are genetically disposed to religious or, in a wider sense, metaphysical beliefs. In this way the evolutionary approach leads to the decline of metaphysics: we are going to explain metaphysics itself as a "natural phenomenon."

This is not to say that we are able to explain *everything* by the means of evolution, that there cannot be dimensions inaccessible to our scientific evolutionary approach. True, we have not yet delved all the spheres of the universe and many aspects of the universe are still unknown to us. Therefore, we might be tempted to speak of an "unknown reality" going beyond our intellectual capacity, something like a "world-immanent transcendence" (Ditfurth 1981, 1987). But this does not mean that such a reality is something supranatural and will remain unknown and unknowable forever. "We will never know" is not a good advice for a scientist (see p. 178). Rather, we should be aware that with respect to modern biology, particularly to the evolutionary approach, we are in a position to get an idea of our own capacities of knowledge and some understanding of our own metaphysical beliefs and their causes lying in our very nature.

With regard to the dualist claim that the mind can be separated from bodily activities and that, therefore, it is something immortal, our evolutionary approach leads to the assertion that this is just a myth. If we are right that mental processes depend on brain processes, then "life after death" is an illusion; an illusion that might have some advantage in a psychological sense—but an illusion and nothing else (Wuketits 1985a). In former times even biologists could believe that the mind is indestructible and immutable and that it is an autonomous substance persisting after the death of the individual. Today's brain research, however, suggests the opposite (Oeser and Seitelberger 1988). Such conclusions may harm religious people. But if one wants to believe in immortality he or she may do it. It is not the task of scientific theories to destroy the people's hope. But one who believes in life after death should be aware that this is a private belief that cannot be substantiated by scientific research. The evolutionist has learned to live without such beliefs.

However, I am aware that my argument, according to which evolutionary epistemology leads to a decline of metaphysics, will look implausible for those who see evolutionary epistemology itself as a metaphysical research program. Indeed, some of the evolutionary epistemologists' claims—at least, some of my own claims in this book—have a speculative character. Despite the fact that science and philosophy always include some speculative elements, I should say that I am not against sound speculation as far as it is apt to promote the discussion. But again, the problem is one of terminology. As I already mentioned (see p. 118), for me metaphysics in its widest sense is identical with *irrational* belief and, thus, particularly identical with religious belief. The question of the origin of religion in human history has moved anthropologists for many centuries within and beyond the framework of the theory of evolution. Evolutionary epistemology leads to a kind of relativism in this context. The argument runs: the content of any religious-metaphysical belief depends on human life, which has a long history (evolution) and cultural tradition. The message of evolutionary epistemology—call it a metaphysical research program, if your want—is that, then, any religious belief can be studied by looking at humans and their history and not by appealing to supranatural principles. This is what I mean by the *decline of metaphysics*: that it has lost the aura of the unknowable. What can be known is not God (or any other alleged supranatural principle) but the origin of human thinking and reasoning about divine forces.

Evolutionary Epistemology and Ethics

If our mental capacities result from evolution and if our mind is just a particular biofunction, then we should think that also our *morality* can be explained in terms of evolution, that it is nothing to be imposed by God but that it has evolved alongside our brain and its increasing complexity.

According to this stance there has emerged what is now called *evolutionary ethics* (for recent discussions see Alexander 1987; Ayala 1987; Mohr 1987; Richards 1986; Ruse 1986; Tennant 1983c; Voorzanger 1987; Wilson 1978; Wuketits 1984c, 1988b). This way of discussing ethical problems has caused many controversies. I do not want to discuss the issue in detail here; my concern is the relation between evolutionary epistemology and ethics. What I want to say at the outset is that this epistemology does not lead to a formulation of *norms*, it can only help us reconstruct the evolutionary preconditions of moral behavior but says nothing about the validity of certain norms that have been developed by cultural evolution and are constrained by sociocultural conventions or, as Shaner (1989) explains, by different *rationales* inherent in different sociocultural systems.

Thus, I agree—and I think that all the other advocates of evolutionary epistemology would agree—to the distinction between *is* and *ought* and to Flew's argument that any theory of (organic) evolution as a purely scientific theory cannot "by itself entail any normative conclusions (conclusions, that is, about what *ought* to be)" (Flew 1978, p. 27). As a scientific theory, evolutionary epistemology contains only descriptive premises, i.e. premises about what *is, was,* or *will be* the case; it does not contain prescriptive premises.

Criticizing some advocates of evolutionary epistemology and ethics (particularly Lorenz, Mohr, and Wilson), Krüger (1987, p. 41) concludes: "What is transported along these lines of thought leading from biology to morality is the traditionally large credit of science, whereas the true premises or the results are of a different origin." What Krüger (like many other critics) has in mind is that biologizing morality may lead to a biologism of the kind of Social Darwinism, because, as he argues, "political views wedded to scientific credibility—this is an unhappy marriage which does not promise reliable offspring" (Krüger 1987, p. 41). This is true. But evolutionary epistemologists are aware of these dangers and try to avoid the *naturalistic fallacy;* that is, the connection between *is* and *ought* or the conclusion that *ought* follows from *is.* Therefore, I do not see any reason for Löw's blatant criticism. Evolutionary epistemology, writes Löw (1984, p. 225), "as a scientific theory . . . comes to an end here. [Evolutionary epistemology] cannot explain why man *ought* not to exploit and destroy nature." Why we ought *not* to destroy nature should be clear: because otherwise we shall have no chance to survive. But this is not the point. As far as I can see, no advocate of evolutionary epistemology is going to support moral norms (*ought*) or even immoral behavior by the means of purely biological premises (*is*); no evolutionary epistemologist would argue that because there *is* a struggle for existence in nature there *ought* to be such struggle (in the literal sense of the word) in human societies. What we are interested in rather is how did humans come to behave in the way they actually do, how are the evolutionary origins of human behavior to be explained and in which way has our behavior been constrained by biological factors. This effort to reconstruct moral behavior does not include any valuation.

The starting point of any evolutionary account of ethics, however, is the insight that morality has a biological basis, that it has developed as a systems property of the brain. In fact, "ethical behavior is an attribute of the biological make-up of humans and, hence, is a product of biological evolution" (Ayala 1987, p. 239). Such statements do not entail any normative assertions. From the fact that morality has developed we cannot conclude that any particular trait of human behavior is good or bad (right or wrong) in an ethical sense. In other words, an evolutionary account for ethics does not support any moral code, but it may help us to understand why such codes have evolved. Or, as Tennant (1983c, p. 291) puts it: the evolutionary approach "may account for the evolution *of* ethics, rather than purport to derive an ethical code from the theory of our evolution." It might be misleading, therefore, to speak of "evolutionary *ethics*": our moral codes are not imposed by evolution, only our genetic disposition to moral behavior. One who prefers to speak of "evolutionary ethics," then, should keep in mind the distinction between "evolution of morality" in a neutral sense and the "evolutionary justification of moral codes." Evolutionary ethics in this second sense has a bad tradition, for it has entailed ideologies like that of Social Darwinism. Spencer's *The Principles of Ethics* (1892) and, even more, some writings by Haeckel (1899, 1905) contain ideas close to this ideology. To avoid any misunderstanding, I want to stress that when I use the term *evolutionary ethics* I do so only to characterize the view that morality has evolved and that there have been biological roots of moral behavior—but that from the evolutionary genesis of our morality we cannot derive right or wrong. I think that most evolutionary epistemologists would agree with such claims.

As I pointed out elsewhere (Wuketits 1988b), the evolutionary approach to ethics has one great advantage. To argue that humans and their morality result from evolution means, to say the least, to admit that our morality has evolved and can evolve further and that moral codes therefore are not fixed forever as unchangeable entities. As evolution generally is an "open process" (chapter 1), a self-planning process that is not determined by eternal laws, the evolution of morality does not prescribe any final goal. Humans themselves are free to find their goals in this universe. Unlike other approaches to explain moral behavior, the evolutionary view, therefore, does not include contentions such as "things are unchangeable" and "the way we act is the best one." Such contentions, legitimatizing the status quo, are ideological claims and have little to do with ethics; rather they harm humankind. The evolutionary approach does not offer any justification of the status quo, but rather can help us to understand under which circumstances humans have created values and norms. True, some traits of our moral behavior may be derived from archaic behavioral patterns and from the drive to survive. If moral codes should regulate the interactions among individuals in a society, then it seems to be clear that these codes have been useful for the sake of survival. To our phylogenetic ancestors it was of certain survival value to believe that moral codes are simply given and therefore objective. And even today many people believe that ethical norms are unchangeable and can be derived from eternal supranatural principles. One who has taken the evolutionary view will dismiss such beliefs and lay the creation of moral norms in human nature. This means that humans are free to change their moral codes; but this also means that humans are responsible for themselves and that there is no supranatural being to which responsibility can be delegated.

Many philosophers have little sympathy for the evolutionary approach to human mental capacities. But if humans result from evolution, then there is no reason to separate these capacities from the evolutionary pathways of humankind. The reader who is willing to accept the evolutionary approach probably will agree to the following conclusions.

1. There is biological grounding for reason; the a priori in the sense of Kant is to be regarded as evolutionary a posteriori (see chapter 4). Descartes's *cogito, ergo sum* is to be replaced by *sum, ergo cogito*.

2. Because our intellect is the result of evolutionary processes, the rationalist's credo in untenable. The same is true of the empiricist's claim that nothing is in the intellect unless it was first in the senses. Our intellect is not a tabula rasa, it is somewhat preoccupied, as it were, by experiences made during

evolution by our phylogenetic ancestors. Evolutionary epistemology therefore goes beyond rationalism and empiricism.

3. There is no need of or, at least, no practical use for the idea of an absolute truth. Our idea of truth is relative to the conditions of living. We may hold a correspondence theory of the meaning of truth but we cannot implement it in efforts to improve the "truth" of any belief. For the latter task, coherence considerations are all we can use. (But "coherence" never becomes the definition of truth in a deeper philosophical sense.)

4. The dualist's claim that mind and body are different categories is to be replaced by a view called *emergentism*, expressing the idea that mental phenomena have evolved alongside organic structures, that these phenomena have evolved as biofunctions that cannot be separated from brain structures and functions. The mind is a systems property of the brain.

5. Like other mental capacities, morality is an outcome of evolution. Thus, we attain to an evolutionary ethics that is not normative, but that can explain how, and under which conditions of living, our moral codes have emerged in the course of evolution.

6. Many traditional philosophical disciplines are challenged by the evolutionary approach. The message of evolutionary epistemology is not to destroy these disciplines but rather to help to develop them into up-to-date accounts for intriguing problems including questions such as, Why do we behave like human beings?

Epilogue: Toward a New Image of Humankind

> Literary intellectuals at one pole—at the other scientists, and as the most representative, the physical scientists. Between the two a gulf of mutual incomprehension—sometimes . . . hostility and dislike, but most of all lack of understanding. They have a curious distorted image of each other. Their attitudes are so different that, even on the level of emotion, they can't find much common ground.
>
> Charles P. Snow

Yet I cannot rest my case. It is important to discuss some of the implications of evolutionary epistemology for an overall perspective on human existence. As the reader might have recognized, this epistemology is not just one of many epistemological schools but rather an attempt to trace back to the *elements* of human nature. So let us see what lessons evolutionary epistemology actually can teach us with regard to our self-conception.

To begin with, let me recall the remarkable and somewhat curious fact that our intellectual life is divided into "two cultures," the scientific culture and the traditional culture (humanities) (On this, see C.P. Snow's still readable essay *The Two Cultures and a Second Look*, 1964). Each has its own terminology and its own methods; nay, each is a different way of seeing the world and our place in it. It has been said that science, as *natural* science, deals with the phenomena of nature—physical law, chemical elements, plants, animals—whereas the humanities are devoted to human intellectual life and its products (culture). This, I feel, is a result of separating mind *(Geist)* from nature. And, indeed, the "mental sciences" *Geisteswissenschaften)* are frequently said to be disciplines having the aim to describe and to understand emphatically; whereas, according to a most common opinion, the (natural) sciences explain phenomena and try to predict with the help of general laws. If it were true that mental phenomena are separated from (human) nature, then, of course, it would be justified to keep apart spiritual and natural sciences. But, as we have seen, this is not true.

Does this now mean that the humanities should develop into natural sciences? We have argued for a naturalized epistemology that "is supposed to give us all the discoverable scientific information about human knowledge that there is" (Stroud 1985, p. 83), so that, after all, we might expect a "fully naturalized mind," accessible to scientific explanation and prediction. And we might suspect that La Mettrie's radical materialism, according to which humans are nothing but machines *(L'homme machine,* 1747), has now been revitalized. Against such claims, however, "the humanistic school was right in one important point, namely in maintaining that the possession of a 'spirit' (in contemporary parlance, 'highly evolved brain') puts human in a very special category" (Bunge and Ardila 1987, p. 6). Evolutionary epistemology does not reduce humans to machines or heaps of atoms, but rather helps to explain their *complexity* as result of complex evolutionary processes.

To stick to the point, we should be aware that the separation of the two cultures, the separation of mind from body, culture from nature, and humanities from (natural) sciences, in short, the "splitting of our world view," is a consequence of our own history, reflecting an old tendency to simplify the world around us and our very nature (Riedl 1985). Remember that our innate perceiving apparatus, consisting of ratiomorphic hypothesis (chapter 4), gives us the advice to calculate the world just for the sake of survival. The emerging rationality, however, has brought humans the dilemma of seeking causes and purposes; and when these causes and purposes (of natural phenomena, of our own life) cannot be found within the visible world, they are regarded as supranatural, coming from outside, so to speak. The splitting of the world view therefore seems to be a result of our cognitive apparatus (Riedl 1985): an apparatus developed for the sake of survival but now capable of self-awareness and transcending, as it were, its biological constraints. Hence, there is the belief that the mind is something supranatural, and that culture, the mind's very creation, is to be separated from nature. This dichotomy, nature–culture, is artificial; in fact, culture is not "unnatural," rather it is one particular expression of human nature.

Evolutionary epistemology leads to a *holistic* picture of humankind, to a holistic self-conception of humans, and thus it may help to establish a synthesis, to see any human being as a unity of "biopsychosocial" factors (Wessel 1988). What is needed indeed is a *holo-evolutionistic* conception of humans (Erben 1980), taking evolution running as a thread through our history, beginning with the origins of humanlike creatures some 4 or 5 million years ago and going to the emergence of rationality. Therefore, one might suppose that a "methodological monism" will be of some relevance (Riedl 1985). But, again, I feel that the critics will reproach evolutionary epistemologists with reductionism. However, this would jump to conclusions that actually do not follow from the evolutionary approach. We are aware that the human mind is a complex phenomenon and that human knowledge is constrained not only by biological factors but depends on sociocultural circumstances, too. However, these circumstances have been produced by brains, and brains result from organic evolution. What I mean is that if we want to get a comprehensive view of ourselves, we should indeed take into account results from different fields of research, from the social as well a from the biological sciences, but we cannot seriously deny that our very origins lie in the processes of organic evolution. Therefore, we should pay attention to these origins; basic patterns of our behavior depend on, and have been developed through, our evolutionary past. Perhaps, some people will think that, in the last instance, evolutionary epistemologists are going to defend the determinist view, but this would be incorrect.

Remember that we have advocated the view of open evolution, which is at variance with the determinist perspective. And remember that at least higher organisms are capable of (individual) learning so that evolutionary programs may be modified. Appreciating this ethological fact and appreciating the human brain's plasticity, we reach a nondeterministic view of humans. Arguing from this point of view, we can emphasize what even a theologian has recently claimed; namely that "through its mechanisms of discernment and learning, the human creature must make its own decisions about what the world system requires, what sorts of responses will best meet those requirements, what norms and limits are which the world imposes. The only authority for the human being's world-constructions and the only sanction for its actions are the authority and sanctions which the human being has discovered and acknowledged" (Hefner, 1987, p. 137). I quote this passage, because, if I have understood it correctly, it expresses the important idea that nobody else but we ourselves are responsible for our actions in the world.

Certainly, for theologians humankind is not the creator, but just the *cocreator* (Hefner, 1987). For the evolutionist, however, humankind is the *creator* of its own destiny. This creation of our destiny indeed is constrained by our evolutionary past—but it is not fully *determined* by this past because our flexible brain allows for learning. Learning in this context implies the possibility of learning from our own evolution. Hence we should learn that any species as soon as it had developed a certain hypertrophy died out—without exception. Remember, for example, the dinosaurs and their hypertrophic size and structure. To be sure, I do not want to compare humans with dinosaurs, but thinking of our nuclear weapons and the rapid development of other technologies I see the somewhat hypertrophic development of our species. But, and this is the most obvious difference between humans and dinosaurs, the great reptiles were not consciously aware of their hypertrophy and had no idea how to handle it. We humans, on the contrary, *are* aware of the great dangers included in our development—and evolutionary episte-mology might help us understand the mechanisms of our development and correct the hypertrophic growth of our technology that, again, is a result of our brain's evolution. As Leinfellner (1984, p. 275) concluded: "Either we learn from our biological and cultural history, or those who do not learn from it are forced to repeat endlessly the mistakes of the previous periods." It is a rather curious situation. On the one hand, we are the first species capable of self-destruction; on the other hand, we are the first species able to determine its own evolution. *Ecce homo.*

Some authors have criticized the evolutionary epistemologists' commitment to questions of culture and *Kulturkritik*. Thus, Wolters (1988) remarked that evolutionary epistemology cannot contribute anything to an understanding of our culture and its crisis, and that *Kulturkritik* should not be present as natural science. Arguments like these express what I have said about the "splitting of our world view:" It is suggested that any question concerning culture and cultural evolution (and its future possibilities or limitations) is a question of social and human sciences. Against such claims I just want to point out that the question of our survival is not—and should not be—restricted to particular disciplines. The question of our future is too important to restrict its discussion to particular disciplines; for example, the social sciences. Certainly, the social scientist can tell us something about possible sociocultural circumstances under which our future can be devised. But this will not be enough.

Only if we go back to our very origins, that is, to our origins as a biological species, should we be able to get some insight into our true nature and develop a view of our further opportunities in this world. To put it this way, our understanding of ourselves including our future depends on advance in our understanding of evolution. Hence, my message is that we should take seriously research in the fields like neurobiology, ethology, and evolutionary biology. Perhaps, some readers will think that these disciplines will not present a *new* image of humans, but rather an old one, a 'biologistic' one, as it was presented hundred years ago by writers like Haeckel. But since Haeckel's times biology has rapidly developed; 100 years ago it was possible, and with respect to Haeckel's blatant biologism justified to some extent, to reject the biological approach to an understanding of humankind. Today this is neither possible nor justified; it is unpardonable to ignore this approach because it tells us much about our past that still is present, as can be seen in many aspects of our behavior.

I have presented evolutionary epistemology as a nondeterminist view compatible with our present understanding of organic evolution. Furthermore, I have sketched it as a nonadaptationist view (Chapter 4); that is, a view taking cognizance of organisms as active systems able to partly determine their own evolution. Conceptions of evolution and evolutionary epistemology established in the nineteenth century and even in recent times have been deterministic and adaptationistic. In contrast to this our view may offer a new understanding of evolution in general and particularly the evolution of cognition including human knowledge, because it is more "organism-oriented," as it were. Therefore, I venture to say that it has become possible to establish a *new* image of humankind. This view has some important implications with regard to *humanism*.

The issue of evolution and humanism has been intensively discussed and some authors have pushed forward to an *evolutionary humanism* (see J. Huxley 1961). Because of bad experiences with Social Darwinism, we should note that an evolutionary humanism is the other way to interpret evolution for human purposes. This is not to say that (organic) evolution itself entails humanism or anything in this context. As we have seen in the last chapter, we have no reason to believe that our moral categories are preestablished, so to speak, in (organic) evolution. But on the other hand, (organic) evolution does not contradict any humanist conception. We humans are moral beings; that is, our social life is bound to moral categories—and there is grandeur in the view according to which (organic) evolution has led to the emergence of a species capable of morality. In fact, evolution does not tell us what to do to fulfill ethical demands; but it tells us that we are members of one and the same species endowed with one and the same cognitive apparatus, so that our (evolutionary) view is at variance with any kind of racism or similar ideology. In this way humanism may be the ultimate concern to anybody thinking about evolution. But what would be more important than a really *human* life?

Unfortunately, it is true that, as Alexander (1987, p. 261) concluded, "only in humans are war and other forms of intergroup competition the central aspects and driving forces of social existence." But, fortunately, it is also true that humans are able to cooperate, able to behave like *human* beings in a narrower sense of the word. It depends on us to increase this cooperative behavior, to move toward a humanist conception of life.

It is clear that evolutionary epistemology does not provide comfort to people whose thinking is deeply rooted in traditional philosophical conceptions. But I have argued that philosophers, if they are really interested in making some progress, no longer can ignore the evolutionist's insight. The insight, however, leads us to the conclusion that humans are neither gods nor created by God, but that they stem from the animal kingdom and that their mental capacities, too, result from evolutionary processes. Thus, we attain to an image of humankind that indeed had been conceived by some naturalists and philosophers more than 100 years ago but, up to now, has not been taken seriously enough. "A century and a quarter after the first appearance of *On the Origin of Species*, the time has surely come to take Darwin seriously" (Ruse 1986, p. 279). This postulate, I think, does not require any further comment. I wish to make only two final points. First, evolutionary epistemology takes a "pragmatic" view of humans. Evolutionary epistemologists ask how humans really behave and what is the true origin of their behavior. In contrast to this program many conceptions of humans are based on an idealization of our species. It has been argued that humans were created in the image of God and that God has been the director of our lives. Also, the human has been pictured as a demigod, having the capacity to change the planet. In contrast to this, from the evolutionary point of view, we attain to the conclusion that we humans cannot change our planet at pleasure. We are part of the biosphere and its complex regulatory systems, so that the biosphere acts back upon our own actions. Hence, one who takes evolution seriously will take nature seriously and know that our actions are constrained by the regulatory principles of the biosphere. One who is not prepared to take this seriously will be surprised at the disappearance of the human species.

Second, following on what I said earlier, evolutionary epistemology rescues something of the old and venerable idea of freedom. It might be an encouraging perspective that we humans, due to our rationality, are the masters of our future evolution. But if we actually want to master our future, we must take into account our past, our evolutionary origins and genealogy. This means that we should grasp our very nature realistically, beyond any illusionism and utopian dreams. "Future evolution," says Simpson (1963, p. 285), "could raise man to superb heights as yet hardly glimpsed, but it will not automatically do so." It depends on us to influence this process toward "superb heights"—or toward our disappearance . . .

I am led, in conclusion, simply to draw the reader's attention to Darwin's speculation: "As natural selection works solely by and for the good of each being, all corporeal and mental endowments will tend to progress towards perfection" (Darwin [1859] 1958, p. 450).

Notes

Prospectus: Approaching an Evolutionary Theory of Knowledge

1. Please note that I am using the term *epistemology* throughout the book in its widest sense; that is, as the study of information-processing mechanisms in the living world and not only as the study of *human* knowledge capacities. For me epistemology is not only a philosophical discipline but a wide field covering different approaches to study epistemic activities.

1. Taking Evolution Seriously

1. The exact date of creation often was discussed. In the seventeenth century, Archbishop James Ussher came to the conclusion that God created the earth on October 23, 4004 B.C. This conclusion, based on biblical chronology, was accepted until the nineteenth century. Only few scholars, among them the eminent French naturalist Georges-Louis L. de Buffon, suggested the idea of a longer duration for the earth.

2. Remember his theory of "pangenesis." According to this theory somatic cells contain particles, which can be influenced by the environment and which can move to the sex cells and thus influence the heredity process. This theory was a mere speculation. Modern evolutionists who have taken a Darwinian view complain of it: "Darwin's theory of pangenesis was an unfortunate anomaly" (Dobzhansky et al. 1977, p. 15). However, the theory demonstrates that Darwin was not a strict Darwinist!

3. By the *epigenetic system*, Riedl means the sum-total of regulatory principles in the genome of a species, a genus, a family, and so on. It is to be understood as a dynamic principle that stores order.

213

2. The Historical Background

1. Mach, however, also was an advocate of "empiriocriticism," according to which we should analyze our experiences to get a "natural conception of the world," free from any metaphysical notions. (A more recent advocate of this position is Zimmermann 1968.)

2. It might be said that Mach and Boltzmann found the Vienna tradition of evolutionary epistemology. This tradition was continued by Konrad Lorenz and Karl Popper, who both were affiliated with the University of Vienna for a time. Now the Vienna School of Evolutionary Epistemology is represented by Erhard Oeser, Rupert Riedl, Günter P. Wagner, and me. (*School* indicates the view defended, not an institution; also, we are not a partisan group or something like that.)

4. Cognition and Reality

1. It is worth noting that Kant intended to prove such a kind of realism based on the idea that things exist in space independent of anybody who has the capacity to know them. This has been called the *metaphysical aspect of realism* (see Stroud 1984). Evolutionary epistemologists argue that the knowing subject is the result of processes that occurred before, and independent of, any knowing subject. At least, this has been a most fruitful working hypothesis, notwithstanding some "deeper" philosophical problems.

5. The Evolution of Human Knowledge

1. The term *irrational* must not be confused with the term *ratiomorphic* (see Chapter 3). Ratiomorphic processes occur at the prerational level, whereas irrationality presupposes the existence of rationality.

6. Evolutionary Epistemology and Culture

1. There is no unanimity among evolutionary epistemologists with regard to sociobiology. Lorenz, as I know from personal communication, simply disliked it; and Riedl (1987d) is most cautious in accepting the sociobiologists' arguments. Other advocates of evolutionary epistemology (Mohr 1983c, 1984; Oeser 1987) have used sociobiological explanations and generally accepted the sociobiological approach. Ruse (1985, 1986) has tried to develop a sociobiologically founded version of evolutionary epistemology. My own attitude towards sociobiology should become visible in the following passages (including the next section).

8. The Challenge to Philosophy

1. Any of the so-called Copernican turns has had an enormous impact on human thinking and thus important anthropological implications (see Thönnissen 1985).

2. Plato's typological thinking, his belief in ideas or "essences" behind the visible world, was one of the weighty obstacles to evolutionary thinking (see Mayr 1982). Popper (1960, 1972a, 1972b), who has characterized Plato's philosophy (and the philosophy of his many followers) as *essentialism*, exposes good arguments against this "antinaturalistic" doctrine, being at variance with the idea of a nondeterministic, "open" universe and having bad impact upon theorizing in the social sciences.

3. According to Jaynes (1985) the postulated duality of mind and body inherent in all dualistic conceptions began 3000 years ago as a duality of consciousness and everything else. Before, this Jaynes argues, there was no consciousness–body or mind–body problem. However, I feel that already primitive humans as soon as they were aware of themselves and the world around them and as soon as they began to consciously reflect upon themselves and the world established the duality.

Glossary

This glossary includes all the basic concepts used in this book and the concepts that have not been properly explained in the text.

Adaptation. The process that changes organs or functions of organisms to make them better suited to a particular environment; also, the adapted organ or function itself. According to a common view, organic evolution leads to adaptations. *See* Darwinism.

Adaptationism. The view that the process of adaptation is one of the major features of organic evolution, so that the claim is made that any organ or function, or behavior in an organism can be explained as adaptation.

Analogy. An inference made to show the similarity between two or more phenomena or classes of phenomena; for example, drawing parallels between organic and cultural evolution. In biology, a concept to characterize functional similarity between organisms that do not necessarily have a common ancestor; for example, the fishlike construction of aquatic vertebrates (*see* Figure 2).

Anthropology. The study of humans divided into particular branches; for example, biological anthropology (the study of human evolutionary history, racial differentiation, and genetic plasticity).

Archetypes. Primordial characters considered as universals. In psychology, basic patterns of experience evoking similar feelings in different persons.

Artifacts. Objects made by humans; for example, tools.

Australopithecines. The earliest representatives of the family Hominidae. They appeared some 4 million years ago in South Africa

and are characterized by an upright posture. Different species of
the genus have been discovered by paleoanthropologists.

Behaviorism. The psychological doctrine that animal and human
behavior is shaped by environmental influences on an organism.
The behaviorists claim that any organism is initially a clean slate
or tabula rasa (empty-organism doctrine).

Biologism. The extension of biological concepts, models, and theories to
other fields, for example, the explanation of social phenomena in
humans using biological templates. *See also* Social Darwinism.

Categories. In Kantian philosophy different types of purely rational
(reasonal) conceptions. The categories are regarded as given a
priori and independent of empirical knowledge. Generally the
term *category* is used to denote different kinds of being or
different classes of objects.

Causality. The relation between different objects or events, where one
results in the other. Generally, the proposition is that every event
has a particular cause. A causal explanation in science seeks the
factors (causes) by which a certain phenomenon is created.

Central dogma. In molecular genetics, the tenet that (genetic)
information flows from the DNA to proteins and not the other way
round. That means that any character and its change in the
course of evolution must be fixed previously in the DNA. The
central dogma contradicts Lamarck's doctrine of the inheritance
of acquired characteristics. *See* Lamarckism.

Central nervous system (CNS). The most complex type of nervous
systems, characterized by a high concentration of nerve cells and
synapses (brain). *See also* Nervous system.

Cognition. The sum-total of processes by which an organism gains
information; that is, processes of perception and memory allowing
for problem solving. *See also* Information, Information processing.

Cognitive niche. An organism's particular horizon (ambient). It is said
that as any organism lives in a particular ecological niche it is able
to gain information about its particular environment.

Consciousness. Generally, a certain brain state in higher animals
allowing for behavioral device, in particular the ability of a human

being to reflect upon itself (*see* Self-awareness). The concept of consciousness is used in an ambiguous manner. In this book, it is used to characterize the human capability of self-reflection. *See also* Rationality.

Cortex. The layer of gray matter, the differentiated zone of cells and synapses in the brain; a major locus of intelligent behavior to mammals.

Culture. The sum of all artifacts, institutions, moral systems, and religious belief systems acquired and transmitted by learning. Culture presupposes a high degree of sociality and complex patterns of communication (*see* Language). It represents an extrasomatic temporal continuum of artifacts and so on.

Darwinism. Darwin's theory of evolution by natural selection. Sometimes the term *Darwinism* is used to characterize particular biologistic interpretations of human life (*see* Biologism). As a scientific theory, Darwinism offers an explanation of evolution beyond any ideological claims. *See* Natural selection, Social Darwinism, Synthetic theory.

Determinism. The view that there is a fixed cause effect relationship between different phenomena. In its widest sense it means that any event in the universe is prescribed by natural laws or by a divine principle. The belief in a determined universe stands in contrast to the notion of freedom.

DNA. Deoxyribonucleic acid, the basic hereditary material of organisms.

Empiricism. The epistemological view that knowledge is gained only through the senses.

Epistemology. The study of (human) knowledge, its scope, and limits. Initially a philosophical discipline, epistemology today is more and more science oriented.

Ethics. The philosophical discipline trying to establish rules for human behavior. It is a normative discipline inventing "good" and "evil" and what humans ought to do.

Ethology. The study of animal and human behavior.

Evolution. The process through which plants and animals (including humans) are changed by the means of natural forces. The concept of evolution expresses the idea that species are not immutable and that today's organisms result from long-term processes. The idea of evolution also has been applied to other classes of phenomena, so that we can speak of cosmic and cultural evolution as well. However, the mechanisms are not the same; the principle of natural selection applies to organic, but not to cosmic or to cultural evolution. *See* Natural selection.

Evolutionary epistemology. The scientific theory of knowledge. It explains all knowledge phenomena in humans and, generally, cognitive capacities in organisms in terms of evolution. The theory has been applied to the reconstruction of the development of scientific ideas. Thus, we can speak of two levels of evolutionary epistemology or two programs: one devoted to cognitive capacities in organisms (including humans) and their biological substrates (sense organs, nervous system, brain); the other characterized as an attempt to establish a theory of the evolution of human rational (scientific) knowledge.

Evolutionary theory. The theory about the mechanisms or causes of evolutionary change.

Fitness. Selective (adaptive) value; "reproductive efficiency of a genotype relative to other genotypes" (Ayala and Valentine, 1979, p. 436).

Fossils. Parts of ancient (extinct) organisms, like bones, that have become mineralized or left impressions in surrounding materials.

Gene. The basic unit of heredity.

Genetic epistemology. The theory of (human) knowledge based on developmental psychology; the study of the development of knowledge in the individual.

Genetic recombination. The mechanism providing the source of variability. It is characterized by a mixing of genes during the process of sexual reproduction.

Genotype. The genetic constitution of an individual organism.

Historicism. The deterministic view of history (*see* Determinism). The belief that there are laws of history and of social development and that there is historical inevitability.

Hominids. The family of the order Primates including fossil and the modern human. *See also* Primates.

Homo erectus. A fossil species of hominids. Fossils have been found in Africa, Asia, and Europe; most are about 500,000 years old; the species emerged about 1 million years ago.

Homo sapiens. The most advanced species of hominids including the Neanderthals and modern humans who appeared about 40,000 years ago. *See also* Neanderthals.

Humanism. An attitude attaching prevalence to human values and rights. Humanism is at variance with the idea of a (pre-) determined evolution (*see* Determinism). It stands in contrast to any ideology that has harmed humankind; for example, racism.

Hypothesis. Any proposition going beyond empirical data. A hypothesis can be tested, however, by empirical findings; furthermore, it must be consistent according to principles of logic. According to Popper's critical approach, any scientific hypothesis must be falsifiable; this is not true to metaphysical hypotheses (*see* Metaphysics). Here, the term *hypothesis* also is used in a metaphorical sense to characterize innate instructions of behavior for the sake of survival (*see* Ratiomorphic apparatus).

Ideology. Any kind of belief including judgments of human social development and instructions with regard to politics. Usually, ideologies start with certain images of human nature and try to substantiate political programs by resorting to scientific observations and theories. Examples for ideologies can be found in every epoch of human history. Ideologists have misused scientific concepts and theories as can be seen, for example, in Social Darwinism.

Information. Broadly defined as knowledge. Thus, being informed about objects, events, and so on means to have some knowledge about these objects or events. *See also* Knowledge.

Information processing. The acquisition, storage, use, and transmission of information. Information processing is a general character of living beings; it depends on particular organs (sense organs, nervous system). Any organism is an information processing system. *See also* Perception.

Innate capacities. Generally, any ability of an individual organism existing before and independent of (individual) experiencing and learning. From the point of view of evolutionary epistemology innate capacities result from evolutionary learning. Experiences by many individuals over many generations have been genetically fixed and thus are the starting point of any individual's experiencing the world.

Knowledge. The key notion in epistemology, in its widest sense, *knowledge* can be defined as a system of observations and ideas about reality or certain aspects of it. In evolutionary epistemology we distinguish between rational knowledge (proper to humans) and prerational (ratiomorphic) knowledge in animals and humans. *See also* Ratiomorphic apparatus, Rationality.

Lamarckism. Lamarck's theory of evolution, particularly his theory of the inheritance of individually acquired characters.

Language. A specific kind of communication; a system of symbols by which humans communicate, by which the members of a social group transmit information.

Linguistics. The study of the system "language," its nature, constituents, and structure.

Materialism. The philosophic-scientific view according to which reality is composed exclusively of material things. Materialism is contrasted by any view whose advocates hold that there is a spiritual, nonmaterial reality.

Memory. Ability of (higher) organisms to recall past states or events; retrieval of past experiences.

Mesocosm. The section of reality that a species is able to perceive. Every species lives in a particular cognitive niche and is able to cope only with the structures of its niche (*see* Cognitive niche). The human mesocosm is defined by the dimensions that have played a certain role in our everyday life. Structures or dimensions beyond the mesocosm are not perceivable by our cognitive apparatus.

Metaphysics. Initially, it was the book after Physics in Aristotle's work. Today, it is the philosophical discipline dealing with phenomena outside the world either perceivable by our sense organs or amenable to theoretical scientific reconstruction. Unlike theories in the sciences, metaphysical doctrines cannot be tested by empirical data.

Mind. An ambiguous notion to characterize phenomena beyond the reach of natural sciences, that is, spiritual phenomena that often have been said to exist independent of material entities. More concretely, the mind is regarded as the complex of capacities involved in cognition, remembering (*see* Memory), thinking, evaluating, and so on. In this book, the mind is regarded as a systems property of the (human) brain.

Mind–body problem. The problem of how material and spiritual phenomena are related. Different approaches to this problem have been discussed. It has been argued that the mind can (should) be regarded as a phenomenon separated from material entities (dualism); also, it has been said that mind is identical with such entities (monism) (*see* Table 10).

Morality. The capability of considering right and wrong (good and evil); a specifically human trait that, however, depends on brain mechanisms and has developed in the course of evolution.

Mutation. A change in the genetic material. Together with genetic recombination, mutations provide sources of variability. *See also* Genetic recombination.

Natural selection. The "driving force" behind organic evolution. According to Darwin's theory, natural selection favors the well-suited varieties and eliminates the others; that is, it leads to a survival of the fittest (*see* Fitness). Natural selection has been said to be an outer mechanism of evolution. The more organismic view of evolution, however, also contains the notion of internal selection; that is the organism itself defines conditions of selection (*see* Organismic constraints; Systems theory).

Naturalistic fallacy. Any inference from is to ought.

Naturalized epistemology. Based on the conviction that knowledge is a natural phenomenon that depends on sense organs and a nervous system, naturalized epistemology relies on research in the natural sciences including psychology. Evolutionary epistemology is a particular type of naturalized epistemology.

Neanderthals. Extinct members of the species *Homo sapiens*, they disappeared some 40,000 years ago. There is evidence that the Neanderthals were capable of self-awareness, including an awareness of death, they speculated about life after death—they developed metaphysical belief systems (*see* Metaphysics) and they used an advanced language as communication system (*see* Language).

Nervous System. A system of cells (neurons) that builds communication channels between receptors (sense-organs) and effecters (organs that produce responses to perceived phenomena). The nervous system is most important with respect to information processing (*see* Figure 5).

Neurobiology. The study of nervous and brain structures and mechanisms.

Ontology. The philosophical discipline concerned with "being"; sometimes related to metaphysics (*see* Metaphysics). Ontology cannot be successfully practiced without reference to findings in the (natural) sciences.

Organismic constraints. The sum-total of functional and construction principles in the life of any organism. According to the systems view of evolution (*see* Systems theory), the evolutionary change of living systems is channeled, at least partly, by these constraints.

Perception. The ability of organisms to "grasp" certain aspects of reality by the means of sense-organs or mechanisms operating analogous to such organs. *Perception* means acquisition of information. *see* Information processing.

Perceiving apparatus. The sum-total of structures and mechanisms that serve for perception.

Phenotype. The appearance of any individual organism; the sum-total of an organism's physical characteristics determined by its genotype and environmental influences. *See also* Genotype.

Philosophy. In the literal sense of the word, it is the "love of wisdom." Generally, philosophy is any critical reflection upon the world and our place in it; any critical examination of fundamental beliefs, knowledge, moral principles, and so on. The subject of philosophy can be natural or artificial objects. However, there is no *one* method of philosophy or *one* particular philosophical world view; rather, there are different schools. Philosophy should not be pursued without reference to the sciences: on the one hand, a philosopher should take notice of the results of scientific research; on the other hand, a philosopher should critically reflect upon the foundations of the sciences and the consequences of scientific research.

Philosophy of Science. The study and critical examination of concepts and theories established in the sciences.

Population. A group of organisms belonging to the same species and living in a clearly delimited space at the same time. *See also* Species.

Primates. The most advanced order of animals, consisting of some 200 species (lemurs, monkeys, and apes) and including the human family (*see* Hominids).

Progress. Advancement or movement toward a certain goal or, in a neutral sense, just advancement without any particular goal.

Proteins. Biological macromolecules fundamental to the structures and functions of organisms.

Psychology. The study of behavior, particularly in humans. Psychology is concerned with all aspects of (human) behavior, including its development in the individual and its specific manifestations.

Ratiomorphic apparatus. The cognitive apparatus at the preconscious level. Those mechanisms of our nervous system that function analogous to, but not identical with, rational operations. It has been argued (chapter 3) that this apparatus works on the basis of inborn "hypotheses" that result from long-term evolutionary learning processes.

Rationality. The capability of humans to reflect upon themselves and their actions.

Rationalism. The epistemological view that knowledge is gained only by the means of reason. Rationalism stands in contrast to the empiricist tradition (*see* Empiricism).

Realism. Generally, the view according to which our knowledge corresponds to objects or events that actually exist; from the realist point of view, we get a true image of (external) reality (naive realism). Evolutionary epistemology leads to a hypothetical realism. Our knowledge, based on innate capacities, is hypothetical knowledge; we calculate external reality on the basis of innate experience–expectation cycles.

Reductionism. Any conviction that certain phenomena can be reduced to other, more simple, phenomena, that for example living systems are nothing else but heaps of molecules or atoms.

RNA. Ribonucleic acid, it directs the protein synthesis. *See also* Central dogma.

Scientific revolution. According to Kuhn (1962), something like a jump in the evolution of scientific ideas that interrupts the phases of "normal science." A paradigm widely accepted up to now replaced by another view.

Self-awareness. Capability of an organism to recognize itself. In a narrower sense human self-reflection based on rational capacities. Self-awareness in this narrow sense includes such phenomena as awareness of death.

Social Darwinism. An ideology based on a false interpretation of Darwin's theory. The extension of Darwin's theory to social phenomena and the conclusion that natural selection ought to be the guiding principle in human social life. *See also* Biologism, Ideology.

Sociality. The capability of socialization; that is the organization of members of the same species building a group and acting in cooperative manner.

Sociobiology. The study of social behavior in organisms. Sociobiologists try to explain social behavior in genetic terms.

Species. Commonly accepted as basic unit of classification. A species consists of populations (*see* Population), its members are capable of interbreeding with one another but not with individuals that belong to other species (although in some cases there might be exceptions).

Symbolism. The creation and utilization of symbols for communication. Symbols are elements of human communication:artifacts, sounds, movements, or expressions of the body or parts of it (gesticulation).

Synthetic theory. A theory of the mechanisms of evolutionary change based on Darwin's theory of natural selection. Synthetic theory explains organic evolution as a result of mutations, genetic recombination, and natural selection (external selection). Also, it is an adaptationistic view of evolution (*see* Adaptationism).

Systems theory. The study of complex systems, that is, structures consisting of different, mutually related elements. One of the central tenets of systems theory is that the whole—a system—is more than the sum of its parts (elements). The systems view is at variance with reductionism. The systems theory of evolution leads to the thesis that (natural) selection is both an inner and an outer mechanism and that evolution is constrained by organismic constructions and functions (*see also* Organismic constraints).

Tabula rasa. "Clean slate"; behaviorists and empiricists have claimed that mind is initially comparable to a blank writing tablet, to be filled with experiences mediated through the senses (*see* Behaviorism, Empiricism) In contrast to the tabula rasa doctrine, evolutionary epistemologists argue that any organism is endowed with innate capacities that, however, can be modified by individual learning (*see* Innate capacities).

Teleology. The idea of purpose in existence. The teleological view regards all natural phenomena as purposeful, developing toward a certain end or goal. The notion of a universal teleology is untenable from the evolutionary point of view. However, it is argued that organisms are teleologically organized in the sense that their parts (organs and their functions) are related to the whole system. This notion of teleology has been called *teleonomy.* Hence, there is goal direction, but no intention that anticipates any end or goal. Only human rational behavior can be characterized as teleological behavior in a narrow sense (goal-intended behavior).

Truth. According to the correspondence theory of truth, (human) knowledge pictures, so to speak, objects or events of external reality. This view has been replaced by a coherence theory of truth. An organism does not necessarily portray external reality in an exact manner, but only generates "schemes of reaction" that must be coherent.

Values. A key notion in ethics, values denote preferences and are created to conduct human behavior. Different societies and cultures are characterized by different value systems. In any case, values express what is estimated to be good or right.

Verbal communication. Communication by the means of a spoken language based on words and not only on optical or acustical signals. *See also* Language.

Vertebrates. Animals characterized by a spine or backbone: fish, amphibians, reptiles, birds, and mammals.

Visual illusion. False perceptual experience of stimuli (*see* Figure 10).

Vitalism. Interpretation of living systems and their particular functions with resort to alleged vital principles or life forces, which have often been conceived as spiritual principles.

Bibliography

Agassi, J. 1977. *Towards a Rational Philosophical Anthropology.* The Hague: Nijhoff.

Albert, H. 1977. *Kristische Vernunft und menschliche Praxis.* Stuttgart: Reclam.

Alexander, R. D. 1987. *The Biology of Moral Systems.* New York: Aldine de Gruyter.

Altmann, S. A. 1973. "Primate Communication." In G. A. Miller, ed., *Communication, Language, and Meaning: Psychological Perspectives,* New York: Basic Books, pp. 84–94.

Amundson, R. 1983. "The Epistemological Status of a Naturalized Epistemology," *Inquiry* 26: 333–344.

Aquinas, T. 1939. *Selected Writings.* London: Dent & Sons.

Argyle, M. 1972. *The Psychology of Interpersonal Behavior.* Harmondsworth, England: Penguin Books.

Austin, W. H. 1985. "Evolutionary Explanations of Religion and Morality: Explaining Religion Away?" In E. McMullin, ed., *Evolution and Creation,* pp. 252–272. Notre Dame, Ind.: University of Notre Dame Press.

Autrum, H. 1971. "The Operational Limits of Animal Sense Organs." In H. Friedrich, ed., *Man and Animal: Studies in Behaviour.* London: Granada Publishing.

Ayala, F. J. 1974. "The Concept of Biological Progress." In F. J. Ayala and T. Dobzhansky, eds., *Studies in the Philosophy of Biology,* pp. 339–354. London: Macmillan.

———. 1985. "The Theory of Evolution: Recent Successes and Challenges." In E. McMullin, ed., *Evolution and Creation,* pp. 59–90. Notre Dame, Ind.: University of Notre Dame Press.

―――. 1987. "The Biological Roots of Morality," *Biology and Philosophy* 2: 235–252.

Ayala, F. J., and J. W. Valentine. 1979. *Evolving: the Theory and Processes of Organic Evolution.* Menlo Park, Calif.: Benjamin/ Cummings.

Ayer, A. J. 1952. *Language, Truth and Logic.* New York: Dover.

―――. 1976. *The Central Questions of Philosophy.* Harmondsworth, England: Penguin Books.

Bacon, F. [1626] 1904. *Bacon's Essays,* ed. by H. Lewis. London: Collins.

Barash, D. 1979. *Sociobiology: The Whisperings Within.* Glasgow: Fontana/Collins.

Barber, C. L. 1964. *The Story of Language.* London: English Language Book Society.

Barker, E. 1985. "Let There be Light: Scientific Creationism in the Twentieth Century," In J. Durant, ed., *Darwinism and Divinity,* pp. 181–204. Oxford, England: Basil Blackwell.

Barnett, S. A. 1970. *"Instinct" and "Intelligence": The Behaviour of Animals and Man.* Harmondsworth, England: Penguin Books.

Barrett, P. H., ed. 1977. *The Collected Papers of Charles Darwin,* 2 vols. Chicago: University of Chicago Press.

Bartley, W. W. 1976. "Critical Study: The Philosophy of Karl Popper Part I: Biology and Evolutionary Epistemology," *Philosophia* 6: 463– 494.

―――. 1982. "Critical Study: The Philosophy of Karl Popper Part III: Rationality, Criticism, and Logic," *Philosophia* 11: 121–221.

―――. 1987. "Philosophy of Biology *versus* Philosophy of Physics." In G. Radnitzky and W. W. Bartley, eds., *Evolutionary Epistemology, Theory of Rationality, and the Sociology of Knowledge,* pp. 7–45. LaSalle, Ill.: Open Court.

Baylis, J. R., and Z. Tang Halpin. 1982. "Behavioral Antecedents of Sociality." In H. C. Plotkin, ed., *Learning, Development, and Culture: Essays in Evolutionary Epistemology,* pp. 255–272. Chichester, England: Wiley.

Berger, P. L., and T. Luckmann. 1966. *The Social Construction of Reality: A Treatise in the Sociology of Knowledge.* Garden City, N.Y.: Doubleday.

Bergson, H. 1907. *L'Evolution créatrice*. Paris: Presses Universitaire de France. English translation 1911, London: Macmillan.

Bertalanffy, L. v. 1968. "Symbolismus und Anthropogenese." In B. Rensch, ed., *Handgebrauch und Verständigung bei Affen und Frühmenschen*, pp. 131–143. Bern, Switzerland: Huber.

———.1973. *General System Theory: Foundations, Development, Applications*. Harmondsworth, England: Penguin Books.

Bickhard, H. M. 1979. "On Necessary and Specific Capabilities in Evolution and Development," *Human Development* 22: 217–224.

Blažek, B. 1978. "On Scope and Limits of Analogies between Evolution and Cognition," *Proceedings of the Symposium on Natural Selection*, pp. 543–558. Prague.

———. 1979. "Can Epistemology as a Philosophical Discipline Develop into a Science?" *Dialectica* 33: 87–108.

Bonner, J. T. 1980. *The Evolution of Culture in Animals*. Princeton, N.J.: Princeton University Press.

Boyd, R., and P. J. Richerson. 1985. *Culture and the Evolutionary Process*. Chicago: University of Chicago Press.

Bradie, M. 1984. "The Metaphorical Character of Science.". *Philosophia Naturalis* 21: 229–243.

———. 1986. "Assessing Evolutionary Epistemology," *Biology and Philosophy* 1: 401–450.

Brandon, R. N. 1985. "Phenotypic Plasticity, Cultural Transmission, and Human Sociobiology." In J. Fetzer, ed., *Sociobiology and Epistemology*, pp. 57–73. Dordrecht, Holland: Reidel

Bunge, M. 1979. "The Mind–Body Problem in an Evolutionary Perspective." In G. Wolstenholme and M. O'Connor, eds., *Brain and Mind*, pp. 53–63. Amsterdam: Elsevier.

———. 1980. *The Mind–Body Problem: A Psychobiological Approach*. Oxford, England: Pergamon Press.

Bunge, M., and R. Ardila. 1987. *Philosophy of Psychology*. New York: Springer.

Callebaut, W. 1987. "Why It Makes Sense to Extend the Genotype-Phenotype Distinction to Culture," *La Nuova Critica* 1–2: 63–83.

Campbell, D. T. 1959. "Methodological Suggestions from a Comparative Psychology of Knowledge Processes," *Inquiry* 2: 152–182.

———. 1960. "Blind Variation and Selective Retention in Creative

Thought as in Other Knowledge Processes." *Psychological Review* 67: 380–400.

———. 1966. "Pattern Matching as an Essential and Distal Knowing." In K. R. Hammond, ed., *The Psychology of Egon Brunswik*, pp. 81–106. New York: Holt, Rinehart and Winston.

———. 1974a. Evolutionary Epistemology. In P. A. Schilpp, ed., *The Philosophy of Karl Popper I*, pp. 413–463. LaSalle, Ill.: Open Court.

———. 1974b. "'Downward Causation' in Hierarchically Organised Biological Systems." In F. J. Ayala and T. Dobzhansky, eds., *Studies in the Philosophy of Biology*, pp. 179–186. London: Macmillan.

———. 1975a. "On the Conflicts between Biological and Social Evolution and between Psychology and Moral Tradition," *American Psychologist* 30: 1103–1136.

———. 1975b. "The Conflict Between Social and Biological Evolution and the Concept of the Original Sin," *Zygon* 10: 234–249.

———. 1984. "Science Policy from a Naturalistic Sociological Epistemology," *PSA* (Philosophy of Science Association) 2.

———. 1987a. "Selection Theory and the Sociology of Scientific Validity." In W. Callebaut and R. Pinxten, eds., *Evolutionary Epistemology: A Multiparadigm Program*, pp. 139–158. Dordrecht, Holland, Reidel.

———. 1987b. Neurological Embodiments of Belief and the Gaps in the Fit of Phenomena to Noumena." In A. Shimony and D. Nails, eds., *Naturalistic Epistemology: A Symposium of Two Decades*. Dordrecht, Holland, Reidel.

———. 1988. "A General 'Selection Theory', as Implemented in Biological Evolution and in Social Belief-Transmission-with-Modification in Science," *Biology and Philosophy* 3: 171–177.

Campbell, D. T., C. M. Heyes, and W. Callebaut. 1987. "Evolutionary Epistemology Bibliography." In W. Callebaut and R. Pinxten, eds., *Evolutionary Epistemology: A Multiparadigm Program*, pp. 405–431. Dordrecht, Holland, Reidel.

Caspari, O. 1877. *Die Urgeschichte der Menschheit mit Rücksicht auf die natürliche Entwickelung des frühesten Geisteslebens*, 2 vols. Leipzig: Brockhaus.

Cassirer, E. 1950. *The Problem of Knowledge: Philosophy, Science, and History since Hegel.* New Haven: Conn.: Yale University Press.

Churchland, P. M. 1979. *Scientific Realism and the Plasticity of Mind.* Cambridge, England: Cambridge University Press.

Clark, A. J. 1984. "Evolutionary Epistemology and Ontological Realism," *Philosophical Quarterly* 34: 482–490.

_____. 1986. "Evolutionary Epistemology and the Scientific Method," *Philosophica* 37. 151–162.

Cohen, L. J. 1973. "Is the Progress of Science Evolutionary?" *British Journal for the Philosophy of Science* 24: 41–61.

Cooney, B. 1978. "The Biological Basis of Mind." *International Philosophical Quarterly* 18: 395–412.

Count, E. W. 1958. "The Biological Basis of Human Sociality," *American Anthropologist* 60; 1049–1085.

Creutzfeldt, O. D. 1979. "Neurophysiological Mechanisms of Consciousness." In G. Wolstenholme and M. O'Connor, eds., *Brain and Mind*, pp. 217–253. Amsterdam: Elsevier.

Crick, F. H. C. 1979. "Thinking about the Brain," *Scientific American* 241 no. 3: 181–188.

Danailow, A., and C. Tögel. 1988. "Konrad Lorenz und die evolutionäre Erkenntnistheorie," *Wissenschaftliche Zeitschrift der Friedrich-Schiller-Universität Jena, Naturwissenschaftliche Reihe* 37: 301–305.

Darwin, C. 1859. *On the Origin of Species by Means of Natural Selection.* London: Murray. Reprint 1958, New York: New American Library.

_____. 1871. *The Descent of Man.* London: Murray.

_____. 1872. *The Expression of the Emotions in Man and Animals.* London: Murray. Reprint 1965, Chicago: University of Chicago Press.

_____. 1969. *The Autobiography of Charles Darwin*, ed. by N. Barlow. New York: W. W. Norton.

Dawkins, R. 1976. *The Selfish Gene.* New York: Oxford University Press.

Deary, I. J. 1988. "Applying Evolutionary Epistemology: From Immunity to Intelligence," *Journal of Social and Biological Structures* 11: 399–408.

Delbrück, M. 1978. "Mind from Matter?" *American Scholar* 47: 339–353.

———. 1986. *Wahrheit und Wirklichkeit: Über die Evolution des Erkennens.* Hamburg: Rasch und Röhring.

Diettrich, O. 1989. *Kognitive, organische und gesellschaftliche Evolution.* Berlin: Parey.

Ditfurth, H. v. 1981. *Wir sind nicht nur von dieser Welt: Naturwissenschaft, Religion und die Zukunft des Menschen.* Hamburg: Hoffmann und Campe.

———. 1987. Evolution und Transzendenz. In R. Riedl and F. M. Wuketits, eds., *Die Evolutionäre Erkenntnistheorie: Bedingungen, Lösungen, Kontroversen,* 258–267. Berlin: Parey.

Dobzhansky, T. 1962. *Mankind Evolving.* New Haven, Conn.: Yale University Press.

Dobzhansky, T., F. J. Ayala, G. L. Stebbins, and J. W. Valentine. 1977. *Evolution.* San Francisco: W. H. Freeman.

Dorsey, G. A. 1925. *Why We Behave Like Human Beings.* New York: Harper and Brothers.

Drummond, H. 1897. *The Ascent of Man.* London: Hodder and Stroughton.

Du Bois-Reymond, E. 1907. *Über die Grenzen des Naturerkennens.* Leipzig: Veit.

Dunn, L. C., and T. Dobzhansky. 1952. *Heredity, Race and Society.* New York: New American Library.

Eccles, J. C. 1970. *Facing Reality: Philosophical Adventures by a Brain Scientist.* New York: Springer.

———. 1979. *The Human Mystery.* New York: Springer.

Edlinger, K., W. F. Gutmann, and M. Weingarten. 1989. "Biologische Aspekte der Evolution des Erkenntnisvermögens," *Natur und Museum* 119: 113–128.

Egidi, R. 1987. "Emergence, Reduction, and Evolutionary Epistemology." In G. Radnitzky and W. W. Bartley, eds., *Evolutionary Epistemology, Theory of Rationality, and the Sociology of Knowledge,* pp. 157–161. LaSalle, Ill.: Open Court Press.

Eigen, M., and R. Winkler. 1975. *Das Spiel: Naturgesetze steuern den Zufall.* Munich: Piper.

Elkana, Y. 1981. A Programmatic Attempt at an Anthropology of

Knowledge. In E. Mendelson and Y. Elkana, eds., *Sciences and Cultures*, pp. 1–76. Dordrecht, Holland: Reidel.

Emerson, R. W. 1894. *Nature, Addresses, and Lectures*. Manchester, England: Routledge.

Engels, E.-M. 1983. "Evolutionäre Erkenntnistheorie—ein biologischer Ausverkauf der Philosophie?" *Zeitschrift für Allgemeine Wissenschaftstheorie* 14: 138–166.

———. 1985. "Was leistet die evolutionäre Erkenntnistheorie? Eine Kritik und Würdigung." *Zeitschrift für Allgemeine Wissenschaftstheorie* 16: 113–146.

———. 1987. "Kritische Überlegungen zur 'kaputten' Erkenntnis- und Realismuskonzeption der Evolutionären Erkenntnistheorie und ein 'Reparaturvorschlag'." In W. Lütterfelds, ed., *Transzendentale oder evolutionäre Erkenntnistheorie?*, pp. 229–260. Darmstadt, Germany: Wissenschaftliche Buchgesellschaft.

Erben, H. K. 1980. "A Holo-Evolutionistic Conception of Fossil and Contemporaneous Man," *Abhandlungen der Akademie der Wissenschaften und Literatur (Mathematisch-naturwissenschaftliche Klasse) Mainz* 1: 1–18.

Farrington, B. 1982. *What Darwin Really Said*. New York: Schocken Books.

Ferguson, E. S. 1988. Biological Memory Systems and the Human Species. *Journal of Social Biological Structure* 11: 409–414.

Flamm, D. 1987. "Evolutionstheoretische Konzepte bei Boltzmann und Mach." In R. Riedl and E. M. Bonet, eds., *Entwicklung der Evolutionären Erkenntnistheorie*, pp. 21–33. Vienna: Verlag der Österreichischen Staatsdruckerei.

Flaskämper, P. 1913. *Die Wissenschaft vom Leben: Biologisch-philosophische Betrachtungen*. Munich. Reinhardt.

Flew, A. 1971. *An Introduction to Western Philosophy: Ideas and Arguments from Plato to Sartre*. London: Thames and Hudson.

———. 1978. A *Rational Animal and Other Philosophical Essays on the Nature of Man*. Oxford, England: Clarendon Press.

Frey, G. 1987. "Die philosophische Bedeutung des evolutionären Erkenntnismodells." in W. Lütterfelds, ed., *Transzendentale oder evolutionäre Erkenntnistheorie?*, pp. 261–284. Darmstadt, Germany: Wissenschaftliche Buchgesellschaft.

Gagliasso, E. 1984. "Una riflessione sul concetto di adattamento." In *Evoluzione e modelli*, pp. 19–103. Rome: Editori Riuniti.

Geertz, C. 1964. "The Transition to Humanity." In S. Tax, ed., *Horizons of Anthropology*, pp. 37–48. Chicago: Aldine.

Ghiselin, M. T. 1969. *The Triumph of the Darwinian Method*. Berkeley: University of California Press.

――――. 1981. "Categories, Life, and Thinking," *Behavioral and Brain Sciences* 4: 269–313.

Glass, B., O. Temkin, and W. L. Straus, eds. 1959. *Forerunners of Darwin 1745–1859*. Baltimore: Johns Hopkins University Press.

Götschl, J. 1987. "Zum Subjekt-Objekt Problem von transzendentaler und evolutionärer Erkenntnistheorie." In W. Lütterfelds, ed., *Transzendentale oder evolutionäre Erkenntnistheorie?*, Darmstadt, Germany: Wissenschaftliche Buchgesellschaft.

Gould, S. J. 1980. *The Panda's Thumb: More Reflections in Natural History*. New York: W. W. Norton.

――――. 1982. "Darwinism and the Expansion of Evolutionary Theory," *Science* 216: 380–387.

Gould, S. J., and R. C. Lewontin. 1984. "The Spandrels of San Marco and the Panglossian Paradigm: A Critique of the Adaptationist Programme." In E. Sober, ed., *Conceptual Issues in Evolutionary Biology: An Anthology*, pp. 252–270. Cambridge, Mass.: Harvard University Press.

Gutmann, W. G., and K. Bonik. 1981. *Kritische Evolutionstheorie: Ein Beitrag zur Überwindung altdarwinistischer Dogmen*. Hildesheim, Germany: Gerstenberg.

Haeckel, E. 1899. *Die Welträthsel: Gemeinverständliche Studien über Monistische Philosophie*. Stuttgart, Germany: Kröner.

――――. 1905. *Die Lebenswunder: Gemeinverständliche Studien über Biologische Philosophie*. Stuttgart, Germany: Kröner.

Haller, R. 1987. "Kommentar zu K. Lorenz 'Evolution und Apriori'." In R. Riedl and F. M. Wuketits, eds., *Die Evolutionäre Erkenntnistheorie:Bedingungen, Lösungen, Kontroversen*, pp. 19–24. Berlin: Parey.

Hefner, P. 1987. "Freedom in Evolutionary Perspective." In V. Mortensen and R. C. Sorensen, eds., *Free Will and Determinism*, pp. 121–141. Aarhus, Denmark: Aarhus University Press.

Hill, O. 1968. "Verständigungsmittel bei Affen." In B. Rensch, ed., *Handgebrauch und Verständigung bei Affen und Frühmenschen*, pp. 31–55. Bern, Switzerland: Huber.

Hinde, R. A., ed., 1972. *Non-Verbal Communication.* Cambridge, England: Cambridge University Press.

Hockett, C. D. 1960. "The Origin of Speech," *Scientific American* 203, no. 3: 88–96.

Hofman, M. A. 1988. "Brain, Mind and Reality: An Evolutionary Approach to Biological Intelligence." In H. J. Jerison and I. Jerison, eds., *Intelligence and Evolutionary Biology,* pp. 437–446. Berlin: Springer.

Holzhey, H. 1983. "Genese und Geltung: Das vernunftkritische Resultat einer Kontroverse zwischen biologischer und kantianischer Erkenntnistheorie," *Studia Philosophica* 42: 104–123.

Hookway, C. 1984. "Naturalism, Fallibilism and Evolutionary Epistemology.," In C. Hookway, ed., *Minds, Machines and Evolution: Philosophical Studies,* pp. 1–15. Cambridge, England: Cambridge University Press.

Horridge, A. 1077. "The Compound Eye of Insects," *Scientific American* 237, no. 1: 108–120.

Hörz, H., and K.-F. Wessel. 1983. *Philosophische Entwicklungstheorie* Berlin: VEB Deutscher Verlag der Wissenschaften.

Hoyningen-Huene, P. 1987. "Context of Discovery and Context of Justification," *Studies in the History and Philosophy of Science.* 18: 501–515.

Hubel, D. H. 1979. "The Brain," *Scientific American* 241, no. 3: 38–47.

Hull, D. L. 1974. *Philosophy of Biological Science.* Englewood Cliffs, N.J.: Prentice-Hall.

_____. 1982. "The Naked Meme." In H. C. Plotkin, ed., *Learning, Development, and Culture: Essays in Evolutionary Epistemology,* pp. 273–327. Chichester, England: Wiley.

_____. 1988. "A Mechanism and Its Metaphysics: An Evolutionary Account of the Social and Conceptual Development of Science," *Biology and Philosophy* 3: 123–155.

Hume, D. [1739] 1972. *A Treatise of Human Nature, Books 2 and 3.* London: Collins.

Huxley, J. 1947. *Man in the Modern World.* London: Chatto and Windus.

_____. 1957. "Evolution, Cultural and Biological." In J. Huxley, *New Bottles for New Wine: Essays,* pp. 61–92. New York: Harper and Brothers.

———. 1958. The Evolutionary Process. In J. Huxley, A. C. Hardy, and E. B. Ford, eds., *Evolution as a Process*, pp. 1–23. London: Allen and Unwin.

———, ed. 1961. *The Humanist Frame*. London: Allen and Unwin.

Huxley, T. H. [1863] 1968. *On the Origin of Species*. Ann Arbor: University of Michigan Press.

Isaac, G. L. 1983. "Aspects of Human Evolution." In D. S. Bendall, ed., *Evolution from Molecules to Men*, pp. 509–543. Cambridge, England: Cambridge University Press.

Jantsch, E. 1979. "Sociobiological and Sociocultural Process: A Non-Reductionist View." *Journal of Social and Biological Structures* 2: 87–92.

Jaynes, J. 1985. "Four Hypotheses on the Origin of Mind," *Proceedings of the 9th International Wittgenstein Symposium*, pp. 135–142. Vienna: Hölder-Pichler-Tempsky.

Jerison, H. J. 1976. "Paleoneurology and the Evolution of Mind," *Scientific American* 234, no. 1: 90–101.

———. 1986. "The Perceptual Worlds of Dolphins." In R. Schusterman, J. Thomas, and F. G. Woods, eds., *Dolphin Cognition and Behavior: A Comparative Approach*, pp. 141–166. Hillsdale, N.J.: Lawrence.

Johanson, D., and M. Edey. 1981. *Lucy: The Beginning of Humankind*. New York: Simon and Schuster.

Kanitscheider, B. 1981. *Wissenschaftstheorie der Naturwissenschaft*. Berlin: De Gruyter.

Kant, I. [1781] 1901. *Kritik der reinen Vernunft*. Riga, Latvia: Hartknoch. English translation London: Bell.

Kantorovich, A. 1988. "The Mechanisms of Communal Selection and Serendipitous Discover," *Biology and Philosophy* 3: 199–203.

Kantorovich, A., and Y. Ne'eman. Forthcoming. "Serendipity as a Source of Evolutionary Progress in Science," *Studies in the History and Philosophy of Science*.

Kaspar, R. 1984. "A Short Introduction to the Biological Principles of Evolutionary Epistemology." In F. M. Wuketits, ed., *Concepts and Approaches in Evolutionary Epistemology: Towards an Evolutionary Theory of Knowledge*, pp. 51–67. Dordrecht, Holland: Reidel.

Kitchener, R. F. 1987. "Is Genetic Epistemology Possible?" *British Journal for the Philosophy of Science* 38: 283–299.

Kitcher, P. 1985. "A Priori Knowledge." In H. Kornblith, ed., *Naturalizing Epistemology*, pp. 129–145. Cambridge, Mass.: MIT Press.

Kluckhohn, C., and W. H. Kelly. 1983. "The Concept of Culture." In M. Freilich, ed., *The Pleasures of Anthropology*, pp. 221–248. New York: New American Library.

Koestler, A. 1959. *The Sleepwalkers: A History of Man's Changing Vision of the Universe.* London: Hutchinson.

Köhler, W. 1973. *Intelligenzprüfungen an Menschenaffen.* Berlin: Springer.

Kornblith, H. 1985. "Introduction: What Is Naturalistic Epistemology?" In H. Kornblith, ed., *Naturalizing Epistemology*, pp. 1–13. Cambridge, Mass.: MIT Press.

Krausser, P. 1987. "Transzendentale und evolutionäre Erkenntnistheorie." In W. Lütterfelds, ed., *Transzendentale oder evolutionäre Erkenntnistheorie?* pp. 334–357. Darmstadt, Germany: Wissenschaftliche Buchgesellschaft.

Krüger, L. 1989. "Ethics According to Nature in the Age of Evolutionary Thinking," *Grazer Philosophische Studien* 30: 25–42.

Kuhn, T. S. 1962. *The Structure of Scientific Revolutions.* Chicago: University of Chicago Press.

Lakatos, I. 1970. "Falsification and the Methodology of Scientific Research Programmes." In I. Lakatos and A. Musgrave, eds., *Criticism and the Growth of Knowledge*, pp.91–196. Cambridge, England: Cambridge University Press.

Lamarck, J. B. de. 1809. *Philosophie zoologique.* Paris: Verdière. English translation 1984, Chicago: University of Chicago Press.

La Mettrie, J. de. 1747. *L'homme machine.*

Lange, K.-P. 1985. *Language and Cognition: An Essay on Cognitive Grammar.* Tübingen, Germany: Narr.

Legge, D. 1975. *An Introduction to Psychological Science: Basic Processes in the Analysis of Behaviour.* London: Methuen.

Le Gros Clark, W. E. 1971. *The Antecedents of Man.* New York: Quadrangle Books.

Leinfellner, W. 1983. "Evolution of Intelligence," *Proceedings of the 7th*

International Wittgenstein Symposium, pp. 161–167. Vienna: Hölder-Pichler-Tempsky.

―――. 1984. "Evolutionary Causality, Theory of Games, and Evolution of Intelligence." In F. M. Wuketits, ed., *Concepts and Approaches in Evolutionary Epistemology: Towards an Evolutionary Theory of Knowledge*, pp. 233–277. Holland: Reidel.

―――. 1985. "Intentionality, Representation and the Brain Language," *Proceedings of the 9th International Wittgenstein Symposium*, pp. 44–55. Vienna: Hölder-Pichler-Tempsky.

―――. 1987. "Evolutionäre Erkenntnistheorie und Spieltheorie." In R. Riedl and F. M. Wuketits, eds., *Die Evolutionäre Erkenntnistheorie: Bedingungen, Lösungen, Kontroversen*, pp. 195–210. Berlin: Parey.

―――. 1988. "Physiologie und Psychologie—Ernst Machs 'Analyse der Empfindungen'." In R. Haller and F. Stadler, eds., *Ernst Mach: Werk und Wirkung*, pp. 113–137. Vienna: Hölder-Pichler-Tempsky.

Lelas, S. 1983. "Naturalizacija teorije znanosti," *Jugoslavenska Akademija Znanosti i Umjetnosti* (Zagreb): 145–167.

Lennenberg, E. H. 1967. *Biological Foundations of Language*. New York: Wiley.

―――. 1973. "Biological Aspects of Language." In G. A. Miller, ed., *Communication, Language and Meaning: Psychological Perspectives*, pp. 49–60. New York: Basic Books.

Levinson, P. 1982. "Evolutionary Epistemology without Limits," *Knowledge: Creation, Diffusion, Utilization* 3: 465–502.

Lévi-Strauss, C. 1969. *The Elementary Structures of Kinship*. Boston: Beacon Press.

Lewontin, R. C. 1976. "The Fallacy of Biological Determinism," *The Sciences* 16: 6–10.

―――. 1978. "Adaptation," *Scientific American* 239, no. 3: 156–169.

―――. 1982. "Organism and Environment." In H. C. Plotkin, ed., *Learning, Development, and Culture: Essays in Evolutionary Epistemology*, pp. 151–170. Chichester, England: Wiley.

Linden, E. 1976. *Apes, Men, and Language*. Harmondsworth, England: Penguin Books.

Linton, R. 1955. *The Tree of Culture*. New York: Alfred A. Knopf.

Locke, J. 1854. *Philosophical Works*, 2 vols. London: H. G. Bohn.

Lorenz, K. [1941] 1982. "Kants Lehre vom Apriorischen im Lichte gegenwärtiger Biologie," *Blätter für Deutsche Philosophie* 15: 94–125. English translation in H. C. Plotkin, ed., *Learning, Development, and Culture: Essays in Evolutionary Epistemology*, pp. 121–143. Chichester, England: Wiley.

_____. 1965. *Evolution and Modification of Behavior*. Chicago: University of Chicago Press.

_____. 1971. *Studies in Animal and Human Behavior*, 2 vols. London: Methuen.

_____. 1974. "Analogy as a Source of Knowledge," *Science* 185: 229–233.

_____. 1976. "Die Vorstellung einer zweckgerichteten Weltordnung," *Philosophisch-historische Klasse Östereichische Akademie der Wissenschaften* 113, 2: 39–51.

_____. 1977. *Behind the Mirror*. New York: Harcourt Brace Jovanovich.

_____. 1987. "Evolution und Apriori." In R. Riedl and F. M. Wuketits, eds., *Die Evolutionäre Erkenntnistheorie: Bedingungen, Lösungen, Kontroversen*, pp. 13–18. Berlin: Parey.

Löw, R. 1984. "The Metaphysical Limits of Evolutionary Epistemology." In F. M. Wuketits, ed., *Concepts and Approaches in Evolutionary Epistemology: Towards an Evolutionary Theory of Knowledge*, pp. 209–231. Dordrecht, Holland: Reidel.

Löwenhard, P. 1981. "Consciousness: A Biological View," *Göteborg Psychological Reports* 11, no. 10: 1–88.

_____. 1982. "Knowledge, Belief and Human Behaviour," *Göteborg Psychological Reports* 12, no. 11: 1–71.

Lumsden, C. J., and A. C. Gushurst. 1985. "Gene-Culture Coevolution: Humankind in the Making." In J. Fetzer, ed., *Sociobiology and Epistemology*, pp. 3–28. Dordrecht, Holland: Reidel.

Lumsden, C. L. and E. O. Wilson. 1981. *Genes, Mind, and Culture: The Coevolutionary Process*. Cambridge, Mass: Harvard University Press.

_____. 1985. "The Relation between Biological and Cultural Evolution," *Journal of Social and Biological Structures* 8: 343–359.

Lütterfelds, W. 1982. "Kants Kausalkategorie—ein stammesgeschichtliches Aposteriori?" *Philosophia Naturalis* 19: 104–124.

————. 1987. "Einleitung: Zur idealistischen Rechtfertigung einer evolutionären Erklärung des Apriori." In W. Lütterfelds, ed., *Transzendentale oder evolutionäre Erkenntnistheorie?* pp. 1–30. Darmstadt, Germany: Wissenschaftliche Buchgesellschaft.

Mach, E. 1886. *Die Analyse der Empfindungen und das Verhältnis des Physischen zum Psychischen.* Leipzig: Fischer.

Markl, H. 1982. "Constraints on Human Behavior and the Biological Nature of Man," *Journal of Social and Biological Structures* 5: 381–387.

Maturana, H., and F. Varela. 1980. *Autopoiesis and Cognition.* Dordrecht, Holland: Reidel.

Maynard Smith, J. 1975. *The Theory of Evolution.* Harmondsworth, England: Penguin Books.

————. 1984. "The Evolution of Animal Intelligence." In C. Hookway, ed., *Minds, Machines, and Evolution: Philosophical Studies,* pp. 63–71. Cambridge, England: Cambridge University Press.

Mayr, E. 1974. "Teleological and Teleonomic: A New Analysis," *Boston Studies in the Philosophy of Science* 14: 91–117.

————. 1978. "Evolution," *Scientific American* 239, no. 3: 38–47.

————. 1982. *The Growth of Biological Thought.* Cambridge, Mass.: Harvard University Press.

Medawar, P. B. 1971. *The Art of the Soluble.* London: Methuen.

————. 1974. "Hypothesis and Imagination." In P. A. Schilpp, ed., *The Philosophy of Karl Popper I,* pp. 274–291. La Salle, Ill.: Open Court.

Medicus, G. 1985. "Evolutionäre Psychologie." In J. A. Ott, G. P. Wagner, and F. M. Wuketits, eds., *Evolution, Ordnung und Erkenntnis,* pp. 126–150. Berlin: Parey.

————. 1987. "Toward an Etho-Psychology: A Phylogenetic Tree of Behavioral Capabilities Proposed as a Common Basis for Communication between Current Theories in Psychology and Psychiatry," *Ethology and Sociobiology* 8 (Supplement): 131–150.

Meyer, P. 1982. *Soziobiologie und Soziologie: Eine Einführung in die biologischen Voraussetzungen sozialen Handelns.* Darmstadt, Germany: Luchterhand.

————. 1987. "Basic Structures in Human Action: On the Relevance of Bio-Social Categories for Social Theory." In M. Schmid and F. M.

Wuketits, eds., *Evolutionary Theory in Social Science*, pp. 1–22. Dordrecht, Holland: Reidel.

Mohr, H. 1977. *Lectures on Structure and Significance of Science*. New York: Springer.

_____. 1983a. "Evolutionäre Erkenntnistheorie," *Biologie in unserer Zeit* 13: 16–20

_____. 1983b. Evolutionäre Erkenntnistheorie—ein Plädoyer für ein Forschungsprogramm," *Sitzungsberichte der Heidelberger Akademie der Wissenschaften (Mathematisch-naturwissenschftliche Klasse)* 6: 223–232.

_____. 1983c. Lässt sich Wissenschaft evolutionistisch begründen?" *Proceedings of the 7th International Wittgenstein Symposium*, pp. 151–160. Vienna: Hölder-Pichler-Tempsky.

_____. 1984. "The Ethics of Science: Compatible with the Concept of Evolutionary Epistemology?" In F. M. Wuketits, ed., *Concepts and Approaches in Evolutionary Epistemology: Towards an Evolutionary Theory of Knowledge*, pp. 185–208. Dordrecht, Holland: Reidel.

_____. 1987. *Natur und Moral: Ethik in der Biologie*. Darmstadt, Germany: Wissenschaftliche Buchgesellschaft.

Monod, J. 1971. *Chance and Necessity*. New York: Alfred A. Knopf.

Morris, R. 1983. *Evolution and Human Nature*. New York: Avon Books.

Müller, H. M. 1987. *Evolution, Kognition und Sprache: Die Evolution des Menschen und die biologischen Grundlagen der Sprachfähigkeit*. Berlin: Parey.

Munévar, G. 1987. "Consensus and Evolution in Science," *PSA* (Philosophy of Science Association) 2: 120–129.

_____. 1988. "Hull, Straight Biology, and Straight Epistemology," *Biology and Philosophy* 3: 209–214.

Oakley, K. P. 1972. *Man the Tool-Maker*. London: Trustees of the British Museum.

Oeser, E. 1976. *Wissenschaft und Information*, 3 vols. Vienna: Oldenbourg.

_____. 1979. *Wissenschaftstheorie als Rekonstruktion der Wissenschaftsgeschichte*, 2 vols. Vienna: Oldenbourg.

_____. 1984. "Evolution of Scientific Method." In F. M. Wuketits, ed., *Concepts and Approaches in Evolutionary Epistemology: To-*

wards an Evolutionary Theory of Knowledge, pp. 149–184. Dordrecht, Holland: Reidel.

———. 1985. "Informationsverdichtung als universelles Ökonomieprinzip der Evolution," In J. A. Ott, G. P. Wagner, and F. M. Wuketits, eds., *Evolution, Ordnung und Erkenntnis* pp. 112–125. Berlin: Parey.

———. 1987. *Psychozoikum: Evolution und Mechanismus der menschlichen Erkenntnisfähigkeit.* Berlin: Parey.

———. 1988. *Das Abenteuer der kollektiven Vernunft: Evolution und Involution der Wissenschaft.* Berlin: Parey.

Oeser, E., and F. Seitelberger. 1988. *Gehirn, Bewusstsein und Erkenntnis.* Darmstadt, Germany: Wissenschaftliche Buchgesellschaft.

Olding, A. 1983. "Biology and Knowledge," *Theoria* 49: 1–22.

Oldroyd, D. R. 1986. Charles Darwin's Theory of Evolution: A Review of Our Present Understanding," *Biology and Philosophy* 1: 133–168.

Oldroyd, D. R., and I. Langham, eds. 1983. *The Wider Domain of Evolutionary Thought.* Dordrecht, Holland: Reidel.

Osche, G. 1987. Die Sonderstellung des Menschen in biologischer Sicht: Biologische und kulturelle Evolution. In R. Siewing, ed., *Evolution: Bedingungen, Resultate, Konsequenzen,* pp. 499–523. Stuttgart, Germany: Fischer.

Perutz, M. 1986. "A New View of Darwinism," *New Scientist* 1528 (October): 36–38.

Piaget, J. 1970. *Genetic Epistemology. New York: Columbia University Press.*

———. 1977. *Biology and Knowledge.* Chicago: University of Chicago Press.

———. 1973a. *The Child's Conception of the World.* St. Albans, England: Paladin.

———. 1973b. *Main Trends in Inter-disciplinary Research.* New York: Harper.

Pilbeam, D. 1984. "The Descent of Hominoids and Hominids," Scientific American 250, 3: 84–97.

Plotkin, H. C. 1982. "Evolutionary Epistemology and Evolutionary Theory." In H. C. Plotkin, ed., *Learning, Development, and*

Culture: Essays in Evolutionary Epistemology, pp. 3–13. Chichester, England: Wiley.

_____. 1987a. "Evolutionary Epistemology as Science," *Biology and Philosophy* 2: 295–313.

_____. 1987b. "Evolutionary Epistemology and the Synthesis of Biological and Social Science." In W. Callebaut and R. Pinxten, eds., *Evolutionary Epistemology: A Multiparadigm Program*, pp. 75–96.

Plotkin, H. C., and F. J. Odling-Smee. 1982. "Learning in the Context of a Hierarchy of Knowledge Gaining Processes." In H. C. Plotkin, ed., *Learning, Development, and Culture: Essays in Evolutionary Epistemology*, pp. 443–471. Chichester, England: Wiley.

Popper, K. R. 1959. *The Logic of Scientific Discovery*. London: Hutchinson.

_____. 1960. *The Poverty of Historicism*. London: Routledge and Kegan Paul.

_____. 1972a. *Objective Knowledge: An Evolutionary Approach*. Oxford, England: Clarendon Press.

_____. 1972b. *Conjectures and Refutations: The Growth of Scientific Knowledge*. London: Routledge and Kegan Paul.

_____. 1976. *Unended Quest: An Intellectual Autobiography*. Glasgow: Collins.

_____. 1984. *Auf der Suche nach einer besseren Welt: Vorträge und Aufsätze aus dreissig Jahren*. Munich: Piper.

_____. 1987. "Die erkenntnistheoretische Position der evolutionären Erkenntnistheorie." In R. Riedl and F. M. Wuketits, eds., *Die Evolutionäre Erkenntnistheorie: Bedingungen, Lösungen, Kontroversen*, pp. 29–37. Berlin: Parey.

Popper, K. R., and J. C. Eccles. 1977. *The Self and Its Brain: An Argument for Interactionism*. New York: Springer.

Portmann, A. 1976. *An den Grenzen des Wissens: Vom Beitrag der Biologie zu einem neuen Weltbild*. Frankfurt: Fischer.

Putnam, H. 1987. *The Many Faces of Realism*. La Salle, Ill.: Open Court Press.

Quine, W. V. O. 1971. *Ontological Relativity and Other Essays*. New York: Columbia University Press.

Radnitzky, G. 1980. "Progress and Rationality in Research." In M. D.

Grmek, R. S. Cohen, and G. Cimino, eds., *On Scientific Discovery*, pp. 43–102. Dordrecht, Holland: Reidel.

———. 1982. "Popper as a Turning Point in the Philosophy of Science: Beyond Foundationalism and Relativism." In P. Levinson, ed., *In Pursuit of Truth*, pp. 64–79. Atlantic Highlands, N.J.: Humanities Press.

———. 1987a. "Cost-Benefit Thinking in the Methodology of Research: The 'Economic Approach' Applied to Key Problems of the Philosophy of Science." In G. Radnitzky and P. Bernholz, eds., *Economic Imperialism: The Economic Method Applied Outside the Field of Economics*, pp. 283–331. New York: Paragon House Publishers.

———. 1987b. "Erkenntnistheoretische Probleme im Lichte von Evolutionstheorie und Ökonomie: Die Entwicklung von Erkenntnisapparaten und epistemischen Ressourcen." In R. Riedl and F. M. Wuketits, eds., *Die Evolutionäre Erkenntnistheorie: Bedingungen, Lösungen, Kontroversen*, pp. 115–132. Berlin: Parey.

Radnitzky, G., and G. Andersson, eds. 1978. *Progress and Rationality in Science*. Dordrecht, Holland: Reidel.

Rensch, B. 1958. "The Relation Between the Evolution of Central Nervous Functions and the Body Size of Animals." In J. Huxley, A. C. Hardy, and E. B. Ford, eds., *Evolution as a Process*, pp. 181–200. London: Allen and Unwin.

———. 1961. "Die Evolutionsgesetze der Organismen in naturphilosophischer Sicht," *Philosophia Naturalis* 6: 288–326.

———. 1971. *Biophilosophy*. New York: Columbia University Press.

———. 1973. *Gedächtnis, Begriffsbildung und Planhandlungen bei Tieren*. Berlin: Parey.

———. 1985. *Biophilosophical Implications of Inorganic and Organismic Evolution*. Essen: Die Blaue Eule.

Rescher, N. 1983. "The Limits of Science," *Proceedings of the 7th International Wittgenstein Symposium*, pp. 223–231. Vienna: Hölder-Pichler-Tempsky.

———. 1986. "Reality and Realism," *Proceedings of the 10th International Wittgenstein Symposium*, pp. 75–85. Vienna: Hölder-Pichler-Tempsky.

Richards, R. J. 1986. "A Defense of Evolutionary Ethics," *Biology and Philosophy* 1: 265–293.

Riedl, R. 1977. "A Systems-Analytical Approach to Macro-Evolutionary Phenomena," *Quarterly Review of Biology* 52: 351–370.

———. 1978. "Über die Biologie des Ursachen-Denkens: Ein evolutionistischer, systemtheoretischer Versuch," *Mannheimer Forum* 78–79: 9–70.

———. 1979. *Order in Living Organisms: System Conditions in Macro-Evolution.* New York: Wiley.

———. 1982. "A Dialectic Approach to Epigenetics and Macroevolution." In V. J. A. Novák and J. Mlíkovský, eds., *Evolution and Environment*, pp. 41–50. Prague: ČSAV.

———. 1984a. *Biology of Knowledge.* New York: Wiley.

———. 1984b. "Evolution and Evolutionary Knowledge: On the Correspondence between Cognitive Order and Nature." In F. M. Wuketits, ed., *Concepts and Approaches in Evolutionary Epistemology: Towards an Evolutionary Theory of Knowledge*, pp. 35–50. Dordrecht, Holland. Reidel

———. 1985. *Die Spaltung des Weltbildes: Biologische Grundlagen des Erklärens und Verstehens.* Berlin: Parey.

———. 1987a. *Begriff und Welt: Biologische Grundlagen des Erkennens und Begreifens.* Berlin: Parey.

———. 1987b. "Grenzen der Adaptierung." In R. Riedl and F. M. Wuketits, eds., *Die Evolutionäre Erkenntnistheorie: Bedingungen, Lösungen, Kontroversen*, pp. 93–104. Berlin: Parey.

———. 1987c. "Leben als kenntnisgewinnender Prozess bei Konrad Lorenz." In R. Riedl and E. M. Bonet, eds., *Entwicklung der Evolutionären Erkenntnistheorie*, pp. 47–57. Vienna: Verlag der Österreichischen Staatsdruckerei.

———. 1987d. *Kultur—Spätzündung der Evolution?* Munich: Piper.

Roederer, J. G. 1979. "Human Brain Functions and the Foundations of Science," *Endeavour* 3: 99–103.

Romanes, G. J. 1883. *Mental Evolution in Animals.* New York: Appleton.

Ruse, M. 1982. *Darwinism Defended: A Guide to the Evolution Controversies.* Reading, Mass. Addison-Wesley.

———. 1985. "Evolutionary Epistemology: Can Sociobiology Help?" In J. Fetzer, ed., *Sociobiology and Epistemology*, pp. 249–265. Dordrecht, Holland, Reidel.

————. 1986. *Taking Darwin Seriously: A Naturalistic Approach to Philosophy.* Oxford, England: Basil Blackwell.

————. 1987. "Evolutionary Models and Social Theory: Prospects and Problems." In M. Schmid and F. M. Wuketits, eds., *Evolutionary Theory in Social Science,* pp. 23–47. Dordrecht, Holland: Reidel.

Russell, B. 1967. *The Problems of Philosophy.* Oxford, England: Oxford University Press.

Ryle, G. 1966. *The Concept of Mind.* Harmondsworth, England: Penguin Books.

Sagan, C. 1978. *The Dragons of Eden: Speculations on the Evolution of Human Intelligence.* New York: Ballantine Books.

Salamun, K., ed. 1989. *Karl R. Popper und die Philosophie des kritischen Rationalismus.* Amsterdam: Rodopi.

Seitelberger, F. 1984. "Neurobiological Aspects of Intelligence." In F. M. Wuketits, ed., *Concepts and Approaches in Evolutionary Epistemology: Towards an Evolutionary Theory of Knowledge,* pp. 123–148. Dordrecht, Holland: Reidel.

Shaner, D. E. 1987. "The Cultural Evolution of Mind," *Personalist Forum* 3: 33–69.

————. 1989. "Science and Comparative Philosophy." In D. E. Shaner, S. Nagatomo, and Y. Yasuo, *Science and Comparative Philosophy,* pp. 12–98. Leiden, Holland: Brill.

Shapiro, H. L. 1974. *Peking Man: The Discovery, Disappearance and Mystery of a Priceless Scientific Treasure.* New York: Simon and Schuster.

Simmel, G. 1895. "Über eine Beziehung der Selectionslehre zur Erkenntnistheorie," *Archiv für systematische Philosophie* 1: 34–45. English translation, 1982, in H. C. Plotkin, ed., *Learning, Development, and Culture: Essays in Evolutionary Epistemology,* pp. 63–71. Chichester, England: Wiley.

Simpson, G. G. 1963. *This View of Life: The World of an Evolutionist.* New York: Harcourt, Brace and World.

Skagestad, P. 1978. "Taking Evolution Seriously: Critical Comments on D. T. Campbell's Evolutionary Epistemology," *The Monist* 61: 611–621.

Smillie, D. 1985. "Sociobiology and Human Culture." In J. Fetzer, ed., *Sociobiology and Epistemology,* pp. 75–95. Dordrecht, Holland: Reidel.

Smith, C. U. M. 1987. "'Clever Beasts Who Invented Knowing': Nietzsche's Evolutionary Biology of Knowledge," *Biology and Philosophy* 2: 65–91.

Snow, C. P. 1964. *The Two Cultures and a Second Look.* Cambridge, England: Cambridge University Press.

Somenzi, V. 1987. "Natura e Cultura: anticipazioni naturali delle innovazioni tecnologiche," *La Nouva Critica* 1–2: 17–25.

Spencer, H. 1870. *The Principles of Psychology. London: Murray.*

_____. 1892. *The Principles of Ethics.* New York: Appleton.

Stanzione, M. 1984. "Epistemologia evoluzionistica: confronti e critiche." In *Evoluzione e modelli,* pp. 193–300. Rome: Editori Riuniti.

Stebbins, G. L. 1971. *Processes of Organic Evolution.* Englewood Cliffs, N.J.: Prentice-Hall.

Stegmüller, W. 1985. "Thesen zur 'Evolutionären Erkenntnistheorie'," *Information Philosophie* 13, no. 3: 26–32.

Stein, E., and P. Lipton. 1989. "Where Guesses Come From: Evolutionary Epistemology and the Anomaly of Guided Variation," *Biology and Philosophy* 4: 33–56.

Stemmer, N. 1978. "The Reliability of Inductive Inferences and our Innate Capacities," *Zeitschrift für Allgemeine Wissenschaftstheorie* 9: 93–105.

Stich, S. P. 1985. "Could Man Be an Irrational Animal? Some Notes on the Epistemology of Rationality." In H. Kornblith, ed., *Naturalizing Epistemology,* pp. 249–267. Cambridge, Mass.: MIT Press.

Stokes, G. 1988. "Mechanism and Method in the Evolution of Science: A Response to Hull," *Biology and Philosophy* 3: 219–223.

Strombach, W. 1968. *Natur und Ordnung: Eine naturphilosophische Deutung des wissenschaftlichen Welt- und Menschenbildes unserer Zeit.* Munich: Beck.

Stroud, B. 1984. *The Significance of Philosophical Scepticism.* Oxford, England: Clarendon Press.

_____. 1985. "The Significance of Naturalized Epistemology." In H. Kornblith, ed., *Naturalizing Epistemology,* pp. 71–89. Cambridge, Mass.: MIT Press.

Tennant, N. 1983a. "In Defence of Evolutionary Epistemology," *Theoria* 49: 32–48.

———. 1983b. "Evolutionary Epistemology," *Proceedings of the 7th International Wittgenstein Symposium*, pp. 168–173. Vienna: Hölder-Pichler-Tempsky.

———. 1983c. "Evolutionary *versus* Evolved Ethics," *Philosophy* 58: 289–302.

———. 1984. "Intentionality, Syntactic Structure and the Evolution of Language." In C. Hookway, ed., *Minds, Machines and Evolution: Philosophical Studies*, pp. 73–103. Cambridge, England, Cambridge University Press.

———. 1988. "Theories, Concepts and Rationality in an Evolutionary Account of Science," *Biology and Philosophy* 3: 224–231.

Thagard, P. 1980. "Against Evolutionary Epistemology." *PSA (Philosophy of Science Association) 1980*, pp. 187–196.

Thönissen, L. 1985. "Kopernikanische Wenden," *Philosophia Naturalis* 22: 294–327.

Tinbergen, N. 1951. *The Study of Instinct*. London: Oxford University Press.

Titze, H. 1983. "Evolutionäre und/oder transzendentale Erkenntnistheorie," *Proceedings of the 7th International Wittgenstein Symposium*, pp. 198–203. Vienna: Hölder-Pichler-Tempsky.

Topitsch, E. 1966. "Phylogenetische und emotionale Grundlagen menschlicher Weltauffassung." In W. E. Mühlmann and E. W. Müller, eds., *Kulturanthropologie*, pp. 50–79. Cologne: Kiepenheuer und Witsch.

———. 1979. *Erkenntnis und Illusion: Grundstrukturen unserer Weltauffassung*. Hamburg: Hoffman und Campe.

Toulmin, S. E. 1967. "The Evolutionary Development of Natural Science," *American Scientist* 55: 456–471.

———. 1972. *Human Understanding*. Oxford, England: Clarendon Press.

Trinkaus, E., and W. W. Howells. 1979. "The Neanderthals," *Scientific American* 241, no. 6: 94–105.

Uexküll, J. v. 1928. *Theoretische Biologie*. Berlin: Springer.

———. 1938. *Der unsterbliche Geist in der Natur*. Hamburg: Wegner.

Varela, F. 1982. "Self-Organization: Beyond Appearances and into the Mechanism," *La Nuova Critica* 64: 31–49.

Vollmer, G. 1975. *Evolutionäre Erkenntnistheorie*. Stuttgart: Hirzel.

_____. 1984. "Mesocosm and Objective Knowledge—On Problems Solved by Evolutionary Epistemology." In F. M. Wuketits, ed., *Concepts and Approaches in Evolutionary Epistemology: Towards an Evolutionary Theory of Knowledge*, pp. 69–121. Dordrecht, Holland: Reidel.

_____. 1985. *Was Können wir wissen? Vol. 1: Die Natur der Erkenntnis* Stuttgart: Hirzel.

_____. 1986. *Was können wir wissen? Vol. 2: Die Erkenntnis der Natur* Stuttgart: Hirzel.

_____. 1987. "Was Evolutionäre Erkenntnistheorie nicht iot." In R. Riedl and F. M. Wuketits, eds., *Die Evolutionäre Erkenntnistheorie: Bedingungen, Lösungen, Kontroversen*, pp. 140–155. Berlin: Parey.

Voorzanger, B. 1987. "No Norms And No Nature—The Moral Relevance of Evolutionary Biology," *Biology and Philosophy* 2: 253–270.

Wächtershäuser, G. 1987. "Light and Life: On the Nutritional Origins of Sensory Perception." In G. Radnitzky and W. W. Bartley, eds., *Evolutionary Epistemology, Theory of Rationality, and the Sociology of Knowledge*, pp. 121–138. La Salle, Ill.: Open Court.

Wagner, G. P. 1983. "On the Necessity of a Systems Theory of Evolution and Its Population-Biologic Foundation," *Acta Biotheoretica* 32: 223–226.

_____. 1984. "The Logical Basis of Evolutionary Epistemology." In F. M. Wuketits, ed., *Concepts and Approaches in Evolutionary Epistemology: Towards an Evolutionary Theory of Knowledge*, pp. 285–307. Dordrecht, Holland: Reidel.

_____. 1985. "Über die populations-genetischen Grundlagen einer Systemtheorie der Evolution." In J. A. Ott, G. P. Wagner, and F. M. Wuketits, eds., *Evolution, Ordnung und Erkenntnis*, pp. 97–111. Berlin: Parey.

_____. 1987. "Der Passungsbegriff und die logische Struktur der evolutionären Erkenntnislehre." In R. Riedl and F. M. Wuketits, eds., *Die Evolutionäre Erkenntnistheorie: Bedingungen, Lösungen, Kontroversen*, pp. 64–72. Berlin: Parey.

_____. 1988. "The Gene and Its Phenotype," *Biology and Philosophy* 3: 105–115.

Washburn, S. L. 1978. "The Evolution of Man," *Scientific American* 239, no. 3: 1466–154.

Watkins, J. W. N. 1974. "The Unity of Popper's Thought." In P. A.

Schilpp, ed., *The Philosophy of Karl Popper I,* pp. 371–412. La Salle, Ill.: Open Court.

Weaver, K. F., and D. L. Brill. 1985. "The Search for Our Ancestors," *National Geographic* 168, no. 5: 560–623.

Wessel, K.-F. 1988. "Der Mensch als biophychosoziale Einheit," *Deutsche Zeitschrift für Philosophie* 36: 97–106.

Whewell, W. [1860] 1972. *On the Philosophy of Discovery.* New York: Franklin.

White, L. A. 1959. *The Evolution of Culture.* New York: McGraw-Hill.

Whitehead, A. N. [1926] 1975. *Science and the Modern World.* Glasgow: Collins.

Wilson, E. O. 1978. *On Human Nature.* Cambridge, Mass.: Harvard University Press.

———. 1987. "The Evolutionary Origin of Mind," *Personalist Forum 3: 11–18.*

Wolf, R. 1985. "Binokulares Sehen, Raumverrechnung und Raumwahrnehmung," *Biologie in unserer Zeit* 15: 161–178.

Wolters, G. 1988. "Evolutionäre Erkenntnistheorie—eine Polemik," *Vierteljahresschrift der Naturforschenden Gesellschaft in Zürich* 133: 125–142.

Wuketits, F. M. 1978a. *Wissenschaftstheoretische Probleme der modernen Biologie.* Berlin: Duncker and Humblot.

———. 1987b. "Die Ordnung der Natur und die Natur der Ordnung." In W. Schäfer, ed., *Evoluierende Systeme III,* pp. 163–172. Frankfurt: Kramer.

———. 1980. "On the Notion of Teleology in Contemporary Life Sciences," *Dialectica* 34: 277–290.

———. 1981. *Biologie und Kausalität: Biologische Ansätze zur Kausalität, Determination und Freiheit.* Berlin: Parey.

———. 1982. "Systems Research—the Search for Isomorphism," *Progress in Cybernetics and Systems Research* 11: 403–407.

———. 1983a. "Herbert Spencer, Charles Darwin, Konrad Lorenz: Historische Perspektiven zur evolutionären Erkenntnistheorie," *Proceeding of the 7th International Wittgenstein Symposium,* pp. 204–206. Vienna: Hölder-Pichler-Tempsky.

———. 1983b. "Evolutionsmodelle in der Erklärung menschlicher Denkstrukturen," *Berichte zur Wissenschaftsgeschichte* 6: 115–122.

———. 1984a. "Evolutionary Epistemology—A Challenge to Science and Philosophy." In F. M. Wuketits, ed., *Concepts and Approaches in Evolutionary Epistemology: Towards an Evolutionary Theory of Knowledge*, pp. 1–33. Dordrecht, Holland: Reidel.

———1984b. "Evolutionary Epistemology—A New Copernican Revolution?" In F. M. Wuketits, ed., *Concepts and Approaches in Evolutionary Epistemology: Towards an Evolutionary Theory of Knowledge*, pp. 279–284.

———. 1984c. *Evolution, Erkenntnis, Ethik: Folgerungen aus der modernen Biologie.* Darmstadt, Germany: Wissenschaftliche Buchgesellschaft.

———. 1985a. *Zustand und Bewusstsein: Leben als biophilosophische Synthese.* Hamburg: Hoffmann und Campe.

———. 1985b. Die systemtheoretische Innovation der Evolutionslehre." In J. A. Ott, G. P. Wagner, and F. M. Wuketits, eds., *Evolution, Ordnung und Erkenntnis*, pp. 69–81. Berlin: Parey.

———. 1986a. "Evolution as a Cognition Process: Towards an Evolutionary Epistemology," *Biology and Philosophy* 1: 191–206.

———. 1986b. "Conceptions of Evolutionary Epistemology," *Acta Analytica* 2: 7–32.

———. 1987a. "Synthetic and Analytical Thinking." *Zeitschrift für Analytische Chemie* 326, 320–323.

———. 1987b. "Evolutionäre Ursprünge der Metaphysik." In R. Riedl and F. M. Wuketits, eds., *Die Evolutionäre Erkenntnistheorie: Bedingungen, Lösungen, Kontroversen*, pp. 220–229. Berlin: Parey.

———. 1987c. "Biology and Human Knowledge: Problems and Perspectives in Evolutionary Epistemology," *La Nuova Critica* 1–2: 5–16.

———. 1987d. "Evolution als Systemprozess: Die Systemtheorie der Evolution." In R. Siewing, ed., *Evolution: Bedingungen, Resultate, Konsequenzen*, pp. 453–474. Stuttgart: Fischer.

———. 1987e. "Evolution, Causality, and Human Freedom: The Open Society from a Biological Point of View." In M. Schmid and F. M. Wuketits, eds., *Evolutionary Theory in Social Science*, pp. 49–77. Dordrecht, Holland: Reidel.

———. 1987f. "Evolutionsmodelle unserer Denkstrukturen bis zum 20. Jahrhundert." In R. Riedl and E. M. Bonet, eds., *Entwicklung der Evolutionären Erkenntnistheorie*, pp. 11–19. Vienna: Verlag der Österreichischen Staatsdruckerei.

———. 1987g. "Hat die Biologie Kant missverstanden? Evolutionäre Erkenntnistheorie und 'Kantianismus'." In W. Lütterfelds, ed., *Transzendentale oder evolutionäre Erkenntnistheorie?* pp. 33–50. Darmstadt, Germany: Wissenschaftliche Buchgesellschaft.

———. 1987h. "Evolution und Adaptation von Erkenntnisprozessen," *Biologische Rundschau* 25: 333–341.

———. 1988a. *Evolutionstheorien: Historische Voraussetzungen, Positionen, Kritik*. Darmstadt, Germany: Wissenschaftliche Buchgesellschaft.

———. 1988b. "Darwinism: Still a Challenge to Philosophy," *Zygon* 23: 455–467.

———. 1989. "Cognition: A Non-Adaptationist View," *La Nuova Critica* 5: 7–17.

Young, J. Z. 1958. "Memory, Heredity and Information." In J. Huxley, A. C. Hardy, and E. B. Ford, eds., *Evolution as a Process*, pp. 281–299. London: Allen and Unwin.

———. 1971. *An Introduction to the Study of Man*. Oxford, England: Oxford University Press.

———. 1987. *Philosophy and the Brain*. Oxford, England: Oxford University Press.

Ziehen, T. 1913. *Erkenntnistheorie auf psychophysiologischer Grundlage*. Jena, Germany: Fischer.

Zimmermann, W. 1968. *Evolution und Naturphilosophie*. Berlin: Duncker and Humblot.

Index of Names

Index of Subjects